The Fire of Faith

The Fire of Faith

The Continuing Story of *The Other Side of Heaven*

The Memoirs of

John H. Groberg

DESERET
BOOK

Salt Lake City, Utah

Visit us at deseretbook.com

First printing in hardbound 1996
First printing in paperbound 2002
First printing of paperbound movie tie-in 2019

Library of Congress Catalog Card Number: 96-78898

ISBN-10 1-57008-290-1 (hardbound)
ISBN-13 978-1-57008-877-3 (paperbound)

Printed in the United States of America
PubLitho, Draper, UT

10 9 8 7 6 5 4 3 2 1

Contents

Acknowledgments

I express my deepest appreciation to my wife, Jean. Without her this book would not be possible. Not only is she a major participant in the events but she also personally typed the manuscript.

I express my deep appreciation to my parents, Delbert V. and Jennie H. Groberg, and to our children (Nancy Jean, Elizabeth, Marilyn, Jane, Gayle, John Enoch, Susan, Thomas Sabin, Jennie Marie, Viki Ann, and Emily Leilani) for their support and help. Special thanks to Jean, Nancy, Jennie, and son-in-law Matt Powell, who have done much of the refining and editing. I am also grateful for the encouragement of many others, including family, friends, and colleagues.

I acknowledge my undying appreciation to the marvelous people of Tonga and other island nations of the Pacific. Through them I have learned from God much of what is important in time and eternity.

This is not an official publication of the Church. I alone am responsible for the views it expresses.

Introduction

The portable radio crackled with excitement as the "Voice of America" announced that American astronauts had successfully circled the moon and were on their way back to earth. It was still dark, a little after 5:00 A.M. in May 1969, in Tonga. My wife and I and our older daughters were huddled around the radio in the central courtyard of our mission home in Nuku'alofa. We listened intently to the voices of the astronauts and the explanations from mission control.

The announcer continued: "In two minutes there will be a brief period of radio blackout as the capsule re-enters the earth's atmosphere. Upon re-entry there will be a very distinct light. Unfortunately this will occur over a stretch of ocean in the South Pacific, near American Samoa, where very few people will be able to see it."

"But we are here," we smiled. "We will see it!"

The voices on the radio went silent. Only static remained. We strained our eyes, looking into the cloudless sky, trying to determine if one star was brighter than the others and might be the astronauts.

Suddenly a brilliant flash of light exploded almost directly overhead. It was not just one point of light but a cluster of colorful flashes. The sparks of color quickly faded as the debris surrounding the capsule burned, leaving one brilliant white band of fire slowly arching across the sky and searing its way towards the sea.

We ran out of the courtyard and down the road to the ocean. What an amazing thing! Men returning from the moon! As we neared the pier we saw a lone Tongan fisherman carrying nets to his boat. We pointed to the bright light moving across the sky and exclaimed: "Look! Men are returning from the moon!"

He looked up, saw the streak of light, and remarked, "I hope they don't scare the fish and ruin my catch."

I could hardly believe it. He wasn't impressed at all. I tried again to share my enthusiasm for this great event, but to no avail. He didn't care. He was concerned about his fishing.

We watched the bright light until the capsule sank below the horizon and into the sea. We listened to the anxious announcer explain about parachutes, markers, helicopters, frogmen, and ships all working in a coordinated effort to pick up the astronauts. "Yes, we have the word. They are safe! They are safe! Oh what a great day for America's space program!"

We were relieved to know that everyone was safe. We turned off the radio and started walking home.

I looked once more to where the capsule from the moon had dropped from view. As I did I saw the old Tongan fisherman slowly rowing out to sea.

I thought of the millions of dollars of modern equipment and the years of engineering genius that had gone into that successful moon venture. What a magnificent triumph!

Then I thought of the lone fisherman silently rowing to his fishing grounds. Like his fathers for centuries before him, he was calm. He knew where the fishing would be best—if only the bright new light hadn't interfered too much.

From where I was standing the faint outline of that lone fishing boat was right in line with the area of the capsule splashdown. Both the astronauts and the fisherman seemed to know exactly where to go and how to get there. I was struck with amazement as I thought of those two separate worlds, which in some ways were so far apart yet this night were so close together. I could relate to each, and I wondered: "Which world am I in? Which world am I more a part of?"

I gazed into the heavens and seemed to feel the answer coming from everywhere: "You are in God's universe. He always has been and always will be over and under and in and through everything. His light permeates all existence and all people, be they American astronauts or Tongan fishermen. Everyone sees by the light of love, understands by the power of prayer, and moves by the fire of faith. All truth, all light, all power, all existence is in God. Through Him is everything; without Him is nothing. Stay humbly close to Him and you will eventually understand and have access to everything."

I felt the warmth of eternal love and the tingling of unlimited possibilities. I also felt very small—like an ant contemplating the sand of the Sahara.

I realized that my knowledge, like that of the fisherman and the astronauts, was still very primitive. Knowledge that endures and saves comes only from God and is obtained through humility and faith, accompanied by obedience and hard work.

To me faith is the assurance that if we believe in and obey God He will answer our prayers, open our vision, give us knowledge, and cause all things to work together for our good. This is the faith I observed among the peoples of the Pacific.

From 1954 to 1957 I served in Tonga as a young missionary. My world then was but a few small islands within Tonga. The experiences of that mission have been recounted in a previous volume entitled *In the Eye of the Storm.*

I returned to Tonga with my family from 1966 to 1969 and served as mission president. At that time my world increased to include all the islands of Tonga as well as Fiji and Niue. From 1969 through 1975 I served as a Regional Representative for the South Pacific. In this assignment my world increased to encompass all the islands previously mentioned plus Samoa, Tahiti, the Cook Islands, the Gilbert Islands, New Caledonia, and the New Hebrides. Then from 1976 to 1978, as a member of the First Quorum of Seventy, I served as area supervisor for the newly created Hawaii-Pacific Islands Area. My world expanded to include all of the Pacific islands commonly known as Polynesia, Melanesia, and Micronesia. This book is about my experiences among these people from 1966 to 1978.

What a choice and increasingly rare opportunity it was to have nearly fifteen years (including my first mission) of close, almost continuous association with the faithful, humble peoples of Tonga and many other Pacific islands. Through them God allowed me to learn many important truths, including the power of love, light, prayer, and faith.

I love God's children everywhere, and have experienced love and faith among people from all parts of the world. No one group of people has a monopoly on these qualities.

I have learned that despite the sophistry of credentialed men and women and the calculating agendas of boards and committees, the real power and influence that bears sway in this world, and which ultimately causes all good to happen, is the humility, the faith, the prayers, the love—indeed the very lives of the meek, those who truly believe in God and act accordingly. Has not the Lord said, "Blessed are the meek, for they shall inherit the earth"? (3 Nephi 12:5.)

The meek are those who believe in God, obey Him, and, like Job, maintain their integrity even though all worldly things may be taken from them. The meek (or believing) continue to fan the fire of faith within them until it consumes all doubt, illuminates all truth, and enables them to accomplish God's will.

I remember an example from Tahiti. We had flown in a private plane from the capital, Papeete, to a small island to hold a conference with the Saints. When we landed, the French officials were alarmed when they found that I was an American and had not received proper military clearance from the authorities in Papeete, because this was an island from which nuclear tests were being monitored. Their frantic calls to headquarters finally resulted in orders that I must leave immediately for another less sensitive island.

The love and faith of the Tahitian Saints who had prepared so long for this conference were not to be easily denied. Darkness was descending and the pilot refused to leave without guarantees of fuel and lights on the next island. The officials could not guarantee them. An argument ensued. The end result was that we stayed. I was put under "military surveillance" in my hotel room until the plane could leave the next morning.

The love and faith and prayers of the local members came through again. The Saints invited the soldiers assigned to "watch" me to bring their buddies and come to the social, including a meal, and stay for the meeting that followed. This would certainly be more interesting than sitting outside a hotel room. Charmed by the local Saints, the soldiers came. They stayed close by me all evening, but gave me freedom of movement and speech. Not only was I able to speak and participate and do all I had come for, but a sizeable part of the local garrison heard the word of God and felt His Spirit as they fellowshipped with the Saints. The love and faith and prayers of those meek members had quietly triumphed again.

The people I worked with in all of the islands knew how to tap into the spiritual power of faith, which at times burned so brightly that it caused otherwise impossible things to happen.

God has all knowledge. We do not. We gain knowledge by acknowledging His hand in all things and being meek enough to learn
from Him.

More than anything else we should be concerned about meekness,
or our standing in God's sight. If that standing is as it should be, nothing else matters. If it is not, nothing else counts.

The key to knowledge, power, progress, joy, and every other desirable thing is faith in the Lord Jesus Christ. I know it is so. I have seen
it work.

How do we gain more faith? We start from wherever we are and
believe a little more and try a little harder.

I look with awe on people of faith everywhere who know that if
they do what is right God will help them. I saw through my experiences in the islands how God blessed the meek and faithful. He extended life, gave revelations, strengthened testimonies, saved souls,
enlarged understandings, dispelled darkness and error, taught truths,
and caused spiritual strength to overcome seemingly insurmountable
obstacles.

I hope you enjoy the examples of the love and faith I saw and experienced among the island peoples.

1

Dedication

Vaipoa, Niuatoputapu
25 February 1969

There was trouble in the air—literally. Tropical storms had raged from the moment we left Pago Pago, Samoa. The heavy, rough seas slowed our progress and made us sick and miserable as we bounced and rolled slowly towards our destination—the island of Niuatoputapu, Tonga. We should have arrived before noon the next day, but it was nearly evening before we saw Niuatoputapu. The captain attempted to get through the reef to the sheltered anchorage on the front of the island, but the seas were too heavy and we were driven back. He tried again, but after a close call with a huge wave he veered the boat away from the front reef and took refuge on the back side of the island outside the reef. The winds were getting stronger, and the waves were heavier and more menacing. We could not land anywhere. It was intensely frustrating, and increasingly dangerous.

We had come to dedicate the chapel in the village of Vaipoa. It had been completed for many months, but permission to dedicate had been delayed because of paperwork mix-ups. I had been very concerned, for I knew how badly the Saints needed the chapel, but I had no authorization to dedicate it.

Then one day when I returned from an exhausting ten-day trip to Ha'apai and Vava'u I had a strong impression to go immediately to Fiji, where I could telephone Salt Lake City about the dedication. My call was referred to Elder Thomas S. Monson. I explained the situation about the chapel in Niuatoputapu and he immediately gave me permission to dedicate it. He said it was the right thing to do, and he would take care of the paperwork.

I returned to Tonga and excitedly announced to my wife, Jean, that we finally had permission to dedicate the chapel on Niuatoputapu. She was thrilled and wanted to be with me for that special occasion. We found a great schedule: the government boat *Aoniu* was sailing from Samoa to Niuatoputapu to load copra and then return to Nuku'alofa. Their loading schedule gave us just the amount of time we needed for the dedication. The *Aoniu* was to arrive at Niuatoputapu midday Monday, so we could have the feasting and dancing that afternoon, followed by the dedication service that evening. We would stay overnight and leave for Nuku'alofa the next day when the crew finished loading the boat with copra.

The schedule seemed so perfect that I felt sure God was blessing us so we could finally fulfill the patiently awaited dreams of the Saints at Vaipoa. Now this storm. Why? I could not figure it out.

We had endured so much discomfort for the last day and a half, and had had such high anticipation of being with the Saints that evening. I was deeply disappointed. I looked at Niuatoputapu. It was right there, yet a crazy storm barred us from landing. How could this be? It didn't seem fair.

Earlier in the day, when we knew we would be late, I had telegraphed from the boat, instructing the branch president to proceed with the feasting and dancing without us. Even though it was storming outside, the members would be safe and snug in the cultural hall. I assured him we would get there as soon as possible and have the dedication that evening. Now this!

I looked at Niuatoputapu and thought back. How many years, how much effort, how much faith had been put into this building? Only the Lord knew. I thought of the stalwart band of Saints, now approaching a hundred members, who for more than thirty years had faithfully waited, hoped, worked, watched, prayed, sacrificed, and gathered money—a shilling here, two pence there, a pound occasionally. Finally they had collected a thousand pounds, an effort worth tens of thousands elsewhere. For years they had been promised a building, but for some reason it had not materialized.

Finally, after tremendous effort, land was officially registered, approvals were granted, and construction began. Everyone on the island, regardless of their religious affiliation, helped with the building. Despite shipping delays, the small chapel had been built rapidly and well.

Then came the paperwork delays. The Saints chose not to use the completed building until it was dedicated. Several times their hopes had been raised only to be dashed by some technicality. They had not complained but rather had exercised faith and patience. They knew their dedication day would come. Their faith was immovable.

On receiving the approval from Elder Monson I had telegraphed the Saints on Niuatoputapu and told them I would be coming on the *Aoniu* to dedicate their chapel, and that Jean and my counselor, President Nau, would come with me. How they had prepared for this crowning event! They had previously telegraphed every detail of their extensive preparations. Now the day had finally come. They were ready and we were here—only not quite, for the gale-force winds and monstrous waves crashing against the jagged coral reef created an impassable barrier.

I looked out over that dark, impenetrable sea of frustration and asked: "Why? Why after all this effort? Why such a storm now?"

We waited, but the storm seemed to intensify. Finally, as the last glimmer of daylight faded from the sky, the captain received a telegram from the authorities on the island stating that we should not try to land, as it was clearly too dangerous.

I felt sick, discouraged, even a little disillusioned. I tried to picture the festivities taking place on shore, about which they had written me. Six huge pigs, 75 medium-sized pigs, and 150 small suckling pigs would be served with an abundance of other native foods to the entire population of the island—close to a thousand people. The chief magistrate would be there. Everyone would be there—everyone, that is, except their mission president and his party, who were waiting beyond the reef, barred by a sea made mad by a frenzied tropical storm.

I paced the storm-tossed deck and gazed at the spray-shrouded island. My heart went out in pain and longing to those on shore. I could see and feel those faithful members, their hearts torn between sorrow and joy. How sad that we could not be together! How unfair that the dedication would be delayed again! How long this time?

I prayed for them, prayed that they would understand and maintain their uncomplaining attitude. As I did so, my mind opened. I saw that they were praying for me, praying that I would understand how much they wanted their chapel dedicated and what needed to be done to accomplish this. A slight chill of fright shivered through me as I realized what I had to do, but their faith calmed me and gave me courage and strength.

Their faith rolled across the sea, through the storm, and totally encompassed me until I finally saw the vision. I had to go ashore. But
how? Their faith was certain—but mine? I looked out over the hissing,
steaming sea that defied any intrusion. What's that? Through the turmoil
and the chaos I seemed to see the Savior walking on other troubled
waters, calming the stormy sea, and saying: "Where is your faith?"
(Luke 8:25.)

Humbly, penitently, quakingly, all of us—those on shore and those
on the boat—united our pleas. "Lord, give us more faith." Then, as a
spark when kindled starts to grow, the flame of faith reached the point
of words. "By the authority of the priesthood, and in the name of Jesus
Christ, and by the humble supplication of faith and prayers for a
righteous purpose; acting as voice for the united faith of many, I command this ocean and this wind . . . to be sufficiently calmed . . . and
the heart of the captain to be sufficiently softened, and the minds of
the police and doctors and officials on shore to be sufficiently relaxed,
so that on the morrow we may go ashore and dedicate this chapel."

The prayers and the faith of that evening—who knows how much
or where from?

I was weak and weary, yet buoyed up by their faith. Now I could
only wait for morning. As I turned to go to my cabin to rest, something drew my eyes again towards Niuatoputapu. I looked and saw, or
sensed, something. What was it? My eyes strained to comprehend.
Yes, something is there. I can see it now—a soft yet penetrating glow
as from a distant fire. The whole island seemed encompassed in a halo
of light. I gazed enthralled. I felt a longing and a bonding, a desire to
be there, to be part of that glow. This desire grew until it became a
fixed determination. I would be there, I would be one with them. I
was sure.

Finally I retired with the fervent plea: "Oh Lord, strengthen my
faith. Help me to be as faithful as the good Saints on Niuatoputapu."

The first light of morning revealed a scene that would test the best
of faith. The wind was stronger, the seas rougher, the gale more terrible than ever. The captain had promised he would try once more to
get through the front reef, which contained the only safe anchorage,
but he was not very hopeful.

As we rounded the eastern edge of the island, the ship was nearly
blown over. The captain ordered the ship to return to what shelter the
back side provided.

It was a desperate situation. We could not get to the anchorage on the front side, and the forbidding reef blocked us from landing on the back side. The shrieking wind and crashing waves were like devils tearing at the very fabric of my faith, now so tenuously stretched between sea and shore. My faith was weakened, yet intact; tried, yet preserved, thanks to the Saints on Niuatoputapu.

Finally, at the moment of greatest despair . . . a slight lull. What's this? The wind is decreasing. The waters are calming!

"Captain, captain. Now?"

"Look at those waves! You'd be dashed to bits. I couldn't risk a lifeboat."

"Then we'll jump in and swim to shore!"

Carefully the good Tongan captain studied the fiery eyes of the young white man who would utter such preposterous words. What did he see? Desperation? Faith? Foolishness? Determination? Who knows?

Slowly the captain turned, muttering something incoherently under his breath. I stood transfixed. I was hardly aware of anything until he said: "It's crazy, but if you are determined and you think you can make it . . . well, no more than two hours. You hear? You be back on board in two hours."

Jean, President Nau, and I raced to the side of the ship as the first mate lowered the small lifeboat into that cauldron of chaos. The telegraph operator shot a message to the radio station in Nuku'alofa, just in time for their noon broadcast, announcing that we were attempting to go ashore. We knew we were coming from a foreign port and had not been cleared by Health, Customs, or Immigration. But the chief magistrate was a friend, and I knew that as long as he was informed, all would be well.

I could feel the tenseness and the determination that literally saturated the space around us. Little did we realize how many others were involved. Hundreds, even thousands, heard that noon radio announcement. Some were only curious, but most added their faith and prayers for our safety.

The distance to the reef was not far, probably several hundred yards. It was low tide, so the reef was more exposed. As we approached the menacing reef with its razor-sharp edges, we weren't sure what to do. Suddenly, as a wave receded, an opening in the reef appeared. It seemed no wider than the launch, but the good first mate, with the steady hand and strong heart of a true Tongan navigator, guided that little craft directly to it.

We entered the narrow opening on the next large swell. We held our breath as we started through the channel. It was not straight! Quick, turn to the left. Now to the right. Careful! Now forward. Watch the swells. Now left . . .

There were never more than a few inches between the side of the boat and the black jaws of that ominous reef. One missed cue and. . . . But there were no missed cues, and there would be none. I acknowledge and praise the steady hand of the helmsman, but angels guided that boat through that channel that day and gently set it down on a stretch of soft white sand in shallow water.

Quickly and gratefully we jumped out of the launch and waded the remaining distance to shore. Then, in the full vigor of eternal youth that comes from faith fulfilled, we raced over sand and rock, mud and grass, through steaming jungle and dense bush, along the best trails we could find. President Nau and Jean were close by my side. Time, precious time, was slipping by. It took most of an hour to reach the chapel, but the word was out. The Saints had gathered.

As we reverently entered the chapel a hush fell over everyone. Talk of tears of joy! Talk of prayers answered! Talk of faith fulfilled! You only had to look into their eyes. They knew it would happen. They were going to get their chapel dedicated! And President Groberg, *their son* who had spent thirteen months with them years ago, was going to dedicate it.

The chief magistrate had received the news midway through a court session. He told the two lawyers that there would be a recess. He came to the chapel in all haste. He was going to be a part of that dedication.

He officially welcomed us to the island. He spoke lovingly of his association fourteen years earlier with Elder Groberg and was especially grateful to greet his wife. He thanked the Church for this wonderful contribution to his island and appealed to God to help the chapel be a light in the ever-constant struggle for greater cleanliness and progress, both physical and spiritual, among his people.

As he spoke I looked around. I was captivated by the beauty of the fine white mats that covered the chapel. Their intricate designs and careful craftsmanship spoke clearly of the love woven into them. The chapel was like a temple reverently prepared to be accepted by God. I wondered who had worked the hardest, the builders in laying the cement and placing the block or those wonderful sisters in weaving those heavenly mats. It matters not. They all gave their best and it was acceptable to the Lord.

When the chief magistrate concluded I greeted everyone and explained that the program would be very short and simple. It would consist of an opening prayer, a song, brief remarks by the branch president, then Jean, then President Nau, then myself, concluding with the dedicatory prayer.

The program went perfectly. As the prayer of dedication ascended to heaven it did not have far to go. I felt the presence and faith of many people—past, present, and future.

I have written elsewhere the words of that dedicatory prayer, which came from heaven, but I mention here a few expressions from it.

Father, we thank thee for this occasion and for this day and for the faith that has made it possible. We know that where faith is, all is possible, and where faith is not, there is nothing. We know that faith is what we must strive for. We know this chapel is nothing but the product of faith and is of no value but as an instrument in teaching faith. Oh Father, protect it. Take it into thy care and into thy bosom and keep it always clean and pure before thee. Bless it to be an instrument to help all who enter herein to be clean and pure and full of faith before thee and thy Son. Help them to have faith in Him, to repent and be baptized in His name and receive the Holy Ghost and endure faithfully to the end of their mortal lives.

With difficulty we concluded our brief, faith-wrought sojourn together. How hard it was to say good-bye! We had overstayed our promise to the captain and must return. The Saints understood. Nearly all the Saints came with us to that distant stretch of pounding surf and sand and rock and reef. As we parted, all eyes were filled with tears. But as I looked into those eyes I saw more; I saw eyes filled with the fire of faith. It glowed as from eternity. Their eyes were conduits of things celestial.

"Good-bye." Softly now. "Good-bye. God bless you all. Thanks for your faith. Keep it burning brightly." I'll never forget that sight. Never.

We had an even harder time getting back to the ship than we had had getting from the ship to the shore. The tide was in more now, so we had to wade and swim farther to the launch. We were totally soaked by the time we reached it. Then the torturous channel ride against swelling seas; then the open ocean; then up the ladder, onto the copra ship. Exhaustion—yet joy. Despite all odds, faith had triumphed.

The captain tried several more times to load copra, and the post office tried to load mail, but it was impossible. Not again on this trip was there any opportunity for any boat or any person to go to or come from shore. Our few hours opened by the powers of heaven to fulfill the faith of those patient, loving Saints was the only physical contact with Niuatoputapu that stormy trip.

The weather worsened and our anchorage was precarious. Niuatoputapu was no place to wait out a storm. A telegram from Nuku'alofa advised the captain to forget the copra and head for Vava'u and seek shelter there, as the gale was getting worse. Even though we were sad to leave, our souls soared in joy as we realized that through the Lord's providence we had slipped ashore, accomplished His mission, and slipped back, right through the very fingers of hell, as it were. And O how Satan raged and tore at us for so doing!

As our boat labored toward Vava'u, Jean and I clung to our bunks and heard the demonic hosts shrieking their defiance, cursing and hissing their madness and rebellion. It was to no avail, though, for the heavenly deed was done. The chapel at Vaipoa was dedicated!

For twenty tormenting hours we were knocked around. Water covered the ship at times and huge waves glared menacingly at us for daring to intrude, yet we were at peace. Just as Enoch saw Noah and his ark "and that the Lord smiled upon it, and held it in his own hand" (Moses 7:43), we knew we were secure in God's hands. What joy to realize that prayers had been heard, faith had been fulfilled, priesthood powers had been acknowledged, and angels had ministered among men and women in far-off Niuatoputapu!

Through the long night I could not sleep but lay musing on the events of the past days. My mind focused on a small chapel, spotlessly clean and beautifully decorated inside and out, and full of love. It literally glowed. No Church money has ever been better spent than the small amount that helped build the chapel in Vaipoa, Niuatoputapu. The building might not last forever, but the fire of faith it helped generate will shine brightly through all eternity.

I closed my eyes and saw those faithful Saints bidding us farewell. They had come under such a variety of circumstances. Everyone was wet and muddy from the hurried journey to the seashore, yet I saw only softness, whiteness, purity, and love. I studied their faces carefully and sensed a glow coming from them. It was hauntingly familiar. Yes, it was the same as the distant fire or halo I had seen over the island the night before. I watched them and saw that light, or fire, continue to grow in intensity until it obliterated all else and projected those Saints forward in a boldness that crossed all barriers. They stood, as it were, surrounded by fire. I knew that their faith, like a fire, had transformed worldly things from one state to another and made the dedication possible.

The fire of faith is a power available to us, if only we will grasp it. How much more we could do if we had more faith! The Lord wants us to overcome our pettiness and build our faith so that our weaknesses can become strengths (see Ether 12:27). All we need to do is humble ourselves and have faith in Him. I know it is possible. I have seen it.

It will be for others to analyze and wonder why things happened the way they did on Niuatoputapu in 1969, but it is for Jean and me to praise God and thank Him for this choice experience. By some calculations a well-planned trip turned into a ten-day nightmare, but the truth is we came to understand things we probably never could have understood in any other way.

Niuatoputapu was never intended to be an easy place. It is a lot like life in a capsule, intended to help us increase our faith. For me it has been filled with those extremes that are so often each other's makers—difficult challenges and unexcelled joy. It has taught me over and over again that the thing of greatest value on this earth is our relationship with our Maker, which is nurtured through faith. He earnestly wants us to increase our faith in Him and in His Son, Jesus Christ, so that we may experience eternal joy.

O that we all might have faith like that which shone from the faces of those patient Saints on Niuatoputapu that special dedicatory day many years ago. May the fire of faith burn brightly in our souls to the eventual consuming of all fears and doubts, thus making all things possible. I know it can.

How did Jean and I happen to be on that assignment to Niuatoputapu? Let me go back to when I returned from my first mission and married Jean.

2

Building and Growing

After our honeymoon, Jean and I rented an apartment in Provo, Utah, and I resumed my schooling. How significantly different my life was as a young married student than it had been just a few months earlier as a single missionary in Tonga! But with Jean's love and patience I weathered the culture shock and was able to graduate in one year.

We moved to Idaho Falls after graduation, where I began working with my father in his real estate business. A few months later, our first child was born. I knew Jean was beautiful, but when I first saw her after the birth of our daughter Nancy she was more than beautiful, she was angelic! To hear the squeal of joy for life coming from our beautiful daughter and to feel the joy of being a partner with God in helping to give that life was more than words can express. I loved my wife, I loved our daughter, and I loved God for giving us the opportunity of parenthood.

After working for a year in Idaho Falls, we went to graduate school at Indiana University. It would be difficult to have a more enjoyable time than we had there. When I graduated with my MBA degree I received several job offers. However, we felt impressed to go back to Idaho Falls and work with my father. I knew I could learn much from him and wanted to make my own contribution to the area I loved.

We arrived in Idaho Falls in early September, 1960, and put a down payment on a small house. A month later our second daughter,

Elizabeth, was born. I had the same intense feelings of love, gratitude, and wonder as I did when Nancy was born. Birth truly is a miracle for everyone concerned.

Dad taught me about insurance, appraisals, loans, and real estate sales. But the thought of building things, especially homes, appealed to me more. Having lived through the Great Depression, Dad was not interested in venturing into that aspect of real estate. But I was young and idealistic and was sure great opportunities were just waiting for those who would take the necessary risks to seize them.

I had no experience in construction and development. Moreover, to get started I would have to borrow more money than I had ever dreamed of. After discussion and much fasting and prayer, Jean and I still felt good about following that course. Thus, with Jean's full confidence and support, I jumped in with energy and enthusiasm. I have learned that once a decision guided by the Spirit is reached you must not hesitate, but must move forward confidently with all your might.

We had been in Idaho a little over a year when I was called to serve as the bishop of our ward. I was surprised; Jean was supportive. I was twenty-seven at the time, so my lack of experience forced me to rely on others and on the Lord, which was a great blessing.

I remember once counseling a middle-aged couple who wanted some help with marriage problems. After they had explained their concerns, they looked at me expectantly, as though the wisdom of Solomon would automatically flow forth. I just smiled at them but could say nothing. Finally they asked, "Well, Bishop, what should we do?"

"I don't know," I responded. "I've never heard of such a problem. Jean and I haven't been married as long as you have, so we haven't gotten to that point yet and I hope we never do."

"In other words, you can't help us?"

"I guess not," I replied. "The only thing I can say is to go home, love the Lord, and love each other. Say your prayers together and thank God for each other. If you still have troubles, come back and we'll try again." They never came back, and as far as I know they did fine.

Another couple had some financial concerns. I told them they should see Brother Hill, our high priests group leader, because he was much more experienced in money management than I was.

"But Bishop," they answered, "we have come to you. You have the keys. You are entitled to inspiration."

"Okay, I'll give you some advice if you promise to do exactly what I say."

"You bet, Bishop, anything you say. We'll do it. We know you have the inspiration."

"My inspiration is to have you see Brother Hill." They were shocked, but they had promised, so they went to see him. He helped them, and they got everything worked out.

Sometimes we tend to make things too complicated. Some people seem to think that bishops have a mysterious gift to say or do things that will magically solve their problems. In my experience bishops are just like other people except they are entitled to revelation and inspiration from the Lord for their ward. I am convinced that much of that revelation and inspiration comes in their ability to tell people with *real conviction* that they ought to love and obey the Lord and love and serve one another. As they do this, it nearly always solves their problems.

Some of our greatest challenges and blessings while I was bishop resulted from the ward's rapid growth. We went from five hundred to around twelve hundred members in about eighteen months. Some weeks the bishopric had as many as twenty new families to visit. Because of limited space, we soon had to hold two sessions of Sunday meetings. Families were assigned alphabetically which session to attend. At one point we had nearly five hundred children enrolled in Primary, which required three separate sessions to fit everyone in. We also held two Relief Society meetings each week. It was a growing and fun time for everyone.

When I was first called to be bishop, the stake president asked me to find a site and build a new meetinghouse as soon as possible. At that time ward members were expected to provide 50 percent of the funding, which could include some of the labor. We earned enough money through fundraisers to purchase the land and began construction in the fall of 1963. That winter broke records for the heaviest snowfall and coldest temperatures. Still, instead of closing down the project until spring, we decided to form extra crews. One crew would shovel the snow and chip the ice away so a second crew could do their regular work. This gave more people an opportunity to get involved. Shortly before the building was completed, the ward was divided.

So many were blessed and so great was the camaraderie that we all experienced an undefined sense of loss as that unifying project came to a close. The beautiful dedicatory service under the direction of

Elder Gordon B. Hinckley gave each who had worked so hard on the building a feeling of fulfillment and vision for the future of our ward.

At about the time our ward moved into its new building, Jean and I moved our growing family into a new and larger home. By that time we had been blessed with two more beautiful daughters—Marilyn in 1962 and Jane in 1964. With each of these births my feelings for my daughters and Jean were deep and wonderful, and I realized anew that they were truly my first priority.

One evening after all our moving was completed, I was alone in the bishop's office, prayerfully going over some names for important positions. I leaned back and was thinking deeply when suddenly, as clear as anything, these words came into my mind: "You will go to Tonga and there preside over a fiftieth anniversary celebration. You will receive further instructions." I could hardly believe it. I hadn't been thinking about Tonga and I put the thought into the back of my mind and said nothing to anyone about it.

Over a year later I had another somewhat strange and unexpected impression. I was at work one afternoon in late April, 1966, when I was suddenly hit by a very heavy sensation and felt that I should go home. I wasn't sure what the problem was but wondered if Jean was all right, as she was expecting our fifth child soon.

When I arrived home, Jean was resting. I asked her if everything was okay. She said she was fine but that I should look at the mail because there was a letter from Salt Lake City.

"What does it say?" I asked.

"I don't know," she replied. "I don't open your mail, but when I saw the envelope I felt a strange sensation."

"Bishops get lots of mail from Salt Lake. What's so unusual about this one?" I asked.

She replied, "Well, this one is addressed to Elder John H. Groberg, not Bishop John H. Groberg. It's something unusual, I know."

I went to the study, found the letter, opened it, and read:

"Dear Brother Groberg:

"We are pleased to extend to you a call to preside over one of the missions of the Church. . . . Your wife is called to serve with you. . . . A seminar for new Mission Presidents is scheduled for June 22, 23, 24. . . . You are both invited to attend. . . ."

It was signed by President David O. McKay and his counselors. There was more, but as soon as I saw the date I ran back to the bedroom and asked Jean, "How quickly can you have the baby?"

"In about three weeks. Why?"

"Good, because we have to report to Salt Lake on June 22. We have been called to preside over a mission." Again Jean was fully supportive and assured me that she knew I could do whatever I was asked to do and that she would be ready to help in every way.

Since no one had talked to us we didn't know what to do or who we could tell. So we just waited. Within a few days we received passport and visa applications for Tonga from Murdock Travel. Soon thereafter we received another letter from the First Presidency confirming my call to serve as mission president in Tonga. We now felt that we could tell others and started to make specific plans. The next few weeks were a whirlwind of activity highlighted by the birth of our fifth daughter, Gayle.

The last sacrament meeting as bishop was full of heartthrobs as we prepared to leave our new building, our new home, and (more touchingly) our many friends and loved ones. As I sat on the stand and looked out over the congregation, I thought, "How good these people are." I realized that during the four and a half years I had served as their bishop I had been young and had made mistakes. How grateful I was for all of those marvelous people who had been so patient and kind, helpful and forgiving. I thought of Jesus, the greatest of all, who loves us and is not only willing but anxious to forgive us. It came to me forcefully that forgiveness and love are inseparable. It is important to live so we can allow His sacred forgiveness to come into our lives. I was overcome with a feeling of deep love towards those loving and forgiving people and towards my Savior. How grateful I was for His example of love and forgiveness and His willingness to make total love and forgiveness a real possibility for all of us. That was my closing message to the ward members. I knew that even though this chapter of our life was over, the love gained, lessons learned, and memories made would last forever.

A few days later Jean and I and our baby daughter, Gayle (five weeks old), traveled to Salt Lake City. The three-day seminar was filled with the Spirit of God. It was worth everything just to be there and receive instruction and support from such great men, indeed prophets of God.

We were especially impressed with everyone's willingness to help with the baby during the seminar. At one time I overheard someone ask Elder Hinckley, "Do you think a young family like that should go all the way to Tonga?" I heard Elder Hinckley reply, "I know they have been called by inspiration and revelation and they will be just fine." What strength that simple yet powerful statement gave me!

Bolstered by the support and goodwill we felt from everyone at the seminar, we returned to Idaho Falls, gathered our other daughters, said our final good-byes, and headed for Tonga by way of Hawaii and Fiji.

Nancy Jean

Elizabeth

Marilyn

JEAN S. and JOHN H. GROBERG FAMILY

Gayle

Jane

— Mission Address —
TONGAN MISSION
Box 58
Nuku'alofa
Tonga, Friendly Island

Family photos from the Grobergs' missionary farewell program.

3

Back to Tonga

Flying to Tonga! It didn't seem possible. I could see the green hills of Fiji below us as we climbed higher and higher. Then the blue ocean came into view. The constant drone of the engines and the warmth of the brilliant sun reflecting off the sea and sky lulled me into pleasant reverie. My mind went back to nearly twelve years earlier when I first arrived in Fiji by boat. Then, I was alone. There was no one to meet me and no one to help me, in fact no one who even knew who I was. What a contrast to my present arrival in Fiji! This time I had my family with me and friends to greet and help me. On my first arrival I had worked and waited for weeks for a boat to Tonga and then spent several trying days getting there. Now we were flying and would arrive in Tonga in just a few hours.

Our three-and-a-half-hour flight to Tonga was full of anticipation, excitement, remembrances, anxiety, wonder, and many other feelings. Eventually Tonga came into view. It looked beautiful. I excitedly pointed out places to Jean and to the children, who chattered in unison, "We're here, we're here!" We circled once, then landed smoothly on the soft grass runway. We were in Tonga.

We received a wonderful reception, with signs, bands, missionaries, and well-wishers everywhere. The retiring mission president and his wife, Pat and Lela Dalton, were most helpful. I was having difficulty speaking Tongan, as it had been nine years since I had left Tonga after my first mission and during that time I had had very little opportunity to use the language.

We went to several receptions and found ourselves in a constant whir of activities over the next two days. We were taken everywhere and introduced to everyone while remembering hardly anything, or so it seemed. After those two blurry days President and Sister Dalton left, and we were on our own. I felt scared, yet excited.

I was not familiar with Nuku'alofa or the main island of Tongatapu, as I had not served there, but I was anxious to get acquainted. The mission seemed to be running well on its own, so I tried not to interfere. One of the former counselors in the mission presidency stayed on as my counselor and helped me greatly by telling me when and where meetings were held. Everyone was helpful. Gradually we began to relax.

We had to adjust to a new home, new schools, a new language, new schedules, new foods, new customs, and many other "news." Jean was a jewel, and no matter what the frustrations were she kept a pleasant attitude. I knew there was a lot for me to do as mission president, but I couldn't put my full effort there until I was sure Jean and the children were all right.

The combination mission home and office was built of cement blocks in a rectangular shape, with each of the rooms opening onto a

The mission home in Tonga.

central courtyard of grass. This courtyard was surrounded by a contin-uous slab of cement that acted as a sidewalk as well as the floor to the various rooms.

One of our main concerns was privacy. To get from one bedroom to another we had to go out into the courtyard area and down to the next door. There were nearly always missionaries or other Church members in the courtyard waiting for interviews or taking care of Church business, so it was difficult to handle family matters without being in the public view.

Our family lived on one side of the mission home and the office missionaries lived on the other but ate their meals with us. Our girls relished the new-found luxury of having "big brothers" around. This more "communal style" of living was very natural for the Tongans but presented some challenges for our family, at least to begin with.

Since the language, customs, and setting were all new to Jean and the children, I knew they would need help in shopping, cooking, get-ting to school, finding friends, and so forth. Acting on some good ad-vice from local leaders, we hired some wonderful Tongan "house-girls" who shared not only their time and talent but also their love. Jean and the children felt comfortable with them, and over time they became like part of our family. Our oldest daughter, Nancy, at seven and a half began helping the office elders with their work and grew to be quite proficient in typing, using the adding machine, and counting money. She became well acquainted with pounds and shillings, deposits, and totals, and learned to balance accounts down to the last pence.

The girls quickly picked up a child's ability in Tongan and found several playmates, both Tongan and English-speaking. Three-year-old Jane attended a kindergarten sponsored by the princess. When I stopped by to pick her up after school she would usually be jabbering away in Tongan with her friends, but when she saw me she would in-stantly turn to her mystified friends and say in perfectly proper English, "Oh, excuse me, I must be going with my father. Good-bye."

We encouraged the children to speak Tongan. However, I began to wonder one evening at supper when one of our younger daughters said, "Please pass the blat."

I looked up and said, "the what?"

"The blat," she repeated, pointing to the bread.

I held the bread and said, "Say, please pass the bread."

There was silence—then the honest effort, "Please pass the blat." I

Playing in the courtyard of the mission home.

then asked her to say "ring" and it came out "ling." She could not pronounce the "R" sound. I realized that since there was no "R" sound in
Tongan ("L" being substituted for it) and no "D" sound ("T" being substituted for it), she simply had not learned those sounds. We immediately started speaking only English in our family gatherings such as
meals and family home evenings. They had plenty of opportunity to
speak Tongan elsewhere and became quite fluent in it, but we wanted
to make sure they could speak English properly also.

I remember working in the office one hot muggy afternoon with
all the doors open in an attempt to catch any vagrant breeze. The air
was thick and heavy and everything was very quiet, when suddenly I
heard a squishing-cracking "splat" followed by an exultant "Got him!"
I walked out and saw one of our young daughters standing barefoot
over a squashed cockroach. When she realized I was there she gazed
up with a look halfway between glee and embarrassment. She carefully slid the dead insect onto the grass with her foot, then wiped her
heel on the grass and ran off to play somewhere else.

I wasn't sure whether to laugh or cry or get angry or do nothing, so I chose the latter. As I returned to my office I mumbled, "Well, she's acclimatized."

Most of the time Jean drove the children the seven miles to school, but occasionally when I was in town I took my turn. We all loved a particular sudden rise in the road that came and went so fast we called it "Tickle Hill." You couldn't go very fast, as the roads were pretty primitive back then, but every time we came to this particular section the girls would laugh and squeal gleefully, "Faster, Daddy, faster!" As we hurtled over the hill (at probably all of 25 miles per hour) our stomachs felt the "tickle" of a sudden up and down. The smiles of children's innocent happiness filled the car and we were all better able to face another day.

We sometimes think we need to take our children on big outings or extra-special events, when often all they want is a nice "tickle hill" experience—something to share together. It's too bad we don't have more "tickle hills" in our daily routines.

As a family we developed a tradition of "special times" with Dad. Each week I would set aside an hour or two to be alone with one of the children doing whatever that child wanted. Each excitedly planned for and anxiously awaited her turn for the "special time." We usually went for walks or bike rides, or went to town to get an ice-cream cone or to buy something small. Sometimes we would do homework together, play games, make cookies, talk in Tongan, or have a geography or history quiz. I always felt this family time was a very important part of my missionary work.

With her white skin and blonde hair, one of our daughters became acutely aware of how different she was from most of her friends. She complained to one of the house-girls, who jokingly told her that if she would stay under a certain light long enough it would turn her hair black. From then on we often found her sitting under this particular light "trying to get her hair black like everyone else's." No amount of explanation could dissuade her from her certainty that the only reason her hair wasn't black was that she had not spent enough time under that special light.

I began to feel an increasing sense of peace about Jean and the children and their adjustment to Tonga. The Tongans loved them, and the feeling was mutual. When we live in an environment filled with honest love we are much freer to give more of our effort to the other

Learning to drink from a coconut
was part of adjusting to life in Tonga.

aspects of the work. I doubt there can be happy life without love, and the more honest the love the more fulfilling the life. I wonder if this isn't the basis of the Savior's statement, "I am come that they might have life, and that they might have it more abundantly" (John 10:10). Isn't He the embodiment of love, and isn't it His great desire that all of us be full of love for one another? I am deeply grateful for all who did so much to show such great love to Jean and those five precious girls, who were such a big part of the mission.

4

Getting Better Acquainted

As the family settled in I began to concentrate on the missionaries and the general Church membership. Since there were no stakes,
the mission president was responsible for all Church activities, including government relations. With thirteen districts, nearly a hundred
branches, close to ten thousand members, and about two hundred
missionaries (including locally called couples) scattered over forty different islands in three separate countries (Fiji, Niue, and Tonga),
speaking five languages, there was plenty to do. I attended district
conferences and missionary meetings, conducted interviews, made
missionary transfers, handled health concerns, worked on legal challenges, attended a constant series of government, social, and diplo-
matic events, and tried to spend adequate time with my family.

All of this, along with the many things I felt I should be doing
but couldn't, combined to put me in a state of discomfort. Having
outside forces dictate what I did and where I went was foreign to my
nature. I was also frustrated with my lack of fluency in the language.
For weeks my frustration increased. I felt I was being pulled in too
many directions.

Finally one day I sat down in frustration and drafted a letter to the
First Presidency. In it I explained that maybe a mistake had been
made. I wanted to be with the missionaries, visit the people, and explain the truths of the gospel, whereas so far most of my time was
spent going to both government and Church meetings, releasing and
sustaining branch and district leaders, and trying to settle all kinds of
problems within branches and districts and among members and mis-

sionaries. I mentioned that there were always several sick or unmotivated missionaries and more problems in the districts and branches than I could possibly deal with.

I explained how I dealt with branch problems in their order of severity. For example, if a branch president quit or ran off with a woman, I felt that took priority and I tried to take care of that right away. The smaller problems, such as disagreements, ineffectiveness, or long tenure in office, had to wait. I mentioned that with nearly a hundred branches and thirteen districts there were so many serious problems that many of the regular problems weren't getting handled at all.

Finally, I explained that since I wanted to do missionary work and seemed unable to do so, maybe the First Presidency could send someone else down to do the branch and district work. This would leave me freer to do the missionary work.

It helped to put my frustrations on paper. I worked the letter over a little and then prayed sincerely to ask if there was anything I had left out, or anything unclear or unexplained. As I prayed, I received one definite impression: "Throw the letter away. It is not your place to counsel the Brethren." I threw it away.

I was still frustrated, but having obeyed the prompting and thrown the letter away I felt I was entitled to know what steps I should take next. I needed to be relieved of this burden of frustration. As I prayed, I began to feel that I must get more help and that the needed help was available right around me. I prayed more and felt an impression to complete the mission presidency by calling a particular district president to fill the vacant counselor position. I also felt impressed to organize an expanded mission council of a dozen good men. I went to ask this particular district president to be my counselor. When I talked to him he mentioned that he had been prepared by a dream the night before and was ready and willing to serve. He also suggested who his successor might be and had several names to recommend for our mission council, even though I had not mentioned this council to anyone. It is wonderful how the Lord works with us when we have enough humility to follow His promptings.

With the call of this new counselor our presidency was complete. We met often and received impressions as to what directions we should move in. We divided the district conferences between the three of us and often assigned district presidents to preside at their own conferences. This relieved the pressure immensely.

In addition to calling good men to serve on the mission council,

A complete mission presidency: (from left to right) Manase Nau,
President Groberg, and Tonga Toutai Paletu'a.

we called exemplary women to serve in the mission Relief Society and
other mission auxiliaries. As we gave all these leaders the responsibility
to travel and train others and handle important details, not only did my
frustration level decrease but also more problems were handled and the
quality and quantity of training increased markedly. In the process all
the participants grew. What a simple, yet far-reaching solution this was
to what a short while ago had seemed an impossible task! I had learned
this same principle before as a missionary and as a bishop, yet for some
reason I had to learn it again.

As I became better acquainted with my counselors, the members
of the mission council, and the district and branch presidents, my respect for them and my confidence in them rose to great heights. I felt
confident they could and would do anything and everything needed
to build the kingdom of God in the Tongan Mission. They were not
only willing but anxious to carry out our jointly made decisions. What
a wonderful thing to work with competent and dedicated people! I
borrowed much strength from their faith, their testimonies, their love,
and their good works. They seemed unafraid of anything, and this
gave me courage to move forward.

One day I was called to a government office to sign a new lease for
some land. As I talked with the Minister of Lands, I learned that I was

the official signatory for all Church property in Tonga as well as the legal representative for all Church transactions. In fact, he told me I was responsible for every aspect of the Church in Tonga. I was surprised. I immediately went home and re-read the letter of call from the First Presidency. Sure enough it stated: "The membership of the Church and its establishments in the mission will be under your presidency. The Saints will likewise need your guidance and counsel, and the branches and other organizations will be officered and maintained under your direction. You are empowered by virtue of the priesthood you hold and this appointment to exercise righteous judgment and set in order the work of the Church within your jurisdiction." I was overwhelmed as the weight of this responsibility sank in.

I was especially troubled with the rocky relationship the Church had had with the government in the past. I decided that I must become better acquainted with all the leading officials of Tonga, including the ministers of Lands, Finance, Police, Education, Foreign Affairs, and so on.

I visited Prince Tungi and Princess Mataʻaho, whom I had known as a young missionary. They would be crowned the next king and queen when the official mourning period for the late Queen Salote ended. Queen Salote had reigned for fifty years and was deeply beloved by her people. When she died in December 1965, a one-year period of mourning was declared. During this time all movies, dances, or other forms of entertainment were outlawed except for those receiving special approval. I also met with the premier and with as many high-ranking officials as I could. As I met and visited with them I was sure they would be fair and helpful.

I wanted to help them also. I knew that the greatest help I could give them would be the truths of the gospel. I took this responsibility personally and determined to help each of them understand the gospel better. I felt the Spirit of the Lord directing these meetings and guiding my feelings. By now I was feeling more and more that this "impossible task" could be accomplished after all. I greatly needed the Lord's help. I learned again the simple truth that "man's extremity is God's opportunity." He does help. I know that.

Over the ensuing months these feelings of confidence were tested time and time again, for as in the lives of most of us some days were up and some were down. Sometimes the weight of responsibility got so heavy that I began to question again whether it could really all be done. God continued to bless me with a sweet spirit of assurance that

He was guiding and helping, but it took prayer and constant effort to maintain that feeling.

I remember a time when someone gave me a copy of a popular weekly news magazine from America. I thought it would be fun to see what else was going on in the world. As I sat down to read it, a thought passed through my mind saying: "You don't have enough time or energy to get the things done that you have been called to do. It would be better not to divert time or energy to other things. It is your choice, and you can do much good either way, but you'll get more of the important things done if you give all of your time and energy to your present calling and for now let other things take care of themselves."

It was not a strong, mandatory feeling, but rather a quiet choice for me in that particular situation. I hesitated for a moment, then closed the yet unread magazine, threw it in the wastebasket, and started planning our next missionary meeting. I never looked back on that decision; I did not keep close track of world events until we returned home three years later.

We did have a small local sheet called the *Tongan Chronicle,* which reported mostly regional news and could be read in a few minutes. If some world event was significant enough, it generally found its way to page two or three, so we weren't totally isolated.

I was grateful the Lord encouraged me to focus my full attention on the work at hand and helped me not to be diverted by outside worldly concerns. I knew that God was in charge of the world and that He had a work for me to do in Tonga. If I did that work, at least that part of the vineyard would be a little closer to what He wanted it to be. He had many helpers on both sides of the veil and I was sure that through them He was very capable of handling the rest of the world.

Choosing to pass up the news magazine was a small but important decision for me. I learned over time that if we concentrate on the assignments God has given us He opens other doors and gives additional light as needed. Has He not promised, "If your eye be single to my glory, your whole bodies shall be filled with light"? (D&C 88:67.)

5

District Conferences

The mission was divided into thirteen districts. District conferences were held four times a year, and I had been told in Salt Lake City that I should try to attend each conference. If I did that, it would take all fifty-two weekends of the year. It often took several days, and sometimes more than a week, just to reach a district by boat. I attended as many as I could, but it was far less than every one. How grateful I was for wonderful counselors who shared in this responsibility!

Each district had several branches. The largest had thirteen. At district conference we met with all the members and the missionaries working in that area. When possible I tried to visit each branch, see their chapel, and meet with the branch president.

On our first conference visit to the Vava'u District the district president told us he had arranged for us to visit all the branches. We started our visits early in the morning at the largest branch. They had a big feast waiting for us. No one can fully understand a Tongan feast until he has seen and experienced one. In traditional Tongan culture, one of the greatest signs of respect you can show others is to give them a large and elaborate feast. Even though things have changed now, much of the history of the islands has been punctuated with periods of drought, famine, and starvation. Thus, in some respects, giving to another person a large feast of food was tantamount to giving them your life.

Tongan feasts are traditionally prepared and placed on large *polas* (trays woven from the huge coconut fronds) heaping with food. Roast pigs, chickens, *ufi, talo,* fish, bananas, *kape,* pineapple, lobster, *lupulu,* coconuts, watermelon, *manioke,* oranges, *faikakai,* and on and on, are beautifully and temptingly presented in a manner that makes the meal a true work of art. There is always much more food than the guests can eat. Some have questioned why so much food is prepared when those eating it can eat such a small part. Let me explain. The best of everything is prepared and presented to the guests first. They eat what part they like, and when they are finished the food is given to the next group, usually the host and his close family. They eat what they want and then the *pola* is passed to the cooks and other helpers. They eat what they want and then the *pola* is passed to the children. After they finish, what little is left is given to the animals. Nothing is wasted.

Along with the feast this branch had speeches, dances, and wonderful music. I thought it was nice to start with a good breakfast, although roast suckling pigs weren't what we were used to for breakfast!

We drove to the next branch, which put on another big feast and entertainment similar to those of the first branch. We found the same at the third branch, then the fourth, and so on. To his credit, the district president had certainly gotten the word out that we were coming, and were the Saints ever prepared! I suggested after a while that we stop the feasts, but the district president said there was no way to do this. It was their way of showing love and gratitude for our visit.

Despite our groaning stomachs, we pushed on and visited eight branches that first day. It doesn't take much imagination to understand how we felt by the time we tried to tinker with the eighth feast that evening! The rest of the branches were farther apart and it took us several days to get to all of them—thank goodness! I learned to be more careful about scheduling.

Occasionally I took Jean and some of the children to conferences. The first big trip for the children was after Nancy's eighth birthday. We took her, Liz, and Marilyn to Ha'apai so Nancy could be baptized there. I had worked in Ha'apai as a young missionary for almost two years. It would be wonderful to see these members again after so many years.

The voyage up was pretty rough and everyone got sick. I began to wonder if taking them was a good idea. However, as we entered the calm waters inside the reef around Pangai, Ha'apai, all the girls were up looking around, enjoying the scenery, and feeling happy to be there. The Saints had a lavish feast waiting for us. It was not only a feast of food but a feast of love. I felt a strong bond of love for these

Just before Nancy's baptism in Pangai, Haʻapai.

good people who had been so kind and helpful to me years before. They seemed to reciprocate those feelings.

We visited what remained of the old house I had lived in as a missionary. Part of it had been torn down (or just fell down, victim of the termites). The Saints had decorated the house beautifully. Memories soared within me as I sat with my family on those mat-covered wooden floors.

After the long trip and the festivities, I could tell the girls and Jean were exhausted, so not long after the sun went down they were asleep. I tried to rest also, but couldn't. There was too much to talk about with too many people. Before long someone came and asked if I could come across the street, where a group of friends were gathered to visit.

I walked over in the pale moonlight and saw not just a few but dozens of men and women sitting quietly around just visiting and enjoying one another. I joined them. We all sat cross-legged on mats on the ground and visited. One hour, two hours, three hours—the time flew quickly. We talked about times past and about things present and about the future. We brought one another up to date on our families and our friends. The night was warm, but a soft breeze joined us and made conditions near perfect.

No one had any desire to pursue his or her own agenda or leave early to do something else. Everyone just wanted to bask in the warmth of each other's genuine friendship. No one even thought to bring up anything negative about anyone's past or present. As I listened and watched and felt what was going on, I realized I was involved in a true miracle: a large group of neighbors, family, and friends, with no one interested in anything except the good of others.

I knew it hadn't always been that way. I remembered times of hurt and anger and of discipline and jealousy. But this evening I felt a totally non-judgmental atmosphere. It seemed as if I was sitting with angels. I saw them as pure, clean, and holy. I realized they were forgiven because they had forgiven. Their soft voices, dancing eyes, patient shrugs, and words of love made the evening a glimpse of heaven.

As I visited with those friends—all of whom had played a big role in my experiences as a young district president—it was as though my mind clicked and recorded in its memory bank a snapshot of feelings, faces, forgiveness, love, and faith that I would never forget. I was with friends, kindred spirits, as it were, bound by the joy of gospel truths. There was not a hint of trying to justify past mistakes or seek present position—not a whisper, not even an inflection of aspersion against anyone—only charity and kindness through the gospel of love and forgiveness.

This was not a group of well-dressed people discussing deep principles from comfortable chairs, but a group of friends—men and women sharing their hearts. No one even wore shoes. Everyone sat on the ground using their voices to convey words, but mostly using their hearts to convey feelings of love and gratitude.

"Tell us about your family," they implored. I told them about Jean and our five daughters. They were excited. "You must have a son. Maybe you will have one in Tonga."

I asked about their families. They told me about them and the other people I knew. They mentioned who had moved away, who had died, who was baptized, who was married, who had babies, and so forth. Occasionally there was soft laughter. Often there were pauses. Always there was love. I looked up at the stars. It seemed as though they were trying to listen in, wanting to be a part of the beauty and love that was spread over that little patch of sand on that small island. Or was it the other way around—were they inviting us to be a part of them?

The thought came to me: "This is how heaven will be. These are friends from years past. We feel close because of the work and the effort we have put forth together for the gospel's sake."

I hope I can always remember that bit of heaven. So often we feel we don't have time to visit and understand others as we should. Maybe in heaven, where there is no time, we can do better.

My desire to always look for the good in others and make time to build relationships increased. I didn't want to be in such a hurry to "get things done" that I delayed getting the most important thing done—developing good, trusting, loving relationships with others. I understood that for this relationship to be as it should be everyone had to feel comfortable in saying whatever was in their heart and know they were not being judged. That is how we all felt that evening.

God feels that way toward us. He wants us to feel that way toward Him. Prayers can only be truly effective in a relationship of deep trust. He already trusts us; it is up to us to raise our level of trust in Him so that honest communication can take place and the relationship can be fully effective. I thought of the relationship between the Father and the Son. What courage, what trust, what faith, what love they had for each other, as exemplified by the scripture: "O my Father, if it be possible, let this cup pass from me: nevertheless not as I will, but as thou wilt" (Matthew 26:39). What an example to strive for and follow!

The next Saturday morning I had the special thrill of taking my oldest daughter, Nancy, into the ocean near Pangai and baptizing her into the Church. What joy! Another bit of heaven! To be again in the sacred *"fanga"* (calm waters) where I had baptized so many in years past—now made even more sacred to us by the first baptism in our own family.

After conference we spent a few days visiting the nearby branches. Each visit to each area had its own pocketful of memories. It was great to meet person after person whom I remembered coming into the Church. Many of these had been "young" people when I last saw them, but were now married and had families to whom they were teaching truth and love. Many had responsible callings and were presiding in power and authority. It was not only a thrill but a strong testimony to the heart-changing power of the gospel.

It was experiences like these that made all the traveling required in the Tongan Mission so rewarding. For me, attending district conferences was one way I could help the Lord "remember those who are upon the isles of the sea" (2 Nephi 29:7).

6

Lavania Veiongo

As often as possible, Jean would attend district conferences with me. One time we had a conference that had us visiting many scattered branches. Gayle was only a few months old, so we brought her along with us. The district president asked Asinate, a sister in her mid-seventies, to travel with us and help care for Gayle.

During our stay Asinate became very attached to Gayle, so much so that when we were ready to return she didn't want to give her up. She had been her helper, guardian, and protector from the sun, wind, and rain. She had put a lot of herself into caring for Gayle, and a very close bonding had taken place. Asinate asked if she could keep her and raise her, but we weren't quite ready to give our children to others to raise (although that custom was still practiced extensively in Tonga). We explained that while we appreciated her help and her desires, we would take Gayle back with us. Asinate was disappointed but understood our position.

She wanted to seal the feeling she had for Gayle in some special way, so she insisted on giving her an ancient royal Tongan name. Lovingly and with deep emotion, Asinate named her "Lavania Veiongo" and ever after called her that. Over the years there were several occasions when the paths of Asinate and Gayle crossed. Each crossing was full of happiness and helpfulness, but I will mention only the last one.

About twenty-five years after this first visit, Jean and I had another opportunity to be in the same area. Naturally we inquired about

*President Groberg with Asinate and
"Lavania Veiongo" (Gayle), November 1968*

Asinate. We were told she was still alive but was now over a hundred years old and had been on her sickbed for several years. Her family said we could visit her if we wanted, but told us she didn't recognize anyone and couldn't say anything.

We drove to the weather-beaten, run-down home where she was being cared for and were ushered into her room. As our eyes adjusted to the semi-darkness we saw the frail shape of Asinate, who looked as old and as worn as her hundred-plus years. Her family gave her great love and devotion as she lay there day after day, month after month, requiring total care.

We talked to Asinate, but she did not stir or respond in any way we were aware of. Her grandniece, already in her sixties, told her who had come to see her, but still there was no response or recognition. We talked to her some more, held her hand, and tried to convey our love, but it all seemed in vain. Finally we felt it best to leave. We thanked the family for their help and their love for this great lady. They asked if we would offer a prayer and leave a blessing on Asinate and on them and their home before we left, which we happily agreed to.

During the prayer, a thought came to me. After I had finished, I returned to Asinate's bedside, took hold of her thin hand, and whispered in her ear: "Asinate, this is Elder Groberg. I bring you the love of your little daughter Lavania Veiongo."

There was a slight stir, then a quiet movement of her lips, "Lavania? Lavania Veiongo? *Malo 'ae omai 'ene 'ofa.*" ("Lavania? Lavania Veiongo? Thanks for bringing her love.") Her eyes opened. I don't know whether they could see, but they seemed to study my face. Then Asinate put her other hand on mine, lifted her head slightly, and repeated the words, "Lavania Veiongo. *'Oku fefe.*" ("Lavania Veiongo. How is she?")

" *'Oku sai.*" ("She's fine.")

" *'Oku ou 'ofa ia Lavania Veiongo. Koe ta'ahine lelie ia.*" ("I love Lavania Veiongo. She is a good girl.")

By now everyone in the household had gathered around in amazement. This was the most Asinate had said or done for months, if not years. Her head returned to her pillow, her eyes closed, and her hand began to release its grip. I felt one more tiny squeeze as she softly breathed, "Lavania Veiongo. *Malo 'e omi 'ene popoaki 'ofa. Tala ange 'oku ou 'ofa ki ai. Lavania Veiongo.*" ("Thanks for bringing her message of love. Tell her I love her.") Then her hands released their grip and there were no more words, only a small, frail form faintly breathing.

We all had tears in our eyes, and we knew something very special had taken place. As I gently released her hand and looked into her face, a whole series of understandings came to me.

I sensed that Asinate was in some way reliving those days of years ago when she carried her little Lavania Veiongo by land and by sea, protecting her from sun, wind, and rain. She was also reliving other days in which she had helped her little Lavania not only as an infant but also as a young child, and eventually as a teenager when they had last met.

It came to me clearly that acts of love and service are never lost and are always close to the surface of things that count. I imagined that Asinate's spirit had been here and there, but when the words "Lavania Veiongo" were spoken something happened that transcended body, mind, spirit, lips, sounds, feelings, and brought them all together in a way that could only happen under the auspices of that greatest of all qualities in the universe—true, unselfish love. In some way that love overcame everything inferior and allowed her to show her recognition and acknowledge her love.

I understood that when we truly love someone completely, when we desire with all our heart to help, serve, and bless another person with no thought of our advantage, even to the laying down of our own life if necessary, something is encoded in our very being that is impossible to erase and that gives a purity of purpose to our lives that rises above all earthly things.

Unselfish love gives us a power and an ability to comprehend and do things that otherwise we could not understand or do.

As these thoughts filled my soul, the central figure of the Savior—the essence of love—seemed to encompass my feelings, and I knew there was a deeper power in His unselfish love or charity for all of us as shown by His atoning sacrifice, which overcame both physical and spiritual death, than we can even begin to comprehend.

For a moment it was as though I walked with Jesus when He visited Martha and Mary at the time of Lazarus's death. The scriptures explain that just before going to the sepulcher "Jesus wept" and the people observed, "Behold how he loved him" (John 11:35–36). Was the love and gratitude He felt for His Father and the love He felt for Lazarus and Martha and Mary not only a prelude to but possibly even a requisite for that great demonstration of power over death, when He cried with a loud voice, "Lazarus, come forth"?

Was it His consummate love that triumphed at that moment? Is love life? Is lack of love death? Is the fulness of love eternal life? When we are full of love are we not full of life, so death (physical or spiritual) has no power over us?

I wondered if the total love Jesus had for His Father and for all mankind, which filled His very being, actually gave Him the power to overcome those terrible trials and pressures, and do that which He otherwise may not have been able to do. He knows the power of love. No wonder He commands us to love God as well as one another. He loves us and knows what power and joy loving one another can bring us.

The scripture "God is love" came to me and I knew it was true. I knew that as a perfected person God is filled with love, thus He is love. As we understand these principles better we will automatically want to have more love and compassion for others.

I thought how marvelous it is that He allows us to participate with Him in this great gift of love and how few of us grasp that life-giving opportunity. I knew that Asinate had done so and I prayed that I could do better than I had done in the past.

August 1973 visit to Asinate at her home in Vava'u:
(from left to right) Gayle, Asinate, Jane, and President Groberg.

All of these thoughts moved through my mind in but a brief moment. Then suddenly I was back in a small home bidding farewell to Asinate and her loving family. As we left that hallowed home I felt we were leaving a sanctuary, or a beautiful temple filled with love. I wished we could stay longer.

We left Vava'u that afternoon and returned to Nuku'alofa for some more meetings. Shortly after returning home from that trip we received word that Asinate had quietly passed away in her sleep. Her last known words: "Lavania Veiongo."

7

Interviews

One of my duties was to interview missionaries, but I was not sure how to go about it. The only examples I had were the few "visits" I had had with my mission presidents as a young missionary. These had been very effective in motivating me to do better, so I decided my interviews should be more like visits than question-and-answer sessions. I hoped to help these missionaries as much as I had been helped when I was in their situation.

Feeling the need for more understanding, I turned to the scriptures and found many examples of interviews. I realized that God uses interviews in a variety of ways. I also realized that for an interview to be effective those involved must listen intently. Joseph Smith referred to his interaction with the angel Moroni as a series of "interviews" (see Joseph Smith—History 1:47). I was sure he had listened intently. I wondered how intently the brother of Jared had listened to the Lord, or how intently Alma had listened to the angel, and especially how deeply the Savior had listened when He said, "Nevertheless, not my will but Thine be done." I was sure that personal prayer was a major type of interview. I became convinced that we could all profit from better and more meaningful interviews.

As all mission presidents learn, interviewing is time-consuming, physically tiring, spiritually draining, and extremely rewarding. I wanted to say the right things in the right way and listen carefully enough to understand the real response, not just the words. This required such mental exertion and spiritual concentration that I had to schedule frequent rest breaks.

In these interviews we reviewed many things and talked about concerns the missionaries had. However, the main thing I tried to do was feel the strength of their desire to put their whole heart and soul into the work. If that desire was strong, I felt I didn't need to know much more; if it was weak, I knew I had to help them get on a better track. Sometimes the most effective interviews were the shortest and most direct. Occasionally I shook an elder's hand, felt the strength of his spirit, looked him squarely in the eye, and simply asked, "How are things going, Elder?" I watched and listened to the response so intently that every fiber of my body strained until peace came and I knew things were all right. This peace came not only from the words being spoken but from the resonance between the missionary's spirit and mine. If that feeling did not come I knew something was not right, and we visited more.

In addition to missionary interviews I had many interviews with other mission officers—district presidents, branch presidents, and so forth. Trying to get the correct facts in interviews, especially on disputes, was always a challenge. I found that if I did my best and kept an open mind the Lord blessed me.

We had many disciplinary councils and many other meetings to try to settle disputes of all kinds. I couldn't handle them alone, but I was blessed with spiritual giants as counselors (see Exodus 18:17–18). How they helped! Many times they would come up with solutions or solve problems in a way that almost took my breath away. I occasionally wondered why I had to struggle so hard when they could just ask a few questions or say a few things and the problem was resolved. I learned that understanding cultures and languages makes a big difference, but I also learned that being in tune with the Spirit makes the biggest difference of all.

I delegated as much as I could, but still found myself involved in an almost unending stream of complex issues. As an example, in a large branch a major dispute had developed between the branch president and the custodian. The whole branch as well as many nonmembers in the village had taken sides. The district presidency had done all they could, but the dispute increased in intensity. The district presidency finally came to me and said they simply could not solve the problem. They officially asked if I would talk to the leaders of the two sides. My counselors, who knew of the situation, said this was one I must handle myself.

I therefore reluctantly arranged interviews—first with the branch president and then with the custodian. As I arrived the whole village seemed to be waiting around for the outcome. I felt terrible, as I sensed there would be big trouble no matter which way the decision went.

The problem centered around who controlled the key to the padlock on the water tank. Some of our chapels had large cement tanks that caught water from the tin roof when it rained. A key was required to undo the padlock to open the pipe and let the water run out. Normally, when there was plenty of rain, this was not a problem; but for many weeks there had been no rain, and water was scarce.

The custodian felt that since he cleaned the tank he should have the key. On the other hand, the branch president felt that since he was in charge of the branch he was also in charge of who got the water. It was not a matter of life and death but rather one of convenience, as the people could haul water from a public well in the next village if they needed to.

I talked to the branch president first. He seemed to have good reasons for his position and did not display a bad spirit. Next I talked to the custodian. Likewise, he had good reasons for his actions and didn't seem to have a bad spirit. Both, however, were very firm in their respective positions. I frankly didn't know what to do. For a long time I thought, pondered, and prayed, but no great inspiration came.

Finally I felt I could wait no longer, so I called both men in. I said I would talk to the branch president alone and tell him my decision. Then I would talk to the custodian alone and tell him my decision, and then I would go home. I asked them not to say anything to anyone about the decision until I had gone. They agreed.

I couldn't figure anything else to do but tell them how I honestly felt. I called the branch president in and told him I believed his story and felt to support him. Then to my surprise I found myself saying: "I have decided to release the custodian"—the branch president smiled broadly, feeling he had won the battle—"but when I do I will also release you as branch president."

He was shocked at these last words, but before he could say anything I said: "Don't worry, I told you I feel you are right, but since I have to release the custodian, I have to release you also. But at least you will have the satisfaction of knowing you were right. The only way you can stay on as branch president is if the custodian stays on as custodian."

He left with a bewildered look. I reminded him not to say anything to anyone until after I had gone. He promised he wouldn't.

Next I called the custodian in and went through the identical procedure. I was sincere because I did believe him. He seemed so pleased when I told him that I would release the branch president, but totally perplexed when I explained that upon the branch president's release he would be released also.

We visited for a few minutes and I told him I was ready to leave, so he and the branch president could tell the others the decision in a few minutes.

As I opened the door to let the custodian out, the branch president was waiting in the hall. He asked if I could wait for a moment while he and the custodian talked. I agreed. A few minutes later the two of them came into the office arm in arm, full of smiles, and jointly announced that they had worked out their differences and no one would need to be released. They apologized for taking my time and assured me there would be no more problems.

I left, and never heard from them again on that issue. It didn't rain for a few more weeks and then we had a series of huge downpours. I have no idea how they worked it out. I suppose each could have told "their side" how they had won, but in kindness to the other person they decided on this course of action.

I felt the Lord was helping me and the branch president and the custodian, as well as many others, to understand how inexorably our progress is tied to the progress of others. I know the world teaches that we rise by stepping on others, but this experience indelibly impressed on me that the only way to rise is by helping others and rising with them.

Another example I remember was an interview that concerned a prominent local Church leader who had been involved in immoral conduct. Wanting to set things straight, the young woman involved with him came in on her own and explained everything to me. She was frightened because the person she named was a powerful man as well as an important Church leader. I asked her to return the next day and wait in the adjoining room while I talked to the man she identified.

When the man came in the next day he denied everything. We talked for a long time and I tried every way I knew to help him come clean. Finally, when I realized he was not going to change his story, I said, "Wait here just a minute." I then opened the door to the next room and asked the young lady to come in.

As soon as he saw her he ducked his head in shame. I simply asked, "Is it true?"

Burying his head in his hands, he replied, "Yes, it is true."

I then said: "We have been talking for more than thirty minutes and you have denied everything. How come you acknowledge it now?"

His answer has remained indelibly impressed on my mind: "Because I didn't think you knew. She told me she wouldn't say anything, and I thought I was safe."

I responded: "I am only a man. What difference does it make whether I know or not? There are only three people who really matter—you, the girl, and God—and all of them know. Whether I know or not doesn't change a thing in terms of eternal consequences."

He had no response, so I continued: "You must not be angry with this girl but rather express gratitude to her for helping set the stage so you could come clean here and now. The scriptures make it clear that there is nothing hidden that will not be revealed sooner or later—at the latest when the Lord comes, 'who both will bring to light the hidden things of darkness, and will make manifest the counsels of the hearts' " (I Corinthians 4:5). I explained how much better it is to voluntarily confess rather than to be compelled by facts to acknowledge something we have done wrong.

We had a good discussion and soon appropriate action was taken. I have watched over the years as both parties with their respective spouses have made wonderful spiritual growth.

From these and many other experiences I came to realize that inspired and inspiring interviews or visits are an integral part of God's plan for our progress and for the growth of His kingdom. I tried as time went on to do much better on both the talking and the listening sides of this divine process.

8

Traveling at Sea

With the exception of Fiji, the only way to get from one island to another was by boat. Most available boats were old and small and often unsafe. Boat schedules were uncertain, which made it difficult to schedule conferences and zone meetings. It was also difficult to transfer missionaries and take care of sick missionaries. We decided that having our own "mission" boat would enable us to travel among the many islands in Tonga and take care of our needs on our own timetable. I had already found an old boat for sale at a reasonable price, and we had many experienced members we could use as a crew.

When we received authorization from the Church we immediately bought the boat. It needed a lot of work, but the enthusiasm of the members for this project was remarkable. Everyone pitched in, and within a few weeks we had a christening ceremony for the good ship *Faifekau* (Missionary). It was about 45 feet long and 10-1/2 feet wide and could carry forty passengers as well as several tons of cargo. We were able to get it fully registered and insured in Tonga.

As with most projects, there were more problems than we had anticipated, but there were also many more benefits than we had expected. First, we were able to make firm schedules and, weather permitting, hold to them. Second, there was a great demand for rides, so except for those on Church business, such as official conference visitors and missionaries, everyone paid his or her own way. As time went on we were happy to find that the boat not only paid for itself but made a small surplus.

Our "mission" boat, the Faifekau *(center).*

For two years the *Faifekau* plied the seas of Tonga and was a great missionary. At first people laughed at us and warned their friends not to travel with the "Mormons," as they wouldn't let you smoke and drink or tell bad stories on their boat. They also said that since the boat's name was "Missionary" they would preach to you while you were on board. Our detractors circulated the story that we had a poorly trained crew, an "over-the-hill" captain, and a very old and unsafe boat and engine.

In the course of two years, however, we did not lose a soul; in fact, no one was even washed overboard in a storm, which was quite remarkable for that time. The reputation of the *Faifekau* and its crew rose steadily, and it came to be considered as among the best in Tonga. To our pleasant surprise we found that people actually preferred to come with us.

During these two years the Tongan economy expanded greatly. The government started a ferry service to the northern islands. Prices and demand were increasing and many new boats were put into the trade. When other options became sufficiently plentiful the need for our boat diminished. We eventually sold the *Faifekau* to a Church member, who developed a successful shipping business. He continued to transport missionaries free of charge.

The purchase and later sale of the boat was a fascinating episode. While we needed it the boat was truly a godsend, but when the need for the boat passed, that special era came to an end.

On one conference trip to Ha'apai when we had the *Faifekau* we took our daughters along. It was a rough trip up, but after fifteen hours we finally arrived. While we were there we had a wonderful dance and an inspirational conference. The captain wanted to return to Nuku'alofa at about 4:00 A.M. Monday, before the seas got worse. We began loading the boat about 3:00 A.M. I reflected again on what a different way of life the Tongans have from ours. Time is definitely of secondary consideration. If the tide and the weather are right, 3:00 A.M. is as good as 3:00 P.M. to load a boat and prepare to leave. How great it was to have our own boat and be able to set our own schedule!

Many were seasick on that voyage, but there was such a feeling of mutual helpfulness that it made the voyage easier. The genuine love and concern Tongans have for each other grows naturally out of their lifestyle. Jean put it well when she said, "This is real life and real help— quite a contrast from the facade of help so often substituted for real help in more 'developed' societies." On that voyage people didn't just think about helping, they helped by holding someone's forehead while they were sick, or by sheltering someone from the cold ocean spray, or by caring for a baby while the mother wasn't feeling well. In turn they were held as they got sick, and sheltered as they shivered from the chill wind and spray. In some ways it was a miserable fourteen-plus-hour voyage, but in other ways it was an opportunity to learn. One of the ways of experiencing joy is to be in a turbulent, painful situation, like a rough sea, and then finally have it end as you arrive and come to shore. Then absence of pain and turbulence is real joy.

As I watched the crew members and others work so hard and so well together through many long and dangerous voyages on the ocean, I had the feeling that one of the reasons why Jesus chose many of his top leaders from the ranks of experienced fishermen was that it is such a demanding occupation. It is fraught with danger, discomfort, the need to work together, the need to follow a leader, the need to be self-reliant, yet the need to rely on God. It requires genuine concern for others, a realization that your life depends on them and their life depends on you. It requires being independent, yet submissive, work-

Tongans and Liz on board the Faifekau.

ing hard any hour of the day or night, and knowing the importance of getting the job done no matter what the costs in toil and hardship. Fishermen know the joys of a full net, the frustrations of an empty one, the tragedies of accidents, the terror of the storm, the joy of calm seas. What better preparation could one have for being a disciple?

We had many terrifying as well as many gratifying experiences at sea. I'm not sure that I ever looked forward to an ocean voyage. I nearly always got seasick. I went because that is what I had to do to fulfill my calling. No matter how physically uncomfortable it was the Lord always blessed me with protection, and no matter what trials we experienced on the way we always arrived safely. More than that, however, He blessed me with feelings, understandings, revelations, and testimonies that probably could not have come in any other way.

9

Riches That Endure

The strength of faith and the depth of spiritual understanding the Tongans demonstrated constantly amazed me. I knew that hard work and extra effort on my part were necessary just to stay close, let alone try to catch up with them. One experience that taught me this came not long after our arrival in Tonga.

I was working in the office one day when a young man brought me a note. It was a request from his great-aunt, with whom he lived, to visit her. It was signed "'Ofa." The note gave an address and said she was always there, so any time I could come would be fine, but she needed to discuss something with me. I told the young man to tell 'Ofa I would visit her the next day in the afternoon.

I remembered 'Ofa and her husband very well. As a young missionary I had been very impressed by this particular older couple. They were always helping the missionaries and others. They had not been able to have children of their own, which I'm sure was a disappointment to them, but there were always other children around their home whom they tended and fed and helped in many ways. I noticed that many times 'Ofa took food to older folks or those who were sick or in some kind of need. She and her husband were very helpful to me also. I was in that area only briefly before being sent to a distant island, but the impression they made on me was deep and lasting.

Now, after many years, I was going to see them again. I wondered about her husband, as the note made no mention of him. I anxiously looked forward to the visit and to seeing what great blessings the Lord had given them during the intervening years. In my mind's eye I imagined them living in a fine house with a beautiful garden and lovely trees and flowers. I realized they would be older now, but I was sure they would be in good circumstances and have many friends to help them.

As I drove to the address, I realized that they were in the same location as before. And as I pulled up to the weather-beaten, tumble-down, coconut *fale* (hut), my vision of a beautiful home and garden was shattered. Why, this was the same house they had had years before, only now it was in a terrible state of repair. The rut-filled roads were the same, the neighborhood was the same, just older. It had been raining, and now there was a light drizzle. Everything was muddy and damp and musty.

I parked on the road close to the house and got out. As I closed the car door, an old woman came out of the house and stood in the doorway. It was 'Ofa. As I walked up the pathway I saw her put out her hand and move it back and forth in a slightly waving fashion. I could tell she was blind. I took her hand, then gave her a big hug. I realized that she had not long to stay in this life, as she had nothing but the frailest body of skin and bones.

"Come in, come in," she beamed. "Let's sit down and talk. It's so good to see you again." Though her eyes were sightless, I was sure she saw. We sat cross-legged on the mat and visited for a long time. She talked about her continuing desire to help the "poor people." Finally she said: "The reason I asked you to come is so I can give you my fast offering. My branch president won't take it, as he says I need it. President Groberg, he has no right to deny me the blessings of paying fast offerings. You are the mission president, you straighten him out. I give this money to you. Please tell the branch president to take it from now on."

She then handed me an old handkerchief tied around some coins she had been saving. I said: "Maybe the branch president is right. Maybe you should be receiving help rather than giving it." She looked at me for a long time and I actually felt she could see me. She was thinking deeply. After a moment she smiled and kindly informed me that, even though her husband had died, she was rich and had nothing to worry about.

I was a little confused, so I began to inquire: Had her husband left her a lot of money? Had she received an inheritance? If she was rich, why didn't she have a better house? She softly laughed and said, "No, no, not like that." I asked if they had ever gone to the temple in New Zealand. "No, we never made it. We often saved money to go to the temple, but ended up giving it to someone else who seemed to need it more." She told me she had recently gone blind. She said it was more difficult now to sew and cook and get around, but she continued to do the best she could to help others. That was her life.

Every physical blessing I felt she should have received seemed to have eluded her. I continued to question her; and when all the facts came out, I said: "'Ofa, how can you say you are rich and you don't have anything to worry about? You have no husband. You have no children. You're blind. You are in poor health. You live in a run-down home. Your roof leaks. You haven't been to the temple. How can you say you are rich?"

She again studied me for a long time and then stopped all of my questions by simply saying: "I am rich because I know the Lord is pleased with my life. Things haven't turned out the way I thought they would, but I know I will be with my husband soon. I know the Lord will bless us some way with a family. I know I have not done all I could do, but I know the Lord is pleased with what I have done."

I recalled what the Lord said so clearly in Doctrine and Covenants 6:7: "Seek not for riches but for wisdom, and behold, the mysteries of God shall be unfolded unto you, and then shall you be made rich. Behold, he that hath eternal life is rich."

We visited a while longer. As the sun began to sink in the west, it sent long shafts of golden beams across the floor of that humble hut. I marveled at the brilliant hue. Finally, I stood and bade farewell to 'Ofa.

As I left, the sun was very low and I realized that a soft transformation had taken place. The golden "huelo 'oe la'a" (afterglow of the sun) had turned the mud into veins of gold; and the run-down hovel into a beautiful mansion. The final rays of the setting sun colored the tattered coconut leaves with an amber-like richness that made them glow and sparkle like precious jewels. What a magnificent close to a beautiful day, heralding a similar close to an equally beautiful life!

As I reached the car I turned and looked back at 'Ofa. Through filmy eyes I saw not an old blind woman but a beautiful angel calmly standing at the door of a palace, quietly waving good-bye, knowing that the sun had almost set. I knew she could see much more than I could.

Later, I prayed fervently to be able to see as 'Ofa saw and do as she did. The vision and feeling of that sacred experience are still with me. "I must do better," I thought. "I must be more helpful. I must seek and find and serve the Lord and others more effectively."

At the close of the year I sent a good-sized check to Church head-quarters for the excess fast offerings the Tongans had gathered and not used locally. Many like 'Ofa wanted to help the "poor people"—who-ever and wherever they were. I continued to contemplate what riches really are and finally started to understand, as 'Ofa and other Tongans did, that they had nothing to do with money and everything to do with quiet helping.

'Ofa has long since passed away, but even today I often think of her. She had sought for and found the riches of eternity. She knew in whom she trusted. Not only has she gone to a great reward, but she tasted some of it while still here. I hope we can all do likewise.

10

Tongan Ways

In order to better understand the Tongan people I think it is necessary to see their point of view on certain issues. Their outlook on helpfulness, "borrowing," keeping track of each other, law-breaking, and Sabbath observance were quite different from what many *palangis* (westerners) were used to. Take helpfulness, for example.

We inherited a large American car that was getting on in years and miles. Its steering wheel was on the wrong (American) side, but the authorities let us use it anyway. There were not many cars in Tonga in those days. Most of the traffic was by foot, horse, bicycle, or horse-drawn cart. Everyone knew everyone's car—especially our large one.

One day after taking the children to school I was returning home along the main road and had just started to accelerate to pass a horse-drawn cart in front of me when suddenly another cart pulled onto the road not far ahead, coming towards me. I could see that there was not enough room to pass the first cart before meeting the oncoming cart, so I pushed on the brakes to slow the car down and pull back behind the cart in front of me. To my consternation the brake pedal went clear to the floor and didn't slow the car at all. Talk about a panicky feeling!

In a split second all sorts of things went through my mind. If I tried to pass I would hit the horse and cart coming towards me: if I didn't pass I would plow into the back of the cart and horse in front of me. If I turned to the left the road was filled with children walking to school, and if I turned to the right there was a large bog of mud and water with some people walking there also.

A decision had to be made instantly. What should I do? I'd like to think I prayed, but I doubt I had time. (I was glad I had prayed and asked for protection before leaving home.) Almost by reflex I sensed a break in the file of people to my right, so amidst yells of alarm and splashing mud and water I swerved to the right and pancaked through the bog, coming to rest in the oozing mud. As the car stopped I looked out the window and saw that the two carts and the car were all in line at the same spot on the road. I could tell that the carts and the car would have hit each other had I not made the last-second turn.

Opening the door, I stepped into the water and mud and found myself surrounded by curious schoolchildren and several adults, all asking what had happened and what they could do to help. I first asked if anyone had been hit and found that by "luck" (translated "special protection") there had been a large enough break in the file of people on the right that the car hadn't hit anyone. The main damage done was getting several people very wet and muddy as the car plowed through the bog. One horse had started to panic, but the experienced driver kept him under control.

What could have been a tragedy turned into a sort of carnival as everyone decided to help get the car out of the mud. Soon many people were pushing and pulling, and inch by inch that laughing, delighted group of Tongans of all ages moved the downed car slowly back onto the road. Would they ever have something to talk about today! "The Mormon car was wounded and helpless in the mud—but we pushed it back onto the road!"

When we got back on the road I lifted the hood and had someone push on the brakes again. I could see the last drop of brake fluid ooze out from a large crack in the brittle brake hose.

Amidst laughter and smiles and good-natured banter I started the car up again and very carefully and slowly followed behind the horse and cart going towards town. The cart driver said he would run interference for me to the mission home.

I thought: "How sweet these people are. One minute their lives are in danger from an out-of-control car, the next minute they are laughing and helping and guiding that same car to its destination several miles away—not a word of complaint or question, only a genuine desire to help."

We soon got another car that was smaller, newer, had the steering wheel on the "right" side, and had brakes that worked.

Tongan "borrowing," or using someone else's things, involves a
very different set of values from what most "westerners" have grown
up with. Here is a good example.

On one occasion an American family came to see me with a complaint. They accused their house-girl of stealing one of their clocks. I
knew the family of this girl and told them I would talk to her.

When I called her in and asked about the clock her immediate response was: "Oh my goodness, you mean they need it. Oh, I feel so
bad. I will put it right back. I guess I didn't do so well. You see, they
have five clocks in their house; one in the kitchen, one in the living
room, one in the bedroom, one in the study, and another in the hall. I
tried to see if they needed them all. I observed carefully and never saw
them looking at or using the one in the hall, which was on a bookcase.
At first I just moved it slightly within the case. No one said anything.
Then I moved it to the end of the shelf. Still no one said anything.
Then I moved it to the next shelf for a few days. No one said anything.
Then I turned it backwards for a few days and still no one said anything, so I felt sure they didn't need it. We don't have any clocks in
our home and we needed one, so I took it home several weeks ago.
I'm so sorry that I didn't find out that they needed it. I'll put it back
tomorrow on the shelf in the hall."

The next day the American family was back again and said the
house-girl had returned the clock but they wanted to know what
Church action we were going to take against this "thief."

I asked them if she had returned the clock willingly when she found
out they needed it. They said she had, but they still "fired" her because
they couldn't trust her. They wanted the Church to take some action
against her to "teach her a lesson." I told them that was not the purpose
of Church discipline. I explained that we wanted to help people repent
(change) by helping them understand and do what is right. It appeared
to me that this had been accomplished. I acknowledged that she
should have asked, and I tried to explain her reasoning, but it didn't
seem to appease them. They still insisted on some "Church action."

By now I was getting a little concerned about their insistence and
asked if there were other problems. They said there weren't, but they
wanted "justice done." When they said that, a thought came to my
mind and I asked them a question: "In your opinion which is worse:
To take something you need from someone after making sure they
don't need it; or to keep something you don't need and not share it
with others who do need it?"

Unable to see the point, they left a little disappointed when they sensed I wasn't going to do what they wanted.

I have thought a lot about the philosophical and moral basis for "Tongan borrowing." I don't have a definite answer, for I know the Lord respects individual property rights. I also know there is a divine principle involving our responsibility or opportunity to share with those in need. Just maybe when we finally understand the principles of "all things in common" and achieve the level of faith necessary to live those laws, we may find that the Tongan approach will need less adjustment than the present *palangi* or gentile one. Of course there is individual selfishness and generosity among all people, and I am speaking only of traditions or customs.

We had our own test on this principle shortly after arriving in Tonga. A young man climbed over the wall of the mission home one night, somehow got into a bedroom where some of our daughters were sleeping, and stole (borrowed) lots of their clothes. One of the girls woke up but was smart enough not to move. When he had his hands full he departed as quietly as he had come. When we heard about it the next morning we were grateful that none of the children had been harmed (which I'm sure was never the intruder's intention). We felt it best not to register a complaint with the officials. We had a nice family discussion about the fact that someone probably needed the clothes worse than we did, so we should not begrudge them that. The girls didn't seem to care, although we tried to emphasize that *they* should never try any "Tongan borrowing."

That was the only physical intrusion into our home that we knew of. However, quite often fewer items came back from the clothes line than were put out to dry. Again we decided that if people needed used clothing that badly, we certainly weren't going to complain.

The Tongans have an amazing ability to keep track of one another. It is more an art or a feeling with them than a science. For instance, few people had telephones in Tonga, but for those who did, the phone system was wonderful. There was a central switchboard operator who generally kept track of where most everyone was who had a phone. She spoke both Tongan and English and recognized voices, so if our children were away from home they would simply pick up the phone and say, "I want to talk to my Daddy." The operator would either ring them through to our home or to my office, or say, "Oh, I believe he is over at Kioa's house. Just a moment, I'll ring him there."

Everyone seemed to know everyone else and usually their whereabouts. There was a prison for law offenders, but it had very light security because there was really no place for escapees to go without being known. As Nuku'alofa got bigger it started to take on some forms of impersonality, although even there everyone was basically part of the town family. I have often wondered if the statement that in heaven "we shall know as we are known" might not have an application more akin to the Tongan cultural experience than to our western, less personal one.

Some "laws" were important to Tongans and some were not. When a law was important to them, they did their best to enforce it. For example, I was in Nuku'alofa one hot day at noon shortly after a large cruise ship full of tourists had arrived. A man crossing a busy street started to take off his shirt, saying it was just too "blankety-blank hot here." His wife replied, "They told us on the ship it was the law to wear shirts in town." He retorted in a rather derogatory way that he would do what he "blankety" well pleased in this "blankety" hot country. As the man got his shirt nearly off, the policeman directing traffic saw him, lifted his bullhorn, and said in his broken English so everyone could hear: "Mister! Put your shirt back on or I'll have to take you to jail!" The embarrassed man put his shirt back on. Several people clapped for the policeman.

Finally a note on Sabbath observance. There was an honest desire to keep the Sabbath day holy and free from commercialism. No boats or planes were allowed to arrive or depart on Sunday. As the tourist industry started to take hold, there were many conflicts and several questions raised as to whether Tonga could continue to hold to these strict standards and see that others did also. I was very proud of the Tongans' making the decision to hold to the strict standard of keeping the Sabbath as a non-commercial day. As an example, Queen Salote received a cable from the queen of England explaining that she was going to visit Tonga and her schedule called for her royal yacht to arrive in Tonga on a Sunday. Queen Salote cabled back and asked Queen Elizabeth if she could arrive on Monday so she didn't have to wait outside the harbor all day Sunday, because the Tongan harbor was closed on Sunday. Queen Elizabeth changed her plans and arrived on Monday. On another occasion the police raided a beach on Sunday, sending home all the swimmers, both foreign and local. I am sure the Lord was pleased with their desire to properly observe the Sabbath and that He blessed them for it.

I have a feeling that in many ways Tongans may be more prepared than many "Gentiles" for some of the truths that are part of eternity.

11

Fijian Gold

The island nation of Fiji with its warm and loving people was an important part of our mission. Its total population and size were many times that of Tonga. The Church population was much smaller, however, as the Church had only been established there for a short time. I had been among the first missionaries to work in Fiji when I waited there for several weeks on my way to my first mission in Tonga.

Fiji was a member of the British Commonwealth, hence many of its people spoke English. Over the years businessmen had imported thousands of East Indians to work in the sugarcane fields. Most of them had stayed in Fiji, and now the population of Fiji was about half Fijian and half Indian. A number of other nationalities lived there also. Our Church membership consisted mostly of Fijians and Indians, but included many of Rotuman, Chinese, Samoan, Tongan, and other backgrounds. They were all wonderful members. The government limited us to six foreign elders, but there were another six native elders also serving in Fiji.

When President David O. McKay had been in Fiji years earlier he looked across the way to a small hill not far from his hotel. He saw an older house near the top of the hill and told those with him, "That is where we will build a chapel." We now have a beautiful chapel on the crest of that hill. It is a near-perfect location, being close to town yet far enough away to be out of the main line of traffic.

Fiji, the only part of the mission we could fly to, had the only international airport in the area, located in Nadi. Fiji also had the only reliable phone system from which to call the United States. I enjoyed being with the people of Fiji, but my visits were usually only a few days at a time. Thus I was especially grateful for the faithful experienced couples who served there. They were a stabilizing influence as they worked with the members in the branches and with the young missionaries.

The Fijian Police Band in Suva was quite famous and played on all important occasions. One day the building they practiced in burned down. Since our building was close to town and had a good-sized cultural hall, they asked if they could rent our facility to practice in it twice a week. We told them we would not accept any money, but would help them out in their emergency. We said they could use our building if they promised not to smoke, drink, or use offensive language there. We often had members or missionaries come to their practices and serve punch and cookies. Many of the policemen were impressed by what they saw and felt. During the two years it took to rebuild their facility more than twenty policemen and their families joined the Church.

Most of the missionary work was done in the two largest cities: Suva on one side of the main island, and Lautoka on the other side. The missionaries had located a few member families in other areas of Fiji. They asked us to visit them.

One of these families lived in a gold-mining town named Vatukoula. It is about halfway around the island from Suva. The family had asked me to talk to their son about serving a mission. They were good members of the Church who had moved from New Zealand. Brother Lelo held a responsible position at the Vatukoula Gold Mine.

He took us on a tour of the mine. It was fascinating to see how they extracted gold from seemingly worthless surroundings. In the nearby hills huge drag-lines dug gigantic buckets of dirt and rocks and emptied them into large trucks. The trucks then came to the refinery and emptied their load of what appeared to be common dirt and rocks into a large crusher. The giant teeth on the crusher smashed everything into small pieces. This gravel was then conveyed to a second crusher, where it came out almost as fine sand.

This "sand" was then mixed with water and run through several more processes, finally being dumped into huge vats full of chemicals and acids, where it was stirred round and round. The mixture went from one vat to another, each containing its own acids and accomplishing its own method of "refining." We walked very cautiously along the catwalks above the vats and noticed that some had a brown-like color while others were more of a rust-red and others a gray color. When the vats and the acids had done their work, the sluicy material entered into some sort of a pressure system that continued the separating process.

Next, the very refined mixture was run through a series of ultra-hot furnaces—so hot that Brother Lelo would not let us even get close to them. He did, however, take us through a heavily secured area to the far end of the long, white-hot furnaces. Here he showed us a spigot-like device through which precious liquid gold fell, drop by drop, into a heavy metal mold which, when filled, was moved to a cooling area where it became an ingot of gold.

He then took us to the safe room where the cooled ingots were stored while waiting shipment to Australia for even further refining.

Jean holding a gold ingot from the Vatukoula Gold Mine in Fiji.

The ingots looked like pure gold to me (and weighed a lot). He let Jean hold one and told her she was holding well over $35,000 worth of gold in her hands.

The tour of the mine and refinery was a lovely experience, but what mainly impressed me was the faithful Lelo family. They had been isolated a long time from other Church members but had kept the fire of faith in the gospel burning brightly in their hearts and home. I interviewed their missionary-age son and found him not only worthy but also willing and anxious to be a missionary. We made the necessary arrangements, and shortly thereafter he received his call to serve in the Fiji District of the Tongan Mission.

I thought a lot about that mine experience, about the missionaries and the local members, about the Lelo family, and what an example of goodness they all represented. Although far from mission headquarters, they were true, faithful, and as precious as gold.

The Lord knows where to locate His mines and how to retrieve His gold. How many truck loads does it take? Maybe a whole mountainside, then another, and another. Even though it may look like common dirt and rocks to us, He knows there is gold there. If we will submit to His will, something marvelous happens. There is crushing, washing, pressure, acids, more pressure, more tests, and even fiery furnaces. In the process the dross, which is of no eternal value, is eliminated and only the precious gold is left. Drop by drop it is gathered, molded, and prepared for even further refinement. In God's wisdom, the refined soul is worth everything.

The scriptures refer to the "refiner's fire," to the dross that must be purged away, and to the day the Lord will make up His jewels.

"For, behold, I have refined thee, I have chosen thee in the furnace of affliction" (1 Nephi 20:10).

"For he is like a refiner's fire . . . and he shall purify . . . and purge them as gold" (Malachi 3:2–3).

"I, the Lord, have suffered the affliction to come upon them . . . yet I will own them, and they shall be mine in that day when I shall come to make up my jewels" (D&C 101:2–3).

If we keep on course we will, with His help, come through that final tap as pure and precious gold—and certainly much more. I was able to see the Fijian gold shine forth even more brilliantly several years later when I returned with Elder Howard W. Hunter, first to make Fiji a separate mission and later to create the first stake in Fiji.

12

Don't Even Think
of Complaining

I'll never forget one early trip to visit the missionaries in Ha'apai and Vava'u. The only boat available was the *Pakeina,* which was known locally as "the rolling tub." It seemed to be built to roll and pitch and toss and keep its passengers in constant discomfort, except when the weather was nearly perfect (which it seldom was). Jean was still nursing Gayle but wanted to come along, so she made arrangements for someone to watch the older girls and decided to brave the rolling tub.

The voyage between Ha'apai and Vava'u turned out to be one of the worst I can remember. I had secured the only so-called room on the boat, which was nothing more than a small enclosure with two narrow planks against one wall and a small rail on the other side, called "bunks." We stayed on deck as much as possible because the air was foul in the tiny closed-in room. The boat left Ha'apai in the early afternoon and rolled and tossed unmercifully hour after hour after hour. I have never ridden a bucking bronco, but I think I know what it feels like.

The roughness of that voyage was unbelievable. We had a few missionaries with us who were being transferred to Vava'u. I have heard of "green missionaries" but seldom seen any. That afternoon, however, we were all literally green from seasickness. I kept thinking that the situation would get better, but as night came on it got worse.

The waves kept crashing across the deck, making it slippery and cold. Even though the air was much better on deck, I felt that for safety's sake we should stay in our bunks. Jean tried to lie down with Gayle on the lower board. I tried to stay put on the upper one.

The rolling and jerking of the boat became so violent that we were often thrown out of our bunks and smashed against the floor and the opposite wall only a couple of feet away. I became quite alarmed, as I simply could not stay put in my bunk. I was afraid I might come crashing down on Jean and the baby if they were thrown from their bunk at the same time as I was thrown from mine.

Because of these dangers and the stuffiness of the room, we decided to brave the deck again. We cautiously went out on the deck, but when I saw how heavy the seas were I began to worry that if a large wave dashed over us, or if we slipped or were slammed against the rail unexpectedly, we might lose hold of one another or the baby. If someone went overboard, it would be all over. It seemed that all of our options were bad.

I finally decided that even with its bad smell and dank air the small room was safer. Even though we might be thrown around a lot, at least we would stay within the walls and not risk going overboard.

The best situation I could think of was for Jean and the baby to stay on the lower bunk. Then I would sit on the floor with my back against the lower bunk, and my feet braced against the opposite wall. In this way I could be somewhat stationary, and when Jean and the baby were pitched to the open side of the bunk they would roll against my back rather than be thrown out on the floor or be smashed against the opposite wall.

Jean and I, as well as the other fifteen or so passengers, were all very sick. Our baby was about the only one who didn't seem to be affected too much by the turmoil. I tried to help Jean and Gayle as much as I could, but they seemed to be doing as well as, if not better than, I was. At times I felt so weak that I worried about fainting.

The floor was hard and wet and cold and my legs and back were cramped from the constant strain and pressure on them. I had been sick for so long that I was sure there was nothing left to throw up, but my stomach kept trying. It was a long, miserable night.

Gayle clung tenaciously to Jean and was able to nurse and sleep on and off during the night. Each time I turned to make sure Jean and Gayle were all right it strained some already tense muscles. I wondered how long I could hold out. All during that long dark night we were in constant turmoil. The pitching boat, the pounding waves, and the shrieking wind tore not only at my comfort but also at my faith, as I wondered why all this was going on.

At one point during the night I turned and looked at Jean and Gayle and felt the trauma and pain they were experiencing. I wanted to get them out of this situation, but there was nothing I could do. "Why did I bring Jean and the baby? Why is this happening? If the Savior calmed the sea of Galilee, why not calm this sea?" On and on went the questions. I was hurting a lot myself, and suddenly a wave of self-pity started to enter my mind.

Right at that moment, however, another influence or feeling flooded my mind. It was as though someone were talking to me—someone who was close to me—someone I knew from somewhere. I couldn't tell who, but I knew it was a faithful woman who knew me and loved me. Her influence filled my mind in a peaceful yet firm way, and I clearly felt the message: "Do not complain. You have no right to complain. You should be grateful for the opportunity of serving the Lord—of helping to build His kingdom. No sacrifice is too great for His sake. Think of what He did for you. Don't complain. Don't even think of complaining."

These impressions filled my heart and mind. What a blessing and comfort they were! I was still terribly uncomfortable, I was still very seasick, my back and legs still hurt, the night was still as dark as ever and the sea was still as rough as ever, but for some wonderfully beautiful reason the thought of complaining entirely left me. Like a cloud of darkness, it had been chased away by an unexpected flood of goodness and light.

I don't want to overstate the situation, but the contrast was so great that I knew I had been helped by an outside force. I closed my eyes and thanked God for His goodness and help and asked for His protection as we continued our voyage. I expressed my deep appreciation for whoever had influenced my thinking so positively that frightful night.

We made it to Vava'u early the next morning. Apart from being stiff and sore and bruised and having touchy stomachs, we were all fine. As Jean stepped onto firm ground with our baby, I noticed her bright smile and her ever-cheerful attitude and I realized that she had not complained in any way.

We held our meetings with the members and the missionaries in Vava'u and eventually returned to Nuku'alofa. Upon returning to the mission office I became involved in myriad things that I felt were important. I began to forget about the feelings of that night—but never did so completely.

Years later, when I was reading some family history my sister Mary Jane and others had compiled, I came across an account of my great-grandmother Elizabeth Susan Burnett Brunt's conversion to the gospel. I had heard bits and pieces before but had not paid too much attention. Now, however, I read her story with great interest.

She was born in London and as a youth went to New Zealand, where she married and had several children. She and her husband heard the Latter-day Saint missionaries in Kaipoi, near Christchurch, around 1870 and were almost immediately converted. She had a strong testimony, but her husband was a little less ardent in his faith. As was the custom in those days, the missionaries asked them to gather to "Zion" (at that time considered to be in the western United States). Accordingly she and her husband began making arrangements to leave New Zealand for Utah.

Their efforts took many twists and turns, but from Elizabeth's point of view the plot was quite simple: since the farm did not sell right away, and since her husband's enthusiasm for immigrating to Utah was not very great, she knew she either had to go on her own or risk never making it to her Zion at all. She did everything she could to sell the farm, but was unsuccessful. She finally informed her husband that no matter what, she and the children were leaving for Zion in one year. Given this ultimatum her husband made some additional efforts to get ready, but he was not too enthusiastic or successful. Exactly one year later this determined woman took her four small children, bought passage on a steamer (via Sydney, Australia) to San Francisco, from where she would make her way to Salt Lake City. She left her husband to settle their affairs in New Zealand and follow when he could.

I pondered on the faith of that young mother with four small children heading out alone from New Zealand to her desert Zion in Utah, a place she had never seen (at least, not with her physical eyes), to be with people she had never met (at least, not that she could remember). Who knows the hardships, the trials, the discouragements she passed through?

One experience she mentioned in her journal illustrates her strength and determination. When the ship docked in Sydney the captain had her and the children stay in some makeshift accommodations on shore while they loaded the cargo bins with grain. The process took several days. She recorded that one night she was awakened just after midnight with a strong impression to go back to the ship immediately. When she arrived, the captain and crew were in the last stages of preparing to sail.

As she took the children to their quarters she heard the captain curse his luck and say, "I thought I was rid of that woman and her four squalling kids." What else she went through we may never know. Obviously she wouldn't have made it without extremely strong faith and almost superhuman effort and determination.

Then something really caught my attention. It was a brief comment that at one point on their voyage from Sydney to San Francisco they encountered extremely rough seas and she and some of the children became very ill. As I read that, the whole picture of that journey flooded into my mind. I could literally see them tossing, both physically and emotionally, on that merciless sea of turmoil. She was alone and discouraged and almost felt to complain, but as she prayed she remembered that she was a member of God's true church and was on her way to Zion. She realized that no problem was too big and no sacrifice too great as long as she achieved her goal and attained her Zion. She promised herself she would never complain, or even think of complaining, and hoped none of her posterity would either.

I was spellbound. I looked at a world map and traced the probable route of her ship. She would have been in almost exactly the same location on the same ocean as Jean and Gayle and I were in—only she was there nearly a hundred years earlier!

I was so overwhelmed with gratitude for the faith of this good woman that I didn't know what to do. I realized there really wasn't anything to do except express my appreciation and increase my determination never to complain about anything I was asked to do in the Savior's cause. I expressed those heartfelt feelings of gratitude through prayer. As I did I felt again some of the same love and peace I had felt on that turbulent ocean in Tonga those many years before.

In my mind I saw again Jean's uncomplaining smile through the night and especially as she first stepped ashore at Vava'u. It melted me to tears. It was a good feeling. As I basked in its warmth I thought I detected a faint wisp of another smile and was confident it belonged to my great-grandmother Brunt.

I have often wondered about Grandma's role in this event, as well as others, since she passed away before I was even born. Her faith was legendary. Her husband eventually came to Zion and they moved to Idaho. They had several more children before he died while working in a Montana copper mine. She raised their eight children basically on her own and then reared some of the grandchildren who had been orphaned when they were very small. I thought of her faith and her determination not to complain and wondered how that feeling got transmitted over the generations.

I thought: "Are there such things as spiritual genes? Are there pools of them that can help shape us, similar to the way physical genes do?" I didn't have an answer, but I was sure that the best thing we can do for our posterity is to be faithful ourselves. I know every person has his or her own moral agency and can accept or reject help offered them. But what a great blessing it is if the "pool" of help we have available contains much of faith and devotion and goodness. We should do our best to build as much goodness and faith as possible in our lives. Not only will it help us now but also it has the potential of being helpful to others down the stream of time. I suppose the early pioneers to the western valleys are as good an example as we know of. What a legacy of faith they left!

Largely because of the influence of my wife and of faithful progenitors, I have tried not to complain—in fact I have tried not even to think of complaining. I have not always been successful, but I keep trying.

13

Return to Niuatoputapu

How intensely I wanted to visit Niuatoputapu! I had labored there for over a year during my first mission and I was anxious to see those faithful Saints again. It was very difficult to find a boat going to Niuatoputapu, but eventually I got passage on the government boat, the *Aoniu*. Although I would have to travel eight days to spend a few hours on land, I knew it would be worth it.

The trip involved a stop in Pago Pago, Samoa. There I was able to visit with a close family friend who had recently been appointed governor of American Samoa. As soon as he heard I was in Pago Pago he sent his driver to bring me to the governor's mansion to stay overnight. The governor was most gracious. He insisted on having me eat as well as sleep in his home, and he put his driver at my disposal for anything I wanted to do.

The governor was meeting with and entertaining some high-ranking dignitaries from Washington, D.C. He introduced me to them and we visited for a while. I mostly just listened, as it seemed these government officials had a lot to say and didn't care to hear much. Mostly, however, they talked about new changes, new policies, new personalities, new positions, new dangers, new weapons, new problems, new methods of adapting to this or that change, and on and on. The tenor of the conversation was quite foreign to me, as I was used to talking about things that never change—truths that are very old, policies that are eternal, personalities and positions that are the same "yesterday, today and forever." We found some common ground, but mostly we were on different wavelengths. They were all very intelligent and very cordial (and maybe a little condescending to a young Idaho farm boy—and a "missionary," at that).

After a magnificent dinner we all retired to a special porch from which the governor said we would soon see one of the most beautiful sights in the world—the rising moon over Rainmaker Mountain. He knew the exact time. As that time approached, our conversation died down and all eyes turned towards the mountain.

It was a somewhat cloudy evening, and as the moon started to rise behind the mountain its reflection was so bright that it seemed to light up the clouds. For all the world, you would think that Rainmaker Mountain was erupting with fire. As these flame-like clouds drifted quietly away and melted into the night, the moon peeked over the mountain to see if all was clear. Seeing that it was, it came from behind the mountain and in one great burst of soft-colored glory rose resplendently into the shimmering Samoan sky.

Except for a few "Oooh's" and "Aaah's" there was breathless silence. I'm not sure you could witness a more spectacular or more beautiful physical sight. The governor seemed pleased that his mountain and his moon had put on such a good show over Pago Pago harbor for his guests.

The governor was leaving the next morning for Apia and then flying to Tonga to meet with the king. He said he would take me with him as it was certainly faster than a boat. I explained that a boat was my only way of getting to Niuatoputapu. He didn't understand why I would want to go to Niuatoputapu.

When the governor and his guests left the next morning he turned the governor's mansion (including the refrigerator, the car, and the driver) over to me until I left later that afternoon. Some of the servants questioned this, but the governor simply smiled and said, "Mr. Groberg is a returned Mormon missionary, so you have nothing to worry about." (He himself was a member of the Church, but not active.)

In the afternoon I had the driver take me to the wharf, where I boarded the boat for Niuatoputapu. What a contrast! I went from space and cleanliness and doting servants to a tiny cubicle, a deck full of grease and dirt, weird smells, and tough Tongan sailors. I felt more at home on the *Aoniu*.

Although the weather was not too good, I wasn't worried as we left on schedule. During the two days it took us to get to Niuatoputapu the weather deteriorated. By the time we got to Niuatoputapu we were into very heavy seas and extremely strong winds. We were able to get to a decent anchorage but this was still far from shore. The launches that came back and forth were having trouble fighting the waves. I jumped onto a small launch that came alongside and we headed for shore.

Our launch smashed into the on-rolling waves. All of us got soaked long before we made the calmer waters of the inner lagoon. I didn't mind. I was well acquainted with hard times on this island, so this seemed an appropriate beginning.

When we pulled up to the old wharf the chief magistrate was there along with about seventy members of the Church and dozens of nonmember friends. What a royal welcome! Emotions were hard to control. Amidst tears and hugs and expressions of love, we made our way to Vaipoa, where the members had scheduled a conference and a great feast.

As I entered the thatched chapel I took a deep nostalgic breath. I smelled again the musty odor of moldy mats, accented by the scent of thousands of fresh flowers and distinctive Tongan oils. I felt the tightness of wet clothes as I sat on the woven coconut fronds that covered the dirt floor. The mosquitoes, the muddy roads, the sound of dripping rain both in and out of the chapel—all seemed deliciously familiar.

As the meeting began, my eyes started to adjust to the semi-darkness of the chapel. I felt some unusual tugs as my heart made some adjustments as well. I looked into the kindly faces of those faithful Saints, felt the goodness of their hearts, and heard them sing, pray, and bear testimony. I was struck with the overwhelming understanding that the progress that counts eternally is not physical but spiritual. I knew afresh that God is no respecter of persons, but loves one as He does the other. I understood that neither time nor place nor circumstance is of any consequence—only goodness of heart, pureness of purpose, strength of faith, and tenderness of love. It was a good feeling.

As I expressed appreciation to the congregation for their goodness and for all they had done and continued to do, I understood a little better what Niuatoputapu had done for me: it had made things so tough that I had to find God—there was no other choice. Yet at the same time the people had been so loving, so kind, and so faithful that it was not overly difficult to find Him, for He was not far away.

I bore my testimony of these truths and of the love the Savior has for all of us. I told how I had learned much about His love and sacrifice right there among them. They knew. There were tears everywhere. My soul was filled with gratitude and renewed determination to do better and be better. I experienced such deep love for these people and for the Savior they had helped me find that for long periods of time I could not speak—I just looked at them. They were very patient. They understood.

I felt their love and faith pulling from me the very deepest emotions of my heart. I understood that as their mission president they now looked to me as their teacher or leader. They seemed to hang on every word, but as I looked into their eyes and saw their testimonies and felt their faith and absorbed their love and remembered their kindness I wondered: "Who is teaching whom?"

The realization came to me that this is part of the beauty of following God's plan and responding to the promptings of His Spirit: we teach and in turn are taught; we care for others and in turn are cared for; we love and in turn are loved; we forgive and in turn are forgiven.

I remembered the Savior pleading with us: "Be ye therefore merciful, as your Father also is merciful. Judge not, and ye shall not be judged: condemn not, and ye shall not be condemned: forgive, and ye shall be forgiven. Give, and it shall be given unto you; good measure, pressed down, and shaken together, and running over." (Luke 6:36–38.)

I expressed my love and gratitude to God for His love and goodness and for the restoration of the gospel, which contains all truth. As I finished and sat down I looked around me at the same old chapel and felt a much clearer understanding of the fact that truth does not change and is not marked by signs of physical progress. It is available wherever loving hearts honestly seek it—regardless of their physical surroundings.

Everyone basked in the spirit of the occasion as we concluded the meeting and began the magnificently prepared physical feast. We ate and visited and reminisced. I asked about those local members I had not yet seen. I was interested in everything told to me. I was pleased by how many had remained faithful and how many new ones had joined the Church over the years. I was surprised to hear of some who had joined and I was equally surprised to hear of some who hadn't yet joined. How happy I was to learn that in several of the families where we had baptized one or two, nearly everyone in the family was now a member. Many nonmembers were present. I sensed how kind and good they were, just as they had been years before when my companion, Feki, and I served there together. It was as wonderful a time as we seem to be allowed in this life. I wished Feki was there. Niuatoputapu didn't seem quite complete without him.

I contemplated the question of why so many good people had

joined the Church and why so many other good people had not. The fundamental understanding of why some people make good choices and others don't seemed to elude me. As we talked I pondered this question and realized that it is not given to us to understand other people's hearts, but it is given to us to understand our own heart—and we can do something about that.

I couldn't fully understand the hearts of those present, but I could understand the love and goodness I felt from them and for them. They made me want to be a better person and to love others more. Maybe that was part of the key to understanding their hearts. If our association with another makes us want to be a better person, that person must have a good heart. If we want to love more fully and more purely as we are around another person, there is something good in him or her.

I understood that as we move closer to the Savior—as we try to be more like Him, sincerely offer our prayers, and honestly study the scriptures—we always want to be better and love more purely and more deeply because He is so good, so loving, so kind, so forgiving. I hoped that as I associated with other people they would feel the desire to be better. I knew that I must not get angry or cause others to feel inferior or unloved or unwanted or unappreciated or of little value. I determined to try harder.

All too soon the time came to return to the boat. The weather had gotten worse and the last barge pulled by a small launch was ready to leave. I said a final good-bye and jumped on the barge.

The seas being rough even inside the lagoon, everyone on board got totally soaked. I didn't mind, as I had never really gotten dry from coming in a few hours earlier. I mainly tried to not lose my footing, which on certain jerks and bounces was a little questionable.

As we moved outside the reef the swells were enormous; we were shoved and pulled up and down and all around. Suddenly the rope from the launch pulling us back to the boat broke, and we were left careening back and forth like a helpless cork. After several tries the rope was re-secured to the boat. Within minutes it broke again. The rope was rotten and weak and there was simply too much force between the launch and the barge. Eventually two ropes were connected and we were finally brought alongside the *Aoniu*.

The trick now was to get on board. The only way was to wait for a big swell that would lift the barge partway up the side of the *Aoniu*, then jump and grab hold of the rail on the side of the boat as people on board reached out and pulled you up and in. You had to time your jump just right. If you jumped too soon or too late the barge would be too low, you wouldn't reach the rail, and you could get crushed between the barge and the boat as you fell.

Most of those around me were skilled and got aboard with what seemed like minor effort. Several were coaching me when to wait and when to jump. Finally, when one large swell lifted the barge well up the side of the *Aoniu,* they yelled, "Now! Jump! Hang on!" I jumped and caught the side rail while two strong pairs of hands from above grabbed my arms and started pulling me up.

Suddenly one of my arms slipped from the grip above, and for a second I was left dangling by one arm. Fortunately the man holding the other arm never wavered nor weakened, and almost immediately someone else grabbed my loose arm. Together they flipped me over the side and onto the deck of the *Aoniu.* I thanked those who had helped me, but they didn't feel they had done anything unusual.

Later, as I reflected about getting on the boat, I thought of the scripture: "In the mouth of two or three witnesses shall every word be established" (2 Corinthians 13:1), and in my own mind I added: "In the arms of two or three strong men, the mission president is brought on board." It may not have been as dangerous as it seemed, since everyone made it safely. Nevertheless I was not used to it, and my heart skipped a few beats at the time.

I didn't have time to panic, but for the brief moment I was dangling by one arm on the side of the *Aoniu* this unusual thought came to my mind: "I wonder what the Brethren would think if they could see me now."

It didn't matter, for I was safe. In fact it seemed strangely fitting to face hardships again on the island where I had learned so much of hardship and pain and trial and their opposites of love and peace and serenity. As I contemplated this a thought came to me: "It would please the Lord if these Saints had a new chapel." I determined to see that this would happen.

As we sailed away I watched Niuatoputapu sink lower and lower into the ocean. I felt a surge of gratitude for protection and for the trials and hardships that make life meaningful and allow blessings and happiness to be enjoyed.

As the island sank below the horizon, I found myself saying: "Thanks, Niuatoputapu. Thanks for the trials and love and faith and understanding you have provided. Were it not for them, I would not be here today. Thanks."

14

A Temple from Heaven

After being in Tonga a few months we were assigned to escort a group of about a hundred Tongan Saints to the New Zealand Temple. Normally the Saints went all the way to New Zealand by boat. This year, however, they only needed to go by boat to Fiji and could fly from Fiji to New Zealand. We met them in Fiji and held a conference there.

There was a great spirit in Fiji, where the Church was growing in numbers and in spiritual strength. The Tongan Saints stayed overnight at the chapel in Suva, where the Fiji Saints fed and cared for them. I have seldom seen such loving concern for a group of non-family members. I realized that this was part of the fruits of the gospel. Just a few generations ago Tongans and Fijians were killing one another in vicious wars; now as brothers and sisters in the gospel they were feeding and helping one another. This is an example of how the gospel can change individuals and families and will eventually change the whole world.

The next day we boarded a plane to fly to New Zealand. The airport and airline authorities kept me busy translating, as very few of the Tongans spoke English. It took a while, but eventually we got everyone on the airplane. The captain and the stewardess asked me to explain all the safety features in Tongan after they had done so in English for the other passengers. It was interesting and even amusing to see our Saints (many of them pretty large) trying to cope with seat belts, food trays, seat backs, and cramped quarters.

We finally got everyone strapped in. As the plane started to move down the runway I could see some genuine fear in the faces of the

Saints. We gathered speed, and as the plane lifted into the air it shuddered and jerked from side to side. I saw wide eyes, clenched fists, and a look of question and amazement on nearly every Tongan face.

I don't believe any of our group had been on an airplane before. They were used to storms and convulsions at sea, but this was a new experience. They didn't know what to expect, as they could not tell where the turbulence and shuddering were coming from.

I assured everyone that we were just fine and the jerks and rolls were simply part of the process of getting into the air. Suddenly we hit some major bumps and jolts as the plane began passing through a layer of storm clouds. There were a few screams—mostly from children—as well as many white knuckles and tense necks, but mostly there was a lot of praying.

It took much longer than I expected for the plane to finally escape the grasp of those buffeting clouds. We eventually pierced the final layer. The plane ceased its bouncing and shuddering and moved smoothly onward and upward into a vast canopy of brilliant blue.

An older widow was sitting by the window next to me. She had had her eyes closed and her fists clenched during the takeoff and the jolting ride through the storm clouds. During all this time her lips had been in continual motion. As the turbulent jerking ceased and the welcome sunlight warmed its way through the windows, she opened her eyes and began to look around. I sensed a feeling of wonder in her heretofore tense face, which softened, then melted into a deep smile. She gazed out the window for some time, then turned to me and asked, *"Kolipoki, 'oku tau 'i hevani koá?"* ("President Groberg, are we in heaven?") (As a young missionary I was called "Kolipoki" because they could not pronounce the other consonants in my name.)

I was going to explain about storms and clouds and airplanes and skies, but sensing her childlike faith and studying her believing eyes I replied: "Yes, we are in a part of heaven. God is here with us. He has brought us through the darkness surrounding the earth and will stay with us to His holy temple. You have nothing to fear." Her whole body filled with a knowing smile as she gently nodded her head in deep appreciation.

After several hours of flying we arrived in Auckland and were met by some faithful Tongan families who had moved to New Zealand. They helped us through Customs and Immigration and took us by bus to a chapel in downtown Auckland. There they fed us a delicious meal. "What a nice thing it is to be a Tongan," I thought. "You have instant family from other Tongans all over the world. This is like a big family reunion."

I was greatly impressed by the helpfulness of the Tongan members in New Zealand. I was also impressed with the desire of the excursion group to get to the temple. Even though there were opportunities to shop in Auckland, not a soul left the chapel until the prearranged buses arrived. We boarded the buses with great anticipation for the final leg of our journey—the several-hour ride to the temple near Hamilton. The weather was fine, and we enjoyed the beautiful green countryside of New Zealand with its rolling hills and thousands of sheep. Some of the Saints dozed a little, but everyone made the driver promise to wake them when we got close to the temple.

It was evening and very dark as we approached "Temple View." Everyone was awake now, and the anticipation among the Saints was so strong you could feel it. There was profound silence as the intensity of anticipation increased with every turn in the road. We slowed down. A mist had rolled in and now hung here and there among the hills and on the road. Finally the Tongan bus driver, who was a member of the Church, announced that after we came around the next bend in the road the temple would come into view. Every neck stretched forward and every set of eyes strained to see. As we rounded the final curve, there, on the brow of a small hill, just above the mist and bathed in brilliant light, glowed the temple with its majestic tower. It seemed to be suspended in space.

So dramatic was the sight, so great was everyone's anticipation, and so vivid was their imagination (or maybe, more accurately, so strong was their faith), that rather than hearing shouts of joy or clapping of hands at the end of the long journey I saw glistening eyes and heard muffled sobs with the reverent words: *"Malo aupito 'ae 'omai 'ae Temipale mei Hevani ma'a mautolu mo homau ngahi famili, malo, malo."* ("Thanks so much for bringing the temple from heaven for us and for our families; thank you, thank you.") They looked to me for some response.

Again I was about to say something to correct what I perceived as their misunderstanding of where the temple was physically located. But as I saw their steadfast gaze and felt their honest faith and deep devotion I thought better of it. Before I answered, I pondered: "Maybe they see things I don't see. I see a physical building that stands on firm ground. But maybe they see a spiritual building—certainly a spiritual power—which in reality is 'the temple,' for the power thereof has come down and continues each day to 'come down from heaven.'"

For a while I said nothing as I tried to see what they saw through their eyes of faith. As I did, I became convinced that through love and sacrifice and deep faith they actually saw as reality things that most of the rest of us miss. Finally I simply said: *"Mo'oni. Ko e Temipale ko e Me'a 'Ofa Mahu'inga 'a e 'Otua ma'a taua. Ta fakaha eta 'ofa he fai 'ene ngaue o a'u ki he ngata 'anga a eta mo'ui."* ("You express the truth. The temple is a most valuable gift from God for us. Let's show our love and gratitude by doing His work and obeying His will to the end of our lives.")

There were nods of affirmation, then a request to sing a song and have a prayer. No mortal can begin to explain the feelings, the sounds, the power, and the spirit that permeated that group of Saints as we covered those last few miles to the temple. Suffice it to say that we weren't in an ordinary bus with ordinary people. We were somewhere else—somewhere in space and time, encircled by the fire of faith and enveloped in a spirit that transcends things mortal and physical.

Finally the bus pulled up to the dormitory and things spiritual and things mortal came back together again as happy, smiling faces greeted us. Our hosts were dressed in white and looked like angels. (And who is to say they weren't? The Tongans knew they were.) And what did those angels see alighting from the bus? Who knows? Whatever it was, they knew it was different and special. There were very few words spoken, mostly hugs and tears and expressions of appreciation for a safe arrival and for a tremendous spirit of love and sacrifice and a desire to "be about their Father's business."

Everyone settled quietly and quickly through only a few hand signals pointing to rooms reserved for various families. When all was under control Jean and I went with President and Sister Heber Jensen to the temple president's home. They treated us very kindly. President Jensen wondered what time our group would like to start in the morning. I said they were planning on the first session at 6:00 A.M.

"They were pretty late getting in. Do you think they will be ready?"

"They will," I replied.

We set the alarm and went to bed. Even though I was physically tired, it was difficult to fall asleep. I kept seeing awestruck eyes and hearing muffled sobs, and feeling deep faith, and hearing songs from reverent choirs of angels. I sensed truths which, though understood, were too deep to be explained.

Somewhere in that element of goodness I must have drifted off to sleep, for there was no question about the reality of the jarring alarm.

After getting ready we left the president's house and started walking towards the temple. The patron housing where the Tongans stayed was to the side below the temple. The sky was not fully bright and there was a light mist hovering over the grass. Suddenly, as though by some silent signal, those faithful Tongan families, all dressed in white, came gliding through the mist, over the grass and up the hill to meet God's temple, which they fully believed had come down from heaven especially for them. As I looked I wondered, "Are their feet even touching the ground?" I wasn't sure then and still am not sure. It was a sight and a feeling beyond words.

At the temple we held a preliminary meeting in the chapel. It was breathtaking to see those beautiful Saints all arrayed in spotless white with their brown faces glowing, their dark hair shining, and their clear eyes glistening. The Spirit of God was present to overflowing. The first song was subdued by tears of joy—"'Oku Mau Fakamalo Kia Sihova" (We Thank Thee, O God, for a Prophet). Then, after a heaven-felt prayer, they burst forth with their specially written and practiced temple song, "Sound Out the Drums of Gladness." It was reverent, but very Tongan.

A group of Tongan members outside the New Zealand Temple.

The Tongans sing so beautifully and with such power that you just want to join in and be a part of it. In Tonga, singing is not a mechanical process but a feeling of the heart. Some of the deepest testimonies I have been given have come as I have been part of a congregation of Tongans boldly singing the songs of Zion, or reverently singing a sacrament hymn. My eyes have often been filled with tears and my heart filled with love and desire as the pure flow of voice, heart, and testimony combine in anthems of praise and prayer. Tongans sing with their hearts, and someway their voices follow. Harmony, color, melody, and depth come as a natural result of emotions felt. The best way to describe the sound of a well-trained Tongan choir is, "a majestic human tabernacle organ." I knew that was what we were hearing that day in the temple.

I spoke first—or at least tried to. I was about as choked up as the rest of the group. We called on several to bear their testimonies. They were so beautiful, so full of faith, that I wondered: "Maybe the temple did come down from heaven for them, as they supposed, or maybe they have taken the temple to heaven. In any event, we are there."

Eventually we gave the needed instructions, concluded the meeting, and started the sacred work of the temple. The day went wonderfully well.

During the day and over the next several days many families prepared to be sealed for time and all eternity. At this point several unusual situations became quite a concern to the temple president. There were some previous divorces, some technically illegitimate children, a few second marriages, many name changes, and a smattering of about every other type of situation that would concern a temple president. Several calls made by President Jensen to the First Presidency resulted in my receiving the assignment to make these decisions with President Jensen. We did our best, and felt that the Lord was pleased with and accepted our efforts.

For the rest of that week Jean and I spent every day with those beautiful Saints in their "temple from heaven." What a glorious week! We spent twelve, fifteen, and up to eighteen hours per day helping in teaching, baptizing, sealing, encouraging, interpreting, explaining, deciding, and so forth.

Towards the end of the week most of the questions or concerns had been resolved and the necessary understandings had been achieved. Everything began to settle into a more comfortable pattern for the temple president and the other workers. Jean and I felt we had accomplished what we were sent to do, so we should now return to our family and missionaries.

The visas for the Tongans were good for two weeks. They wanted to spend this whole time at the temple. Jean and I explained to them that we needed to leave, but they could on their own do a great amount of important work for their families and others.

We got packed and ready, but just before our car was to leave I felt a strong desire to go to the temple once more. There wasn't time to attend a session, so I quietly went alone up some stairs to a landing from where I could observe the session in progress. As I did, I remembered an experience from the first Christmas after we were married.

We had made plans to spend the holidays with Jean's folks in southern California. A few weeks before Christmas I received a call from Brother Gordon B. Hinckley. He asked me what I was doing during Christmas vacation. I told him we were planning on visiting Jean's family in southern California, and he replied in a very pleasant, somewhat teasing, yet firm manner: "You just thought you were going to California. Actually, you are going to spend the holidays in the Salt Lake Temple helping to prepare some important temple presentations in Tongan."

"I guess you're right," I replied. We had a good visit and I received my instructions.

Jean was wonderful about the change in plans and said I should do what I was asked by those in authority. Thus when the Christmas break came Jean went to California and I went to Salt Lake City to work on the temple project. I spent many long hours in the Salt Lake Temple and did a lot of memorization and other work. Elder Richard L. Evans and Brother Gordon B. Hinckley helped a lot and gave me and the others involved much good advice. The final product was sent to the New Zealand Temple to help the Tongan Saints who might be able to travel there. I enjoyed working with everyone involved in the project, especially Elder Evans and Brother Hinckley. I was not surprised when at the next general conference, in April 1958, Brother Gordon B. Hinckley was sustained as an Assistant to the Twelve.

When we finished the 1957 project there were still a few days before school started, so I made a hurried trip to Los Angeles, where I had a wonderful, though short, visit with Jean's family and other relatives. Never once did she complain that we could not be together that first Christmas.

Up to the time of the New Zealand experience I had not thought much about my participation years earlier in preparing the presentation for the use of the Tongans in the New Zealand Temple (although many from the excursion group had made comments about it). As I climbed those stairs, however, and saw a familiar face and heard a familiar voice, a quiet thrill swept over me. As the clear, beautiful sounds of Tongan were spoken in a way I could no longer speak, explaining the life-giving truths of the gospel, I was struck with a sense of amazement and gratitude that totally immobilized me. For a moment I wondered, "Where am I? Where are those words coming from? Who is saying them?" It was as though they were coming from another world. And in a sense they were.

In one brilliant flash my mind raced through all eternity and seemed to encircle all truth and all knowledge. I knew that nothing in this life really was very important except teaching and living and sharing the truths embodied in the gospel of Jesus Christ. What a vision! I understood better the great blessing of service to others. I thought of all those who had helped and who continued to help daily in temple service in Tongan and in many other languages. I thought of all those who had taught and continue to teach the gospel of Jesus Christ in Tonga and throughout the world—or throughout the universe, for that matter. I thought of the Savior, who made all this and much more possible. I could not move; I could only weep and wait and watch and listen and love and feel—feel things so deep and so eternal and so real that physical surroundings gave way to their spiritual counterpart and I knew I was in a temple "come down from heaven."

Eventually I began to sense my physical surroundings again and remembered that the car was waiting and we had to leave for the airport. As I walked back to the car I thought of Jean and her not having complained those many years ago. That brief separation had now turned into an indescribable blessing. Here we were together at the New Zealand Temple with many loving Tongan Saints. I felt closer to Jean than ever and caught just a glimpse of the majesty of her worth and eternal character. I understood that any inconvenience or sacrifice asked of any of us, if cheerfully given, is always repaid in ways we cannot begin to comprehend.

As I heard and felt unspeakable things, I knew that any effort to teach the truth, any honest testimony of Jesus borne in a proper way, any love truly given, or any "sacrifice" unselfishly made, is recorded in heaven (see D&C 62:3) and will be brought back to us with unfathomable interest at some time, in some way, and in some place. I real-

ized that this applied not only to our lives but also to the lives of all
those who are influenced or will be influenced for good by any of our
efforts. The phrase "one great eternal round" kept going through my
mind as I slowly returned to the outside world and the waiting car.

The temple president later wrote and told me of his great surprise
and joy at how faithful the Tongan group was and how much temple
work they were able to accomplish. They attended every session the
entire second week.

When I arrived back in Tonga I quickly became involved with
other mission responsibilities, and the temple experience began to
move farther from my immediate memory. Still for several nights in a
row, as I moved from waking to sleeping, I seemed to see beautiful
brown-skinned people dressed in spotless white, gliding across a car-
pet of grass, ascending through a light mist to a temple come down
from heaven to meet them. Somehow I knew it was more than a
dream.

15

Developing Missionaries

One of the interesting challenges we faced was the great number of people who wanted to serve missions. Up to now all native missionaries had served locally. Since there was a relatively small population base and a limited number of islands in the mission, we knew that we would soon reach saturation. As we prayed and pondered about this we felt certain that our assignment was not only to take the gospel to nonmembers but also to help prepare future leaders for God's kingdom. The best way we knew to do this was to see that every young man and the young women and couples who so desired could serve a meaningful mission. We knew this missionary experience would strengthen their testimonies and build a solid base from which future righteous families would spring.

As we continued to wrestle with the issue of over-supply we were led to set stricter requirements for those called to missionary service. We required that the potential missionaries have their own clothes, scriptures, and a certain amount of money before they applied. We also asked that they learn several discussions, memorize certain scriptures, have a history of activity in the Church, such as tithe paying, fasting, helping those in need, and otherwise showing a sincere desire to be a missionary. Some members of the mission council felt the requirements were too high and might discourage some from serving. For a while there was a dip in the number of new missionary applications. As soon as the standards were well understood, however, they began to be complied with, and the number of new missionaries began to rise again.

Several districts qualified one hundred percent of their young men of proper age and sent them to us for missionary service.

To establish an orderly method of integrating these waves of new missionaries we organized our own training program (something like the Missionary Training Center of today). We held a one-week session every three or four months, thus spacing the arrival of new missionaries to three or four times a year. This way we had more stability in companionships and weren't forced to make so many transfers. On a rotating basis we asked the district and branch presidents, most of whom were returned missionaries, to help teach the sessions of these missionary training meetings. They loved it and as a consequence understood better what was expected of the new missionaries and did an even better job of interviewing and preparing missionaries.

As a mission council we wanted to be sure that the members and the missionaries each understood their duties and performed them properly. We wanted to be certain that the members lived their religion fully so the new converts would be well assimilated into whatever branch they were baptized in. Over time, sacrament meeting attendance moved to the eighty percent range (and often higher). Hardly ever did a new convert become inactive. It took constant effort to maintain the high standards, but through hard work on the part of many wonderful leaders the standards were not only maintained but also raised. You could not have more faithful members nor more obedient missionaries.

Over ninety percent of our missionaries were local. I was grateful for the handful of American missionaries we had and felt they were some of the best in the world. I was delighted to help train future leaders for Utah or Idaho, but felt a special fulfillment in training future leaders for Tonga, Fiji, and Niue.

The mission council asked the members to furnish *all* the clothing, food, and housing needed for the single missionaries and wherever possible also furnish spending money for personal things such as toothpaste. Cash was difficult to come by at that time in Tonga, so each family largely "paid" for their son's or daughter's mission by housing and feeding other young missionaries. Many blessings flowed from this. As the members housed and fed and clothed the single missionaries they felt closer to them, became more a part of their activities, and furnished them with more referrals.

We also experienced few discipline problems. As the members

became more aware of who the missionaries were and what they were supposed to be doing they were more willing to help them. For example, if members saw missionaries even looking like they might do something wrong, the members immediately spoke to them, and if the elders or sisters continued in questionable actions, the members reported their concerns to me or my counselors. I remember one branch president reporting that he didn't like something he observed in his branch. I asked him what it was, and he replied: "Well, a few weeks ago Elder T . . . met a young lady in our ward. The first week he sat on the row behind her. The next week he sat on the other end of the row she was in. And last week he sat right next to her. I don't like the trend." Needless to say, a transfer was made.

At first the Church Missionary Department requested a type-written list of the names and dates of the local missionaries desiring to serve. From that list they sent each one a separate letter of call. As time went on, however, they asked for more and more information until eventually they requested the complete missionary form, including pictures, signatures, and medical forms. The local staff and leaders were as cooperative as possible, but filling out forms was difficult for them, as the basic nature of Polynesian culture relies on oral rather than written information.

Some simply still could not understand how writing things down in a foreign language on a strange form helped someone receive inspiration. To them, being right and doing right was what gave validity to their work. I remember when one faithful leader told me: "Our Father in Heaven, who is aware of each sparrow, surely doesn't check any file on us or on any of His numberless children before giving them assignments or answering their prayers. He knows us all and interacts with us according to that knowledge and not according to some printed form." I explained that God had infinite knowledge but we were still mortal and were not yet able to comprehend all things. They asked why not. I realized I was fighting a losing battle, so I just told them to fill out the forms as required and reminded them that "to obey is better than sacrifice, and to hearken than the fat of rams" (1 Samuel 15:22). They did the best they could.

Before long, some of our local elders received calls to serve in other countries. They expressed sorrow at not being able to serve in Tonga, but they were obedient, went where they were called, and served well.

We still called our own local couples according to our needs. (Later this would also be transferred to the central Missionary Department.) It should be noted that the social and economic situation in Tonga was very different then from now. At that time very few people worked for wages and nearly everyone did subsistence farming. Thus, other than missing family and friends, it didn't make a lot of difference to a young couple whether they farmed "at home" or on some distant island. Since families still generally built their own homes with the help of others, this also could be done virtually anywhere, including a small island they may be assigned to labor on. Many of these small branches had homes for missionary couples already built. I don't want to minimize the faith or sacrifice of the couples called on missions, as they did leave family and friends and spent their time in missionary rather than personal pursuits, but it wasn't too much of a problem financially.

Most of the couples called served in a branch calling—in the husband's case, usually as branch president. While on their mission they diligently studied the gospel and taught and fellowshipped investigators and the few less-actives there were. They always returned home full of the Spirit and much better founded in the gospel.

The calling of local couples was one of the most tender and inspirational things I did. I remember once being in Ha'apai and observing a fairly young couple with two small children who participated happily and enthusiastically in the conference. I felt impressed to talk to them about going on a mission and having the husband serve as a branch president in some small, struggling area.

When I called them in they were all prepared to go, having received the same witness of the Spirit that I had felt. The wife looked to be close to her time to deliver their third child. I asked when the due date was and they said in about three weeks. I suggested that they report to the mission office in two months so they could get the new one here and the wife could get some of her strength back.

I was surprised when just a little over a month later my secretary said that Brother and Sister Taani were there from Ha'apai ready to start their mission and receive their first assignment. I called them in. She had obviously had the baby. I told them I hadn't expected them for another month and asked if everything was all right. They smiled and said: "Oh, yes, everything is just fine. Our baby came a few days early but only lived one day. We buried him under the big tree in our front yard. It was a beautiful service."

I replied: "I'm sorry to hear that. Maybe under the circumstances we should postpone your mission call for a while."

They looked up almost in shock. "Oh no, President. Naturally we were sad to lose our baby son, but were grateful to have this mission call to look forward to. We know he is in the celestial kingdom, and we want to get on with our mission immediately so we can better prepare ourselves to be with him one day. Please let us start now."

I have seldom felt such honest, childlike faith. I felt impressed to set them apart right then and there. As I did I had the unmistakable feeling that another spirit was participating and approving of all that was done. There were muffled sobs and tears of joy as blessings were given and received.

As I said "amen," a strong impression came to me and I knew exactly where they should be assigned. We all sat quietly for a few moments as we wiped away tears and gained our composure. Finally I spoke: "You are a special family. The Lord has rewarded you and will continue to reward you for your faith. Be assured that you do not go on this mission alone. I am now ready to give you your assignment as to where you ought to serve."

Before I could say any more they both looked at me and said, "We are happy to go to Matuku and stay as long as you say. Do you have any other instructions?"

I tried to not act surprised. Matuku was exactly the place that had come to my mind as I concluded the setting apart. Even though I had not yet told them where they would serve, I perceived that it had been put in their minds at the same time it had come to mine. I looked at them in wonder. Yes, Matuku, I thought. Not only a place to live and serve but a place for a faithful family to continue to demonstrate their love for the Lord by serving others and thus moving ever closer to their goal of the celestial kingdom. "No," I said, "I have no other instructions except to remain faithful and humble and work hard and be obedient." They said they would.

As they left I closed the door and fell immediately to my knees, thanking the Lord for such faith and for allowing me to be a tiny participant therein. I thanked Him for giving me this extra confirmation that the original inspiration to extend the call as well as all the events that followed were indeed from Him. I was grateful to know that He sanctioned our efforts and that He blessed in such marvelous ways those who obediently responded to such calls.

I watched this couple carefully during their mission. They served wonderfully. When their two years were finished they returned home with a new baby boy—happy and fulfilled and well on their way to their goal. I wish we could all have such faith in the Lord and such great love for Him. I wonder at times if faith in Him and love for Him aren't really the same thing.

I often think of this wonderful couple and hundreds of others like them. I also think of the single missionaries and their families. As I do I feel to exclaim: "God bless you and your family forever." And He has, and He does, and He will. I know that for sure.

16

Niue

Niue is a relatively small island located east of Tonga about halfway to the Cook Islands. It was the third area of our mission. The only way to get there was on the *Tofua*, a ship from New Zealand that made a monthly circuit through the islands. It took over a week of travel in order to spend about six hours on Niue. Niue has its own language, which is about halfway between Samoan and Tongan but is substantially different from either. Niue (which earlier had been named the Savage Island because of problems some early European sailors had there) was governed by New Zealand as a mandated territory.

After Feki Po'uha, my former missionary companion, had finished his mission in Tonga, he went to Hawaii to help build the Church College of Hawaii, the Polynesian Cultural Center, and several chapels. He married a girl from Niue and they had a young family. They were now living in Niue, and Feki was serving as the district president there.

What a joy it was to see Feki and his family waiting at the wharf when we arrived on our first visit to Niue. His smile was as broad and wonderful and sincere as ever. One of life's greatest thrills is to meet old friends, especially when they have continued active in the gospel. It had been nearly eleven years since Feki and I had seen each other. I think I know a little how Alma felt when he was reunited with the faithful sons of Mosiah (see Alma 17:1–2).

Feki and his wife, Foli.

We spent a busy six hours learning about Niue and the Church situation there. At that time we had six branches, several hundred members, one large chapel, several smaller chapels, and eight missionaries. We drove completely around the island, met with many of the members, interviewed all of the missionaries, and still had time to reminisce with Feki about many past experiences. What a glorious and fulfilling visit we had in that distant part of the mission! I was impressed with the members and the missionaries. Even though they were far from mission headquarters, I felt comforted that they were in Feki's capable hands.

When Elder S. Dilworth Young toured our mission he wanted to visit Niue. We boarded the *Tofua* in Samoa for Niue. Unfortunately the weather turned bad at Niue and, because of the risks involved, the captain would not allow passengers to go ashore. We stood on the deck and looked across the span of churning ocean to the island. We could see a large group of Saints gathered on the hill behind the wharf

dressed in their "Sunday best," ready to welcome a General Authority
to their island, anxious to feast upon his inspired counsel. They had
prepared a feast of their best food to show their love and appreciation.

We pleaded with the captain, but he would not relent. He felt it
was too dangerous for passengers to get into the wildly bouncing
launches that went between the ship and the wharf. He allowed
launches from shore to come alongside and load and unload mail and
cargo. It was a great disappointment.

I asked one of the men working on a launch to ask Feki to come
to the ship. Within half an hour Feki came, with his huge smile and
pleasant manner.

We visited for nearly an hour. Elder Young gave him some wonderful counsel and advice. I learned a great deal from it also. When the
boat was ready to sail on to Vava'u it was hard to say good-bye to Feki.
We were grateful, however, that he was able to take our love and Elder
Young's love, instructions, and teachings back to the Saints on Niue.

17

A New King

The new year (1967) brought the end of the official mourning period for Queen Salote, who had passed away in December of 1965. Although many continued mourning, plans and preparations could now begin for the coronation of the new king. The official coronation was announced for July 4, the king's birthday.

The king and queen left for England to get the proper red velvet and ermine robes and have their royal crowns fitted, and so forth. Jean and I received a special engraved invitation to attend the actual coronation as well as all of the related ceremonies and celebrations. The "Official Dress" prescribed for the "Gentlemen Invitees" was listed as "Uniform or Morning dress." I had never heard of a "morning suit" but felt no concern, as to me my "uniform" was a regular missionary suit.

As the time of the coronation drew nearer it seemed that everyone in Tonga was getting into the spirit of this huge once-in-a-lifetime event. After all, it had been nearly fifty years since the previous coronation, and the new king was still relatively young, so who knew how many years it would be until the next one?

A few days before the coronation we found out that I must have a true "morning suit" in order to be admitted. A regular suit was unacceptable. A morning suit consisted of a top hat, a special pair of gray pants, and a certain type of gray pin-striped jacket with tails. I checked everywhere I knew and there simply were none available in Tonga. I appealed to the person in charge of allowing the guests in. While he was understanding, his instructions were clear and he felt he could make no exceptions.

I was in a real quandary. I knew how much it meant to the members of the Church to have "their" mission president participate in the actual coronation ceremony. Yet I also knew I could not go unless some miracle happened. I had visited the king and queen soon after our arrival in Tonga, mainly to officially let them know I was back in Tonga. (They already knew, as very little escapes their attention.) I now wondered about talking to them directly, but I decided that would not be proper.

Then, just three days before the coronation, I heard that a group of Tongan members of the Church from New Zealand had chartered a plane to come to Tonga for the coronation. I quickly called the mission president in New Zealand. He got in touch with Percy Harris, one of the men who had been so helpful with our recent temple group. When he understood what the situation was he just said, "Leave it to me." I gave him my measurements.

The next day the chartered plane from New Zealand arrived. Percy had brought what must have been the last morning suit in New Zealand. It fit perfectly. What he had done to get it I'll never know, but he did it. I know it took lots of faith and prayers but it also took a lot of work on Percy's part.

I immediately went to the Secretary in charge and told him to leave my name on the list for the coronation ceremony. He was amazed and wondered how I could have gotten the suit. When I explained what had happened he looked at me with an unbelieving gaze and said, "Wow, what kind of a church do you belong to, anyway?" I took a few moments and told him "what kind."

What an experience—to almost miss the coronation and thus disappoint so many wonderful Saints through carelessness in not having the proper dress! It was a good reminder that carelessness could cause us to be left out of a vitally important event. The five foolish virgins in the New Testament parable appear to be careless, which caused them to miss the wedding feast. I wondered how we might feel someday, when invited to special events in eternity, if we could not attend because of carelessness or inattention. It would be terrible if because of apathy or procrastination we were not properly clothed. I determined to be more careful about proper preparation.

The coronation day arrived. I donned the famous morning suit and top hat, Jean wore formal dress, and we went to the ceremony. Many members were waiting in the crowds outside the walls of the palace grounds. As we walked to the gate and presented our card we

*President and Sister Groberg ready for
the coronation ceremony.*

could see many of them pointing and whispering: "That's our president and his wife. They are friends of the king and queen. They have a front row seat." How glad I was that my oversight had been corrected—mostly by the faith and hard work of others.

The coronation was held in the small private chapel of the royal family that is on the grounds next to the palace. The Royal Chapel was of Victorian architecture and matched the palace. The interior was lined with exquisitely carved woodwork. The whole chapel had been beautifully refurbished for this auspicious occasion. The relatively small size of the chapel severely limited the number of people who were able to attend the actual coronation, and we found that our reserved seats were indeed "front and center."

The coronation itself was a lovely religious ceremony conducted by a leading Methodist minister. I don't know where they got the exact ceremony, but the Bible was used liberally and many phrases sounded familiar to me. The Tongan words were beautiful and meaningful. If lived up to they would make any king a wonderful ruler.

During the ceremony everyone was very reverent and quiet, including the crowds outside. However, when the crowns were placed on the heads of the king and queen and the last "amen" was said, a designated person opened the back door of the chapel and announced that a new king had been crowned. Immediately the whole island erupted in cheering and shouting and singing praises. Cannons went off; older women and men as well as others danced with wild abandon; and a scene of joy and happiness ensued.

We emerged from the small chapel into a sea of smiles and almost unbelievable exuberance. When all the special guests were seated in their designated places on the palace front lawn, the main doors of the chapel opened. With the royal crown on his head and ermine-bordered, red velvet robes trailing from his massive shoulders, His Majesty King Taufa'ahau Tupou IV stood before his loyal subjects. Then, descending the red carpeted stairs he stepped onto the royal pathway of tapa cloth held in place by Tongan women seated respectfully along both sides. Queen Halaevalu Mata'aho, in equally royal attire, and their four children followed after the new king as they moved regally to the veranda of the palace. There they stood and waved to everyone as literally miles of schoolchildren paraded by, all in their respective school uniforms, waving and shouting *"Tue! Tue!"* (Hail! Hail!) to their new king.

The lid that had been put on merrymaking for the past year and a half had finally come off, and as it did it blew sky high. For hours, group after group of villages or churches or businesses came by with their offerings of food, cloth, money, kava, tapa, and many other gifts. It was truly a national celebration.

Jean and I milled around the palace grounds mingling with ambassadors, generals, admirals, governors, prime ministers, leaders of other churches, and heads of state from all over the world. I was surprised at the number of dignitaries there who turned out to be Latter-day Saints. I was also concerned when some of them turned out to not be as strong as I had hoped, at least as far as the Word of Wisdom was concerned.

It was fascinating to see and hear the massive numbers of schoolchildren, as well as entire villages, colorfully costumed alike, the children dancing and singing in perfect unity and harmony.

National Geographic magazine had a crew there capturing all the events of the coronation in beautiful color for their March 1968 issue. They did an excellent job of recording the scope and grandeur of the celebration.

*Newly crowned King Taufa'ahau Tupou IV leaving the coronation
(the royal palace is in the background).*

Later we drove to the king's summer palace. The villages along the way had constructed large gateways of beautiful flowers and intricate designs for the king to drive under. The roads through the villages were carpeted with thousands of yards of new tapa cloth. For the past several months we had awakened to the hauntingly beautiful tap-tap-tap of this bark-based cloth being made.

Warships had been sent from many nations in honor of the occasion. They seemed to fill the harbor of the Friendly Islands as they nestled together. The evening of coronation day, thousands of school-children participated in the ancient *Tupakapakanava* ceremony. They lined the entire length of beach on the Nuku'alofa shore and on the small islets in the harbor. At a given signal they all lit torches that burned for hours, outlining the islands with a shimmering glow against the night sky. The weather was calm, the sea like glass. It reflected the torches, and the warships ablaze with lights strung all about their masts and decks. This calm scene of striking beauty was punctuated with a gigantic fireworks display, shot forth in a coordinated effort from the visiting warships. The fireworks were spectacular enough as they burst overhead, but when combined with the reflection in the calm sea and the beauty of the torches lining the entire shoreline, it was truly a once-in-a-lifetime sight.

The next few days were as a country gone wild in the delirium of joy—for they now had a new king! I wondered about the rejoicing that will take place when our heavenly King comes to reign on earth.

The gifts given the royal couple were amazing by any standard. And what great feasting took place! It was estimated that thirty thousand pigs met their fate on the feasting tables. The mission Relief Society officers, with Jean's help, had made a beautiful quilt for the queen. It had a replica of the royal crown quilted in the center. Toward the end of the celebrations Jean and I and the mission Relief Society officers presented the quilt to the queen at the palace. She was most gracious and expressed her sincere appreciation and her willingness to help Jean and the Relief Society in any way she could.

The mission council had previously shown their support and respect by making a formal presentation of a huge pig and a large kava plant to the king. He was appreciative.

Jean and I were happy to have been able to represent the Church. The Saints were delighted to be able to tell their friends and neighbors, "Our president and his wife were in the very room with the king when he was crowned." We attended all of the major coronation events and felt that the Church was thus recognized in a way that put the past behind everyone and opened new relationships and new opportunities for us and for all of Tonga.

18

Relationship with Headquarters

Our relationship with headquarters in Salt Lake City was quite simple. I reported to a member of the Quorum of the Twelve, designated as my "first contact." During the first half of my mission that was Elder Thomas S. Monson. During the second half it was Elder Howard W. Hunter. I was given a mission budget for the normal operating costs of the mission, but any large or unusual expenses, such as a new chapel, went through this first contact, who got the needed approvals.

Once a year we were invited to attend a mission presidents training seminar for the mission presidents in the Pacific, which was conducted by our first contact. We met in a central location, such as New Zealand, for a few days of instruction and inspiration. In addition, once a year a General Authority came from Salt Lake City and spent a week or so with us. During this time he would go to most parts of the mission and meet with the members and missionaries. We called this a mission tour.

Since we had no stakes in our mission, all administrative decisions regarding members and missionaries were left to me. Anything outside our mission, such as a group going to the temple in New Zealand, required approval from our first contact.

Our communication with Salt Lake City was almost exclusively by mail. There was one plane per week to and from Tonga, so if all the connections went right we could receive an answer to a letter in three to four weeks. If there was an emergency we could use the telegram or even telephone Salt Lake City from Fiji.

The only Church materials we had translated in the Tongan language were the scriptures and a few missionary tracts. Consequently we called several local people to form a translation committee. They were some of the hardest workers I have ever seen. They came faithfully to the mission office several nights a week and translated lessons for the priesthood, Relief Society, Sunday School, Primary, Mutual, and so forth. This was done on a Church service basis with no pay.

Since we didn't have the time or capability to translate many lessons we chose a few of the most appropriate lessons from some older English-language manuals and designated specific chapters of scripture for the other lessons. As far as I was concerned, the best lessons came from the scriptures, but our translation committee members were so humble and faithful and prayerful that the lessons they translated were very good.

After they translated a lesson, copies were made to distribute to the various branches. The copies were run on our Gestetner machine (like a ditto copier). The quality of paper was marginal, the printing was rather poor, and the typing errors were many, but the spirit of sacrifice that accompanied those lessons hallowed them. I never heard a complaint about them. People overlooked the mistakes and poor printing quality and felt the love and sacrifice of their friends who had put forth so much effort to get the lessons to them.

Since we didn't have as many experienced members in Fiji and Niue as in Tonga, we didn't have translation committees there. They did the best they could with the English manuals.

Communication was often late or uncertain. For instance, once we received a letter from Salt Lake City asking us to go to Christchurch, New Zealand, for a seminar for all mission presidents and their wives from Australia, New Zealand, and the islands. Even though it was written six weeks earlier, by the time we received it we had only a few days to get to New Zealand. We learned to keep our schedules very flexible.

The seminars for mission presidents were inspirational and helpful. After them, Jean and I felt we understood better what was expected of us, but more than that, we felt we had friends who knew what we were talking about and understood our concerns.

Elder S. Dilworth Young and his wife, Hulda, were assigned from Church headquarters to tour our mission after finishing a similar tour in Samoa. He asked me to meet him in Samoa at the end of his tour there and we would begin the tour of the Tongan mission by taking the boat from Samoa to Niue, Vava'u, and Nuku'alofa. Jean and I flew to Samoa on the designated day. When we arrived Jean stayed in Apia with Sister Young. I went with some Samoan elders who drove me to a meeting where six zone leaders from Samoa were scheduled to meet with Elder Young.

We arrived at the chapel shortly before Elder Young and the Samoa Mission president did. As they entered the room I stood at attention with the Samoan zone leaders. Elder Young went around the circle, shook hands with each one and asked us to give our name and where we were laboring. I was the last in line. When he came to me I responded, "I am Elder Groberg and I am laboring in Tonga."

"What are you doing out of your mission?" he shot back.

"You asked me to meet you here," I replied.

"Why would I do that?"

"Well, you were going to tour our mission."

"Then where is your mission president?"

"I am the mission president."

"How do I know that? You are far too young. Do you have any proof?"

By now I was really sweating. We didn't wear name tags in those days, and my wallet and passport were back in town with Jean. I couldn't figure out what to say next. I looked imploringly at the Samoa Mission president, who finally let the ruse out with a stifled smile. When I realized the joke I finally relaxed and smiled, as did Elder Young. But he really "had me" for a while.

Jean and I instantly loved Elder and Sister Young. Elder Young had an endless supply of stories to tell. We were willing listeners and he always seemed to have the ability to lead me on right to the last minute.

One night as we were sailing, Elder Young said he had always wanted to see the Southern Cross in the night sky, but was not sure which stars formed it. I suggested that we ask the ship's captain. The captain came out on the deck and not only pointed out the Southern Cross but also gave us a fascinating personal tour of many of the constellations in the night sky of the Southern Hemisphere. Brother Young often referred to that beautiful night on the South Pacific ocean when a courteous ship's captain pointed out the Southern Cross. He made wonderful applications to the heavens and the stars and God's sure hand in guiding us if we will but follow the proper "stars."

After the disappointment of not being able to go ashore at Niue,

President S. Dilworth Young (center) with Tongan Boy Scouts.

we finally arrived in Vavaʻu. What a reception we received there! The
wharf was lined with schoolchildren dressed in their crisp green and
white uniforms, singing "We Thank Thee, O God, for a Prophet" to
the accompaniment of a wonderful brass band. Not only the Youngs
but also the passengers and crew on the ship were overcome by the
magnitude of the outpouring of love as well as the smiles and laughter
of those beautiful Tongan children.

Elder Young turned to me and asked if other General Authorities
had ever participated in something like this. I told him a few had. He
said, "I have often heard of the deep love President McKay has for
Tonga, and now I can see why."

We sailed on to Tonga; after a few days there we flew to Fiji and
finished the mission tour. Elder Young's parting suggestion was: "Keep
on doing whatever you are doing now."

Our visitors from Salt Lake City were limited in number, but we
appreciated all those who made the extra effort to get to Tonga. There
was a nice hotel in Nukuʻalofa where guests who came could stay. The
mission home was full to overflowing with our family, but we hosted
visitors for meals at the mission home with our family.

Tonga was still "out of the way" and thus we were mostly left
alone. On balance I suppose that was a blessing. We always knew we
could receive help from our first contact in Salt Lake City if we needed
it. We also realized that Tonga was as close to heaven as Salt Lake City
was.

19

The Lord's Purposes
Made Known

During the first part of our mission I kept myself very busy doing the things that *obviously* needed to be done. Because of this I likely did not spend enough time planning and contemplating the things that *really* needed to be done. I was working hard and putting forth great effort, but for some reason after many months I felt uneasy. It was as though something was missing—something very important, something without which the full progress God desired for the mission could not be realized.

I puzzled over this uneasy, partially vacant feeling. I sought answers in fasting and prayer, but to no avail—at least not for some time. As I persisted, however, I found myself spending more and more time reading, studying, pondering, and praying over the scriptures. The uneasy feeling began to slowly recede. The time spent reading and pondering the scriptures was like taking a voyage to a beautiful land. I remembered with fondness and anticipation the peaceful truths I had previously learned. I wanted to learn even more. I had a great desire to quietly and reverently and without pressure "feast upon the words of Christ," for I knew that they surely would "tell [me] all things" I should do (see 2 Nephi 32:3).

Each day I asked the staff not to disturb me for a period of time. To begin with it was half an hour, then one hour, then two hours, often more. I learned so much and received such direction and insight on how the Lord wanted to move the work forward that for the rest of my mission I seldom spent less than an hour a day with the scriptures, and often much, much more. Many years after my mission I heard of a statement attributed to Martin Luther in which he purportedly told his aides: "I have so much to do today, I must spend an extra hour in scripture study and prayer. See that I am not disturbed." I can certainly relate to the feeling and testify to the efficacy of that principle. I continued to hold regular meetings, attend conferences, conduct interviews, and travel as needed. Now, however, these things seemed more effective. I also noticed that much more of importance seemed to get done in the same amount of time.

Often my study time was in the afternoon when others were resting. One afternoon near the end of 1967 a strong impression, seemingly unrelated to what I was reading, came into my mind. The impression was that I should remember something I had previously been told and do something about it. I couldn't remember anything. I tried to dismiss the feeling and go back to scripture reading, but the impression was strong and persistent. I struggled for a while. Then suddenly I remembered sitting in the Twenty-sixth Ward bishop's office in Idaho Falls and hearing the words: "You will go to Tonga and there preside over a fiftieth anniversary celebration. You will receive further instructions." The remembrance was so real and so vivid that it startled me. I became quite concerned, for I realized I was now serving as mission president in Tonga and to this point I hadn't even thought about a jubilee celebration, let alone done anything about one.

From that moment on, the thought of holding some sort of a jubilee celebration never left my mind. I began asking everyone about their recollections of what happened in Tonga fifty or so years ago. I wrote to the Church Historian's office in Salt Lake City. They sent me what brief historical entries they had about the early days of the Tongan Mission. At first it was very confusing to me. It appeared that the work in Tonga had started sixty-four years earlier with missionaries coming under the direction of the mission president in Samoa. The Tongan Mission had been started . . . then stopped . . . then started again . . . then almost stopped again . . . then miraculously continued through what might have appeared to be an oversight. At times laws had been passed against the Church, but through divine providence they were not enforced and were eventually repealed.

As I studied the maze of events that had brought the Church to where it now was in Tonga, I became increasingly fascinated. I sent letters to the families of the former mission presidents and asked them for pictures, along with any other information they might wish to share with me. The more information I received, the more clearly I could see the hand of the Lord guiding and directing the course of the Church in Tonga over those years.

I visited with older men and women, both members and non-members. They shared some of the most faith-promoting incidents I have ever heard. Few things have strengthened my testimony more than reading and studying and talking to others about the course of the Church in Tonga.

The time had arrived to celebrate all that had happened thus far in Tonga. It was to be a jubilee to honor the faith and diligence of many wonderful Saints over many years. It was also to help strengthen the faith of the current members and to openly acknowledge, to members and nonmembers alike, God's hand among His covenant people in the island kingdom of Tonga.

I now had a general idea for a jubilee celebration but wasn't sure about the specifics. Then one day an office elder, while doing some cleaning in a musty back room, found a box containing some old letters and files. He asked what he should do with it. Normally I left those decisions to the office elders, but I felt different about this. I told him to bring the box to my office, where I would look at the contents and decide.

When the old box was put on my desk, it seemed that it ought to be burned or thrown away. Water had seeped onto the box from somewhere, causing considerable rot and an offensive musty smell. Nevertheless I started looking through the box. After the first few water-ruined files I found a veritable treasure trove of letters in perfect condition. In chronological order dating from the early 1900s to the late 1930s I found correspondence between the First Presidency and several mission presidents in Tonga. Many of the letters were from the Church Presidents personally. A shudder of excitement and anticipation ran through my mind and body as I began to read. I was sure I would find information from these letters that would give me clearer direction on the jubilee.

Once I began reading those marvelous historic letters I could not stop. I read and read, hardly wanting to eat or sleep or do anything else. Among the letters were numerous requests for money to build wooden living quarters or chapels. Usually the requests were granted, at least partially. I remember one letter from President Joseph F. Smith saying that the request for a thousand dollars to build a chapel was more than they could send, but he was sending eight hundred dollars and felt that in some way the mission president could make that do and maybe get a few more local donations.

I was touched by a personal letter from President Heber J. Grant wherein he told of a widow from western Wyoming coming to visit him. She told him her son had been in Tonga for nearly four years, and during all this time the neighbors had been good to help her get the crops in, but now she wondered if it would be all right to have her boy come home and help with the harvest in the coming fall.

President Grant wrote the mission president and said in essence: "I realize that years of service alone is not reason to conclude a mission and I don't want to tell you what to do, but I was touched by Widow J . . .'s visit and request. If you feel all right about it, you might consider releasing Elder J . . . from his mission so he could help his mother get the crops in this fall." The mission president noted on the letter that Elder J . . . was released right away and returned home in time to help his widowed mother with the crops.

There were dozens of such exchanges, some very faith-promoting, some rather sad. Some letters told of missionaries who had died of typhoid fever and were buried in Tonga, and some told of missionaries who had been sent home because of moral problems. I was often brought to tears by the feeling of love and personal concern conveyed by the prophet. I sensed how, like the Savior, the prophet truly cared for each person involved.

Some of the most fascinating exchanges resulted from letters sent by mission presidents to the First Presidency telling about their personal struggles. One such letter from the 1920s contained the sentence, "Even though we have several hundred members in Tonga, I'm not sure there are even ten who would have the faith to cross the plains." (I thought: "This letter was probably written in a 'down moment'; how happy I am that I felt impressed not to send the letter to the First Presidency that I wrote several months ago.") A reply from the First Presidency came saying that, if the situation was that bad, maybe the mission should be closed again and Tongan Church affairs transferred to Samoa. It said they would send further instructions as well as steamship tickets for the mission president and his wife to return to the States in the near future.

From some handwritten notes it was obvious the mission president didn't know what to do about that response. He called some of the faithful Saints and they fasted and prayed. He then sent a more encouraging letter. Several months later he noted on his copy of the first response. "Tickets and Instructions never arrived—Tongan Mission saved."

I was fascinated by everything I was learning and all the relationships I was seeing, but I still could not put my finger on just what event we were to celebrate or how or when. To me a jubilee connoted fifty years from some event; at least, that is what I understood from the scriptures. Nothing I had read so far seemed to quite fit. Then one day it happened.

A letter arrived from the widow of the first full-time mission president in Tonga. The handwriting was shaky, but in essence she said: "I am sending a picture of my husband and me as you requested. Also I felt impressed to send you some of my husband's writings along with some of my own recollections of the very early days of the Tongan Mission."

I could almost feel my fingers tingle as I started reading the enclosed sheets. There were some discouraging entries telling of problems and concerns—of deaths of elders through disease and illness and of unfaithfulness of missionaries and members alike. There was a vivid description of a serious epidemic sweeping Tonga then, which was moving the native population towards extinction. The members didn't seem to be spared, and the mission president wondered if he should visit the sick members and thus expose himself and his family to the deadly diseases. He wrote about the local people being afraid even to bury their own dead, and of the government hiring hardened sailors from passing foreign ships to dig graves and bury the dead.

Most of the entries were very depressing. He mentioned that the First Presidency had told him to use his own judgment, to pray diligently and do what he felt best even if that meant leaving and "waiting for another time when the situation may be better and the Tongans may be more receptive."

Then I came to some writings telling about events in November 1918. As I began to read this section my eyes started to cloud over, my arms began to tremble, and my whole body started to shake. This faithful man in effect said: "I feel that if the Church is to move forward in Tonga, we must not fear death nor disease nor opposition. Accordingly I am calling the first all-mission conference for November 1918. The faithful will come regardless of the problems."

He then gave a brief report of the conference, which for some reason had not been mentioned (or at least I had not noticed it) in any of the histories I had seen thus far. In summary the report said: "What a marvelous conference. It would be hard to feel a greater spirit than we had. The Saints from all over the islands came together

and bore testimony to one another and listened to me. Some said if
they were going to die they would like to die together. But the Spirit of
prophecy fell on me and I told them that neither they nor the Church
would die here, but rather grow and become a strength in many
ways." He then noted that he felt this conference was the real beginning of the Tongan Mission. He wrote of the love and the faith of the
local members (you could feel his own love and faith). He said that
even though he knew there would be more trials ahead, he had the assurance that things would eventually work out and the Church in
Tonga would become a powerful influence for good among many.

It was almost as though I was with him and the Saints in November of 1918. Their faith seemed like a fire glowing through eternity. I
said out loud: "Yes. And there will be another conference, a golden jubilee, fifty years later in November 1968. You and all the faithful
Tongans will see that your faith and efforts have been justified and
your sacrifices have been accepted. The rock cut out of the mountain
without hands which you so nobly gave your all to has rolled forth
and become a powerful influence for good in Tonga (as well as in
many other lands). Your faith will be remembered and sanctified and
passed on in purity to the next generation!"

I could hardly contain myself. I literally shouted for joy. I wanted
to tell my counselors and the missionaries and everyone; in fact, I
wanted to tell the whole world! I ran and found Jean and told her the
great news. I called my counselors, the mission council, all the missionary leaders, and many others to a special meeting to tell them of
this miraculous discovery. They gathered and listened with great anticipation. When it was all explained they were as excited as I was, if not
more so. I knew the jubilee could not fail.

Accordingly, we set November 1968 as the date for the Fiftieth
Anniversary Golden Jubilee Celebration to commemorate the beginning of the Tongan Mission as represented by that original conference
of faith. We decided the jubilee should be a missionary conference.
We would have feasting, dancing, and conference sessions, but our
main emphasis would be on missionary work.

As we met and excitedly discussed the prospects for the conference another thought entered many of our minds at the same time. I
knew exactly what several others were thinking, but they were too respectful to say anything and silently waited for me to be mouth for
what we all felt. I looked at each one and quietly started speaking:
"We have nearly a year to plan and prepare for this divinely inspired
jubilee event. Do you believe the Lord would allow a stake of Zion to

be standing in Tonga by November 1968?" Every heart seemed to skip
a beat at that thought: A stake! A real stake of Zion! Maybe . . . Yes. Of
course. Why not? We can do it if the Lord wants it—and we think He
does.

You have never seen a happier or more enthusiastic group of men
and women than those faithful leaders who left my office that evening.
I stayed behind to be alone for a while and to thank God for making
His will known so clearly. I also thanked Him for giving me some initial preparation and then reminding me to think about this momentous jubilee to which we now so eagerly looked forward.

Committees were formed and began working. We divided everything up among many anxious and available hands: programs, food,
invitations, dances, announcements, official protocol, and on and on.

Over the next few months miracle after miracle occurred. Doors
formerly closed were opened and things previously unknown came to
light. Several "old members" were found who either had memories of
that original conference in 1918 or had heard about it from their parents or grandparents. An unstoppable outpouring of the Spirit occurred as person after person came forth and volunteered to help in
unusual and important ways. Soon every detail began to fall into place.

I wrote to Elder Monson and told him what we were planning.
Our thought was to have this jubilee for Tonga, and we did not antici-
pate outside help or attendance. The only thing I asked for was to
have Ermel J. Morton (former missionary, translator, and school prin-
cipal in Tonga) come to Tonga and write a short history of the Tongan
Mission. I was deeply grateful to the Lord for guiding me through
enough history to establish the right time and the right event for our
jubilee, but I felt it best to turn the actual compiling and writing over
to others. To our delight this request was approved.

We contacted the king and queen and got a commitment from
them to attend our celebration on 28 November 1968. Things began
to move rapidly. The committee met every week and heard reports
and coordinated activities. Of course, we had to keep everything else
going, such as proselyting, district conferences, interviewing, training
members and leaders, building chapels, keeping the schools running,
and spending time with our families. It was rather easy to mesh all of
these things together, for each of our children, along with everyone
else in Tonga, was caught up in the enthusiasm of this greatly anticipated event and wanted to do all they could to help. The Lord had
made His will known. We had received further instruction. We were
now on our way.

20

The Fire of Faith

In preparation for the jubilee we invited Church members who so desired to share with the mission presidency and the mission council stories of faith from their heritage. Many came. These accounts were never given in a boastful or elaborate way but always in a quiet, simple manner, merely stating the facts and the outcome, much like the stories of faith found in the scriptures. Selected examples were shared with the general membership at district conferences and other meetings so that all might know of the sacrifice and faith upon which our present blessings were based. I knew how difficult it was to be a member even ten years before this, so I could appreciate how difficult it must have been two or three decades before that. The following experience is representative of the many examples of faith during those early years of the Church in Tonga.

Tonga[1] came from a religious family. His father was a part-time preacher in their local church, and, as most Tongans did, Tonga went to church each Sunday. One day some Mormon missionaries came to his village. His father invited them to visit in his home. When the missionaries told about their belief in modern prophets and additional latter-day scripture, the father became angry, ceased to listen, and refused to allow them in his home again. He warned his family against "those Mormons," and specifically forbade Tonga to ever be in the same house with them.

---

1. This man's story has been previously published using the name "Finau," which name he used at one time. In Tongan, the word *Tonga* means "south." Also it is the name of the country and is a common name for a person.

A seed had been planted, however. "If there were prophets and scriptures to guide the people in former days, why not today?" Tonga wondered.

He knew he could not hear more about these concepts and this religion at home, so he followed the elders and found what homes they were visiting and when their meetings were scheduled. He told the missionaries of his dilemma of not being able to be in the same house with them. He asked them to sit close to the door and speak loudly so he could sit outside in the shadows and listen. This went on for several weeks until word got back to his father, who became very angry and vehemently denounced "those Mormons" and again strongly forbade Tonga to even listen to them.

Tonga wanted to be respectful to his father but also wanted to learn more about the gospel, as he had felt a calm spirit of peace when he listened to the missionaries' teachings and testimonies. Unfortunately, every time he talked to his father about the Church his father beat him. For several months there was a fierce conflict between father and son.

Finally, Tonga announced that he was old enough to be on his own and that he was determined to follow the dictates of his own conscience. The father was furious and began beating him again. Tonga refused to fight back. When the father's strength was spent he looked at his bruised son and asked if he had learned his lesson yet. Tonga calmly replied that he would follow his conscience and do what he felt was right in the sight of God.

Tonga sought out the missionaries and asked if they would teach him openly to make sure he understood the important doctrines of the Church. They agreed, not knowing that each meeting resulted in another beating for Tonga. Finally, when Tonga was convinced that he understood the main doctrines and when he had prayed and received his own witness, he asked the missionaries to baptize him.

They were understandably hesitant, as the problem with his father was well known by now. Tonga explained that he was of age and could make his own decisions. After much prayer the missionaries felt they should baptize Tonga, since he had so much faith and understood the doctrines so well. The missionaries still felt some fear and trepidation, but by prior arrangement they met Tonga Friday evening on a secluded section of beach. They were all dressed in white and began to wade out into the ocean to get to a spot deep enough to perform the sacred ordinance of baptism.

Even though others were not told of the time or place, somehow the word had gotten to Tonga's father several hours before. In anger or desperation or both, he told his oldest son to "teach Tonga a lesson." Encouraged by his father and drunken with anger, Tonga's older brother got a large stick and headed for the beach.

He arrived at the beach just as the baptism was finished and Tonga and the two elders were wading back to shore. In an anger-emboldened rage, he uttered a blood-curdling scream and headed straight toward the threesome who were now in fairly shallow water.

The two elders heard the scream, looked up, saw the stick and the charging brother, and quickly ran away. They yelled at Tonga to follow them, but he quietly shook his head and simply stood there, his eyes full of peace. He raised his head and looked straight at his brother. The elders reached land and took cover in some nearby bushes just before the brother reached Tonga. When the brother saw that Tonga would not run but waited calmly for him with a look of perfect seren-ity, he hesitated for a moment—but only a moment. Then with a curse of anger he took the last couple of splashing steps, lifted his large stick, and sent it crashing across Tonga's back. Tonga still did not move. Again and again the stick smashed into his back, tearing his shirt and exposing huge red welts oozing with blood and pain. At last an extra heavy blow crumpled him to his knees, then another and an-other left him sprawled face down in the water.

An exultant cry rent the air, and the enraged brother staggered to shore and disappeared uncertainly down the trail. He had "taught Tonga a lesson" and left a seemingly lifeless form floating partially sub-merged in the gently rolling ocean.

The two elders who had witnessed all this came from their hiding places and ran quickly to where Tonga lay in the ocean, barely mov-ing. They were grateful to see he was still breathing. They lifted him from the water and were sickened by what they saw. Getting beaten severely enough to raise welts and blood and tear fabric is painful enough, but to have that raw flesh submerged in salty ocean water and sand was more pain than they could comprehend. They shuddered. They wondered whether Tonga also had some broken bones or other unseen injuries.

Tonga could hardly move, so they each took an arm, lifted him up, and dragged him stumblingly to shore. As they got well onto land, Tonga spoke for the first time and asked where they were going.

"To the hospital, of course," they replied. "We must get those wounds treated and see if there are any broken bones. You may have some serious back or rib problems."

"No," said Tonga. "Not yet. I have only been baptized. I have not received the gift of the Holy Ghost nor been confirmed a member of The Church of Jesus Christ of Latter-day Saints—God's kingdom on earth. See that log over there? Take me to it, let me sit down, then confer upon me the gift of the Holy Ghost, and confirm me a member of the Church. I want to be a full part of God's kingdom now."

"We'll do that tomorrow. You need to get some medical treatment now."

"No," Tonga replied firmly. "Do it now. Who knows, you may be right, there may be serious physical problems, I may not even make it to the hospital or I may not be alive tomorrow. I am in pain, but mostly I just feel numb. I am, however, in full control of my feelings and I want to become a full member of God's kingdom now—please."

The two elders looked around, sensing possible danger. They saw no one else. They looked at Tonga and saw a fire of faith and determination coming from his eyes that overpowered the burning of his wounds. They sat him down on the log, laid their hands on his head, and by the power and authority of the priesthood of God gave him the gift of the Holy Ghost, confirmed him a member of The Church of Jesus Christ of Latter-day Saints, and under the inspiration of God gave him a special blessing that no permanent physical damage from the beating would afflict him.

As they took their hands from his head there was calmness in their eyes—no more furtive glances at the surrounding bushes, only tears of gratitude for the faith of a committed Tongan Saint in these latter days. Finally they got him to the hospital, where he was checked, given some care, and released with the admonition: "You were lucky this time. You have no life-threatening injuries or broken bones, but don't get into a fight like that again." (The doctors and nurses were of course not aware of the details.)

Tonga stayed with the elders that night, but the next day he wanted to return to his home. They went with him and found his father, who, still filled with bitterness and anger, commanded him to leave and never return. Tonga's older brother was nowhere to be found. The missionaries made arrangements for Tonga to live with a member family.

Tonga was eventually reconciled with his father and his family. His

father apologized to him and sought his forgiveness, telling him that
his mind had been darkened at the time. Tonga willingly, even anxiously, forgave him. Several family members, including both his father
and his brother, later joined the Church. Tonga became a school-
teacher. He was always active in the Church. He married, raised a
wonderful family, held many positions of responsibility in the Church,
and proved to be a blessing to thousands of people over decades of
time.

Tonga's back carried physical scars throughout his life; his soul,
however, remained unscarred by anger or desire for revenge.

As Tonga told me this story he used such detail that, even though I
was not physically present when the events transpired, I felt in one
sense that I was. I saw clearly in my mind's eye everything as he explained it. I still felt the same fire of faith in his eyes that had burned so
brightly and been felt so keenly by those missionaries many years ago.

I thought of good parents who work hard to leave an inheritance
of stocks and bonds or houses or other forms of worldly wealth to
their posterity—which beyond a reasonable amount is usually lost and
often becomes a stumbling block rather than a stepping-stone for their
posterity. I thought of the heritage of faith Tonga passed on to his posterity.

I wondered: "Why don't we spend our time and energy leaving a
heritage of faith which will last forever? It is just faithfulness! There
really is nothing else of value to leave. Brilliance loses its luster, physical strength wanes, earthly beauty fades, worldly riches lose their
value. Only faith and love remain. Why don't we realize that and act
accordingly?"

As I heard these marvelous stories of faith, I realized that these
Saints displayed an unusual ability to recognize the difference between
the important and the vital. For Tonga it was important to get medical
help, but it was vital to receive the gift of the Holy Ghost and be confirmed a member of the Church. He could tell the difference. The
Prophet Joseph Smith showed that, while it is important to make a living, it is vital to keep our covenants. Enos's example taught that it is
important to pray, but vital to receive forgiveness of sins. I thought of
the Savior's life. Through Him we know it is important to live, but
vital to love, so we can really live forever.

The stories I was hearing showed that when the vital is taken care
of, the important automatically follows. If we always keep our covenants (do that which is vital) all else will work out as it should. I

hoped I could always sense the difference and pay whatever price was required to achieve the vital.

As I heard these stories I wondered: "What value do we put on our membership in God's kingdom?" Do we understand that it is important to be a member but vital to gain a testimony of the Savior and His atoning sacrifice? Do we know that it is important to feel sorry for the things we have done wrong but vital to truly repent, bring the Savior into our life, cast our burdens on Him, and receive His forgiveness? These early Saints knew.

There were hundreds if not thousands of examples of such faith. We did not record them all, as most of them should rightly remain with the individuals who experienced them and with their families.

I sensed, however, that the Lord felt good about a representative few being brought to the attention of other Tongans through conference talks, so they could know upon what foundation they were built, from what heritage they came, and of the fire of faith that burned in their ancestry.

21

Is Your Faith Sufficient?

During a school vacation we took the children with us in the mission boat to a conference in Ha'apai. We had a rough trip up but made it safely. On our return trip the seas were rough, but since we had a skilled captain and crew I felt no undue alarm. The boat jerked and twisted all afternoon, but toward evening we were only slightly behind schedule. So far, so good. But the worst part of the journey lay ahead, as we had to cross the open ocean during the night.

The waves were large, the wind was strong, and the night was dark. I felt myself involuntarily shudder a little. I prayed that the captain and the crew would perform their duties properly. I looked at Jean and the children and hoped the captain knew what a precious cargo he was carrying. I looked in his eyes and sensed that he felt the weight of responsibility.

We bounced and rolled through the night. Occasionally I thought I heard unusual sounds from the engine room. About halfway through the night, at what seemed the very darkest hour, I heard a fearsome, elongated sputtering, a coughing sound, and then silence. The engine had quit!

The boat had been battered badly enough with the engine going full bore. Now, with no engine, there was nothing to pull us through the mauling onslaughts of the angry waves.

I heard cries of alarm. Soon the captain and crew seemed to be everywhere. Clanking and complaining came from the engine room.

The boat was small and it didn't take much for everyone to hear and know what was going on. A broken shaft? A jammed cylinder? A faulty fuel pump? Every possibility was checked, but to no avail.

After what seemed an eternity the captain came to me, grim-faced, with the unwanted news. "We don't know what is wrong. We have tried everything we can think of, but we can't get the engine going again. What should we do?"

I looked at him and replied: "You are the captain. You are the one I should ask. You've got to do something. The ocean is getting wilder, and we will be in real danger if we just sit here."

"I know all that," he replied. "What I am saying is, we don't know what to do. We have plenty of fuel. The engine simply won't start. Therefore I have come to you for advice. You are the mission president. Your family is on board. It is dangerous and will get worse. You tell me what to do."

I looked into his eyes. They were calm, and expressed deep trust. He had the faith that somehow I could help him out of that dangerous situation. Quietly I said, "Give me some time. When I'm ready, I'll let you know."

I had been in many tight situations, but never one quite like this. It is one thing to be in danger yourself, but it is quite another to have your wife and children in danger too. I felt responsible, not only for them but for everyone on board. I wanted some time and space, but there was precious little of either on that small, crowded boat. I struggled to find peace. I prayed for faith and understanding. That was hard to do on a boat bouncing wildly in a hellish cauldron of raging elements. All around me I heard the pleading of anxious voices. I felt the closeness of panicky feelings. What should I do? I wondered if more depended on me than I could deliver? I knew I had to exert sufficient faith to find out what God would have us do. He was our only hope. I asked everyone to pray for help and deliverance.

As I prayed, I kept thinking of Jean and the girls. "I shouldn't have brought them," I thought. "Why didn't we stay in Ha'apai longer? We knew the seas were bad."

Then I thought: "We were making good progress until the motor quit. Why did it quit now, with my whole family aboard?"

An unwanted thought flashed through my mind. "If you die tonight, at least all of you will go together."

Nancy, Jean, Liz, and Marilyn on board the Faifekau returning from Ha'apai.

"No," I cried. "That's not it. We're going to make it."

"Then exercise more faith. For it will take power to start the engine, and the only power available to you is faith. Do you have sufficient faith?"

"Do I?" I wondered. "Do I?"

I don't know how long my own struggle went on. Quite a while, I suppose. I went through questions, concerns, and rationalizations. I felt a deeper love for Jean and the children than I ever thought possible. In a similar manner I felt a love for Heavenly Father and for the Savior that cannot be explained. I struggled for a long time. I felt myself getting weaker, yet strangely at the same time getting stronger. I came to know that fearful night that faith is a real power, not just a great motivator and revealer and strengthener and guide. It is all of those things, but it is also much more. Faith in the Lord Jesus Christ is an eternal, endless power as great as any power in the whole universe. Finally, a calmness came to me that made the whole of that terrible night worth it. I called for the captain. "Yes?" he said, with anticipation.

"Go through the regular routine again for starting the engines. Things will be all right."

With faith, all the crew went through the standard procedure for starting the engine. Soon there were clangs and clanks and muffled shouts. Then some sputtering. Then that joyful sound of a diesel engine coming to life, running smoothly, and gradually gaining power. The crisis was over; we were moving again.

I heard a collective sigh of relief. The seas were as rough as ever, but the boat was moving, guided by a skillful and faithful captain. I thanked those around me. I asked them to express their appreciation to God for His kindness to us that night. I exchanged a look of deep love and trust with Jean.

For me, sleep had fled. I spent the rest of the night trying to adequately express my love and appreciation to the Lord and absorb the great lesson I had experienced. As hard as I tried, I felt my efforts were still inadequate. I tried to understand what had happened but could only see it partially—"as through a glass darkly" (see 1 Corinthians 13:12). I realized that to exercise faith unto life takes great effort. Sometimes it may take more effort than we want to expend—yet we must. While I hope I never have to go through a night like that again, I was grateful for the experience.

With the first light of day we could see the low silhouette of Tongatapu in the distance. We were on course—we would be home in a few hours. We had been saved. I looked at the captain. I was deeply grateful for his skill and courage and for that of the crew also, but I was even more grateful for their faith and obedience.

If we are willing, God will bless us all with adequate opportunities to expend the effort necessary to increase our faith. We may not always enjoy those circumstances, for they may involve danger, illness, death, disaffection of a loved one, or something similar. I don't know what each person's individual opportunity to develop faith will be, but I do know that it is possible to gain more faith if we are willing. I know that with God's help we can develop deeper faith—in our Heavenly Father and in His Son, Jesus Christ. Sufficient faith has enough power to allow us to continue our journey home through the night, even though we may have been temporarily stopped for some reason.

Jesus lives and has all power. As we exercise faith in Him we tap into that infinite power. The motor of our lives may be temporarily down. At times we may be surrounded by raging waves and hissing seas and stinging winds. But if our faith in Him is sufficient He can power us safely to our destination.

22

Missionary Harvesting

In Tonga everyone was expected to grow their own food. All the leaders, including the king, had gardens. Supplying food was considered a patriotic duty. There were regular garden inspections by government officials. Sometimes it didn't rain for weeks or even months, which caused shortages of food. During one of these "lean" periods people began complaining about the large number of "Mormon missionaries" who were eating great quantities of food but not producing any. This negative whispering campaign spread rapidly and began to seriously affect the work. Sometimes when the missionaries approached a home to talk to the people about the gospel they were met with the question: "Why don't you go raise a garden and be helpful in these hard times instead of just talking?"

I met with the mission council to discuss what to do about this situation. There were such sharp differences of opinion that the council requested that I make the final decision. They promised to follow whatever I proposed. I asked them to fast and pray with me and promised that in three days I would announce a decision.

During this time I reviewed my notes of their various suggestions, talked to many missionaries who were "on the firing line," consulted with several government officials, and visited leaders from other churches. Finally I felt I had done enough "homework," so I took the issue again to the Lord in prayer. I received my answer and knew what to do.

We met as agreed, and I explained that the Lord was most interested in seeing that His work move forward among the Tongan people. He knew how best to do that. What I would propose might be different from what they were used to, but it would be the best thing for the work in Tonga at that time.

I proposed that we set aside one day a week (there were no formal "preparation days" for missionaries at that time) and on that day the missionaries would do missionary work in a different way. The elders would put on their work clothes and do gardening as a district or as a zone, and the Sisters would do weaving or *tapa* beating. All missionaries would spend at least half a day in this type of physical labor, then spend another few hours helping the families they were staying with. In the evening they would put on their missionary clothes and resume their regular proselyting activities. I also proposed that as a mission we rent certain parcels of land for these "missionary gardens." I asked the missionaries to make these gardens the best and most productive in their communities.

The missionaries were soon "hard at work," and missionary gardens began to "bloom" in many locations. Several were awarded prizes by the government inspectors. The whispering campaign against "those lazy Mormon missionaries" took on a new flavor as the village gossip became: "Have you seen the Mormon missionary gardens? They are the best around, and the work they do and the food they raise is unbelievable."

Before long when the missionaries came to a door they were met with: "Oh yes, come in. Tell us about your garden." What had started as an impediment to the work was in just a few short months a great bonus. The missionaries accomplished more in six days than they had in seven. They also enjoyed better health. The work flourished.

In a few years imported food became more common, grocery stores became a way of life, people got jobs, and money became the medium of exchange. Thus the "missionary gardens" were gradually phased out and the work moved forward without them.

It has always been a testimony to me that the Lord knows what is best at a given time in a given country under given circumstances. Had we held rigidly to the standard line, the progress we experienced would not have occurred.

23

A Missionary Jubilee

In September 1967 we were asked by our first contact to accompany the next group of Tongan Saints to the New Zealand Temple in October and to attend a mission presidents seminar in Auckland, New Zealand, at the same time. As we planned for this trip, Jean announced that in March of 1968 we would have another addition to our family. Everyone was excited. News of this type travels rapidly in Tonga, and soon it became common knowledge. The queen said that after five girls it was about time we had a boy and he would be her Tongan boy. I thought, "A new baby, hopefully a new stake, a golden jubilee, more missionaries, more baptisms, more growth of the kingdom: What a year 1968 is going to be!" (Little did I know *what* a year it would be.)

Since we had asked the members to concentrate on missionary work in preparation for the jubilee, Jean and I felt we should set an example. We systematically invited each of the leaders in the government to our home for a nice meal and a gospel presentation and discussion. We showed the wonderful film "Man's Search for Happiness" so many times that we almost memorized it (and really wore it out). These meetings were wonderful experiences, and we made many lasting friendships as a result. I not only explained the gospel to all these leaders but also explained our intent regarding the jubilee. We received not only their approval but their enthusiastic support for the jubilee.

These meetings did not result directly in many baptisms, but they created goodwill and led indirectly to other baptisms. The members and missionaries were aware of these meetings. They were especially proud of the fact that top government leaders were coming to the mission home. This increased their desire to do more friendshipping themselves.

Anticipation of the jubilee brought about a big increase in all aspects of missionary activity. The youth requested an all-mission dance festival as a fellowshipping opportunity. It was a huge success, with several thousand participating. Branches, districts, and auxiliaries thought of and held many fun, innovative, and effective missionary activities. Our baptisms started moving up from about fifty a month to sixty and occasionally into the seventies. The enthusiasm and buildup to the jubilee was all-pervasive and continued to increase every day.

The missionaries asked if I would speak to selected groups of investigators who had received all of the discussions but were still unsure. Although I mostly bore my testimony and said the same things the missionaries did, the synergy of being together helped many make the final decision for baptism. Even though it took a great deal of my time it was very rewarding and I was happy to help the missionaries.

In October we accompanied the next group of Saints to the temple in New Zealand. Most of them were going to the temple for the first time. As with the first group, the Saints exhibited deep reverence and awe as the temple came into view. This time we had most of the unusual situations worked out ahead of time, so the work at the temple went very smoothly.

After getting the group started, Jean and I left them and went to the mission presidents seminar in Auckland. What a wonderful seminar! We reviewed with Elder Monson our plans for the jubilee, a possible stake, and many other things. These seminars made us feel so good. Interestingly, despite all the good suggestions made, all the papers handed out, and all the programs discussed, I really only remember one thing from these seminars: we knew that the Brethren loved us and were our friends. They cared and would do whatever they could to help us and ease our burdens.

I tried to convey that feeling to my children, my wife, my missionaries, and all with whom I worked. Facts and figures and programs come and go and have a way of changing so rapidly that they often have little relevance after short periods of time. However, the feeling of knowing that someone really cares about you, that someone loves you, that someone is your friend and sincerely wants to help you—this lasts forever and does more good in the long run than all the programs

in the world. Sometimes I have wondered if the main value of programs is as a format around which we can show our love and concern
for others.

At the conclusion of the seminar Jean and I went back to the
temple and spent two more days with the Tongans. Things were going
smoothly, but I noticed that they were all doing "temple file names."
Even though I was very happy for them and felt a great spirit of service among them, something that I could not then identify began to
bother me.

After much time, prayer, and contemplation I finally understood. I
was able to see clearly what should be done. After the temple group
returned to Tonga I called a special meeting of all who had been to the
temple.

I began by commending all those who had gone to the temple and
acknowledging their faith and sacrifices and determination to do what
is right. I then made reference to the upcoming jubilee and the sacrifice of the early Tongan members during those trying years. I explained my feelings about how we should honor them, and all of our
ancestors, by living the gospel as they did and as they would have us
do. An important part of that is passing on to our children the faith
they passed on to us.

Then, feeling inspired by a higher source, I said that in addition to
being strong members there was another important way that we could
honor our ancestors, which I would explain to them. They were all
ears. I asked how many "*palangi* names" they had done work for in the
temple. They responded that they were nearly all *palangi* names, as
that is what the temple gave them. I then asked how many Tongan
names they had done work for.

A profound silence came over the entire congregation. A spirit of
introspective pondering prevailed. Their eyes lit up, and they were
filled with the spirit of Elijah. They began to understand the same message I had previously received. They immediately wanted to know how
to go about getting names of their Tongan ancestors to the temple.

We went through the various steps needed to accomplish this,
such as proper research and correctly filling out the forms. They
grasped the concepts and were eager to start.

This meeting opened a whole new vista of service for the jubilee
celebration. Right then and there we set a goal to have hundreds if not
thousands of Tongan names ready for the following year's excursion to
the New Zealand Temple. Nearly all of these names would be their

parents and grandparents and other relatives who had been faithful in the past, those we were trying to honor in the jubilee.

This was the first time we had discussed that aspect of honoring the early Tongans. As the meeting came to a sweet and spiritual close, I sensed some smiles from beyond and felt a stamp of approval for this new effort.

As the feelings from that meeting and the information given there spread throughout Tonga, many started working on genealogical research. Over the next nine or ten months there were probably about as many deceased Tongan family names prepared for temple work as there had been in the previous fifty years. It was wonderful to see how enthusiastic everyone was on this as well as other aspects of the jubilee. The next temple group, which left about a year later, spent their entire time at the temple doing work for Tongans.

The year 1968 rolled around. The enthusiasm for this jubilee year was almost beyond belief. It continued to amaze and please me to see how so many different aspects of the work began to be understood and implemented as a result of the decision to hold this jubilee celebration. I was sure that, like the jubilee itself, these new initiatives were from heaven.

Preparation for the jubilee celebration brought a new emphasis on genealogical research.

24

A Tongan Baby

As the time for the birth of our baby drew near there was a heightened degree of excitement among our daughters, the missionaries, and the people around us, both members and nonmembers. My mother flew to Tonga to help during this special time.

Around the middle of March, Jean, my mother, and I attended the wedding of premier Tu'ipelehake's daughter Fusipala to the noble Hahano. We had felt a special friendship with this couple. For a wedding present we gave them a set of the standard works of the Church. They seemed to appreciate it.[1]

On Saturday evening, March 16, our branch commemorated the founding of the Relief Society with a lovely meal, a special program, and a display of handiwork by Relief Society members. Most of the branch was there. When we returned home Jean was very tired and soon asked that we notify Dr. Niumeitolu (the Tongan medical practitioner who had agreed to help with the delivery of our baby) that her labor had started and that she felt the time was very close for the birth.

Missionaries went to his house and informed him. He said he would meet us at the "pay ward" of the hospital. We left our daughters with their grandmother, took Kesaia, one of the house-girls, and went to the hospital. The hospital facilities were not what we were used to, but the lack of "things" was more than compensated for by the caring attitude of the people.

---

1. Years later Princess Fusipala joined the Church.

The "pay ward" was an older, wood frame home with four rooms that were used as "semi-private" rooms for patients who paid a small fee for their use, as opposed to the crowded public wards in the main hospital. As we entered the room I noticed a single light bulb dangling from the ceiling. I asked where the delivery room was. The doctor laughed softly and said, "Wherever you want. Will that table do?"

The room had several open windows with no screens, so anyone passing by could look in. As the night was warm, Kesaia fanned Jean and rubbed her back. The nurse kept watch over the open windows and tried to keep people, mosquitoes, moths, and flies away.

The doctor checked Jean and said it would be several more hours. I held Jean's hand and talked to her for a while, but wasn't sure what my place was. The nurse and Kesaia seemed to know just what to do, so I tried to stay out of their way and visited with the doctor. Time wore on, and eventually the first inklings of dawn began to chase the darkness away. It had been a sultry night and the nearly cloudless sky promised another hot, humid day.

The doctor looked at his watch. "I think it will still be several more hours before your wife delivers. As you know, I am a lay preacher in the Methodist church, and I have a sermon to give in a village a few miles from here. I believe I can go home, finish preparing my sermon, go to the village, give my sermon, and be back before the baby comes."

I responded: "You haven't checked Jean for some time. Why do you think it will be several more hours?" He replied that he had helped a few *palangi* women in their deliveries and they always yelled and screamed and carried on when the time got close for delivery, whereas he had hardly heard a murmur from Jean. I said, "But my wife is no ordinary *palangi* woman. Please check her again before you leave."

When he checked Jean he was startled and said: "You are right. She is very unusual. I think the baby will be born very soon. I may have to miss my preaching assignment."

"Thank you for staying," I replied. "I have a feeling you will be blessed for your willingness to sacrifice your sermon. In fact, I feel that even though you haven't had as much preparation time as you would like you will not miss your appointment but will give one of your best sermons." I suggested he could use in his sermon some of the religious principles we had been talking about. He just smiled and went about his work.

Things started to happen very fast. Just as the sun finally filled our little island with light and life that peaceful Sunday morning, a faithful mother gave that final painful effort, and light and life began anew as a precious soul made its mortal appearance amidst gasps of joy. "It's a boy!" A few well-placed spanks brought forth those heaven-sent squeals of life. A new day had begun.

There were smiles everywhere. I held Jean's hand, kissed her perspiring brow, and again gazed into her angelic face. She had once more passed through the valley of the shadow of death and emerged triumphant—shining in the brilliance of God's approbation. How could I be so fortunate to have such a wonderful wife?

The doctor and the nurse got things cleaned up, then weighed the baby on an antiquated basket scale. The doctor proudly said: "Mr. Groberg, you have a healthy ten-pound baby boy. You also have a remarkable wife. Everything will be fine. The nurse knows what to do, so if it's all right with you I will leave now. I think if I go straight to the church I can get there in time to deliver my sermon."

"Thank you," I replied. "Go with our love. I know God will bless you." [2]

I bowed my head and thanked God for the safe arrival of our son, for Jean's well-being, and for all the other help given us. I asked God to help the doctor deliver a good sermon. I'm sure he did. I mused over the events of that early morning. Because of its location on the International Dateline, Tonga is the first land to welcome each new day. It seemed significant that our son not only had arrived on but also had ushered in that special Sabbath. I thanked God with all my heart for the miracle of life—especially for the life of His Son that made all other life possible.

I thought of the five of us spending the night in that plain, wooden building with no modern facilities or instruments. I realized that the vast majority of humanity has started life on this earth under somewhat similar circumstances. I pondered another birth in a very unpretentious setting which, though far away in time and place, was very near to me in reality and importance. I felt the warmth of love from Kesaia and the good doctor and the nurse. I wondered if God,

---

2. While the good doctor and his wife have not yet joined the Church, their son has and is a faithful member. I have felt that just as the doctor unselfishly helped God bring physical life to our son, so God graciously granted spiritual life to his son. What wondrous opportunities both of those births open up.

who allowed Simeon and Anna to hold the infant Lord, might also have allowed other faithful souls to help in that most important of all births? I jotted the following down:

> Was there a caring midwife there,
> Or only Joseph's tender care?
> If angels sang with joy and praise,
> Might some have helped in other ways?
> Did some instruct that special pair?
> Or—was it for them alone to share?

No matter how it happened, I know He came. I know He lives and loves and saves and forgives and guides and blesses. I know He accepts our efforts of love and sacrifice and blesses all His children with opportunities to help their fellow beings live, both physically and spiritually. I felt the weight of responsibility to teach our son that his life was meant to serve others and thereby show his gratitude to God for the precious gift of life. Oh, how I hoped I could be equal to that task of training and helping! I felt that this young boy, a child of promise, would do all he should, for he had arrived safely under difficult circumstances in the mission field. I sensed that much more lay ahead, but for now I was swallowed up in the wonder of it all—life and light and love from God; one eternal round.

Elder Thomas S. Monson (center) visited Tonga
shortly after John Enoch's birth.

After knowing that Jean was well and with her blessing I returned home and shared the happy news with my mother and our daughters. Everyone was excited! You can imagine what the main topic of discussion was among the Saints at church that morning.

A few days later I wrote a letter to my dad and family in Idaho expressing some of my feelings. Following are excerpts from that letter.

"21 March 1968
"Dear Folks,

"Time moves on and that which we dreamed of is reality and that which was reality for so long is as a dream, and the line between dreaming and reality grows ever thinner—especially as one dreams for things pertaining to righteousness.

"I have had some very poignant thoughts and feelings of late in regard to birth and life and opportunity and eternity and family. For so long we had no son and dreamed of the day when we would. Now we have a son and the times we dreamed of having one are only dreams. . . . One sees, if not clearly at least more clearly than before, how only love and sacrifice and a humble heart—true willingness to live by 'every word of God'—are of any importance. All else is but a test of this willingness.

"Anything man can do, God can do better. Our purpose is to show Him we are willing to listen and obey and work hard in His cause of righteousness. If we do this, someday we may partake of the fulness, which includes all we can see and feel and hear and touch and think of—everything conceivable and more, much, much more. All of this is based on righteousness, humility, and living the gospel of Jesus Christ every day, having full faith and confidence in God and in Christ Jesus, the Savior of *all* the world.

"All blessings come from Him and through faith in Him, all is possible. I have come to realize strongly that faith is the agent whereon the wheels of spiritual progress turn. If only we can have enough faith, everything—literally everything—is for our best good. Lack of faith is the greatest lack anywhere; thus faith—true abiding faith in Christ and through Him in Our Father in Heaven—is by far the greatest need of each of us individually and the whole world collectively. And that is expressed in obedience, love, and unselfish sacrifice. . . .

"Mom has been so good to help. She is indeed an angel. I do believe she has as much sense of what is important as any angel anywhere.

*Queen Mata'aho invited the Groberg family to visit the royal palace
so she could meet John Enoch (in Jean's arms).*

"As she moves around comforting, helping, and working I realize more than ever that angels in heaven are just people with clear understanding, people who know the beginning from the end and who, living in eternity, can see clearly those things of value and those of no value. Thus they are motivated by and act according to those eternal principles which are of most worth—love, sacrifice, help, and so forth. Mom has this understanding, so I see very little, if any, difference between her presence here and that of an angel. Thanks for lending her to us. It is so good to have everyone home and happy. We appreciate your sustaining support.

"Love,

"John and family."

25

I Know, I Know

Everything appeared normal, so Jean and the baby returned home from the hospital in a few days. The missionaries and members were anxious to help. We felt a great outpouring of love from everyone.

When the baby was ten days old he broke out with a severe case of infant impetigo. The calamine lotion the clinic at the hospital gave us had no effect on the sores. A visiting Peace Corps doctor gave us some antibiotic that cleared up the rash, but just when things seemed to be back to normal the baby suddenly developed a very high fever and started throwing up. We didn't know what to do. After a few days he improved, so we thought no more of it. As soon as we relaxed a little, however, his fever soared and he started throwing up again. Then in a few days he returned to a more normal state. By now we were quite worried and wondered what would happen next.

These well-sick cycles continued and our concern grew. My mother kept changing her flight plans, not wanting to leave until she knew the baby was well. She was truly an angel of mercy, staying up late at night with the baby many times so we could get some rest.

One of his "well times" fell on Easter Sunday, and we took him to the Liahona Branch. In both Tongan and English I gave him a blessing and the name of John Enoch Groberg. (This was the name of my grandfather, who served a mission to Sweden, married, and was left a widower at the birth of their third child. He, too, died a year later.)

Our five little girls were a precious part of these events. One morning our sparkling Marilyn, age 5, confided: "I really do know why baby John Enoch is better. It's because every time I said my prayers I asked Heavenly Father to please make him better, and Heavenly Father listened to my prayers and so He made our baby better!" Sister Liz, age 7, quickly reminded Marilyn that she wasn't the only one who prayed for him: so did she and others, and the folks at Liahona even fasted all day and prayed for him.

During another of his "well times" the queen invited us to visit her at her summer palace so she could meet Mom and the girls and John Enoch. With a soft royal smile she said, "See, I told you that you needed to come to Tonga to get your boy!" She has continued to maintain a special interest in him.

Elder Monson came to tour the mission at this time. He was magnificent in motivating and inspiring those great young missionaries. We were pleased and grateful that the baby seemed well during his visit. Elder Monson must have had some spiritual premonitions, for he confided in my mother that if the baby had further problems we should not hesitate to take him immediately to the United States.

When we finished our meetings in Tonga we flew to Fiji and met with the missionaries there. Elder Monson then caught a flight to New Zealand and I prepared to return to Tonga.

Elder Monson was complimentary and supportive and his visit uplifted me. I only wished I could feel as good about the health of our new son. I tried to convince myself that things would be all right—after all, we were on the Lord's errand and He does watch over His servants and their families. But something kept me feeling uncomfortable. In the morning, as I prepared to go to the airport, I received a very disconcerting call from Jean. She reported that the baby had developed a high fever and was constantly throwing up. She said he was listless and would not eat. She was very concerned.

I left for the airport immediately, as though that would get the plane there faster. Prayers were my main source of solace as I anxiously waited. Just before they called my flight, a Fijian airport worker came over and said there was an emergency phone call for me. I ran to the phone, not knowing what to expect.

The phone call was from Elder Monson, who was in a barber shop in New Zealand and had had a feeling that he should call and inquire about our baby. I explained the new concern and tried to be as optimistic yet as honest as I could. He was thankful I was on my way back to Tonga. He assured me of his faith and prayers and those of the Brethren and repeated what he had told my mother—that if necessary

I should not hesitate to send Jean and the baby to the United States for help. I thanked him for his sensitivity to the Spirit and for his faith and prayers and those of the Brethren. I had a feeling we would need every ounce of help available. As I hung up the phone the waiting airport employee anxiously ran me to the plane, whose pilot he had prevailed on to wait for me.

Though the flight to Tonga took only a few hours, emotionally it seemed to take forever. Why this setback? How I prayed for our son and for Jean! When I finally got to the mission home things were even worse than I had anticipated. Not only did John have a high fever but also his formerly healthy body was now a sickly yellow color and he was vomiting severely. I knew he was in serious trouble.

I called some of the elders and my counselors and we gave him another blessing. Doctor Tapa, the head doctor in Tonga, took our case personally and visited our home several times. He was the most professionally qualified doctor in Tonga and did everything in his power to help. Despite all he and others did, the baby continued to get weaker.

The euphoria of a few weeks before was replaced with a heaviness of spirit that settled as a pervasive somberness on all of us. The housegirls and my mother did the best they could to keep some sort of schedule going with our daughters. Jean, of course, was terribly torn, but she kept up remarkable courage and equanimity considering all the demands on her strength, both physical and emotional. My counselors and the missionary assistants said they would keep the mission running, so I should not worry about that but should spend all the time I needed with my son. Everyone wanted to help in every way they could.

Despite the faith and love and prayers of so many, the baby's condition continued to worsen. The oppressive feeling that shrouded us was unrelenting and got heavier and darker each day and seemed determined to smother and crush all light and life and hope. I wanted to battle this dark force but didn't know how. All our prayers and faith and blessings hadn't seemed to change anything. What more could I do?

Eventually Jean and I stayed exclusively in our bedroom, where we kept an around-the-clock vigil over our sick son. He was sinking fast. We took turns sponging his forehead, fanning his fevered body, and trying to force water down his little throat with an eye dropper. He had long since become too weak to nurse. We prayed and cried and held him and did all we could, but none of it seemed to have any effect. He continued to get weaker and weaker.

Occasionally Jean left the room to check on the other children, but for the most part we spent our time with our precious son of promise who now seemed so close to expiring. I lost track of days and nights and seldom left the side of our little boy for any reason.

Once when Jean stepped out for a while I came close to "touching bottom." The baby had just thrown up the tiny dropper full of water I had given him. I was so discouraged, I almost stopped struggling. I wondered, "What's the use? The end seems inevitable. Why struggle more?"

I placed him on a blanket in the middle of the floor and sat next to him. For long moments I looked into his eyes. What did I see? I saw sunken eyes studying me, pleading with me as though to say, "I'm your son—help me!" It nearly tore me to pieces and I wanted to cry out: "I want to help you. Just tell me how! What more can I do? Just tell me!" I caressed his little arms and legs, now so very thin. I noticed the top of his head had sunken way down, and his beautiful, loving eyes had fallen deep into their sockets. He lay very still—too still: not crying, not moving, just looking at me—our only son lying so quietly, hardly breathing. I sensed that he was very close to leaving. I groaned inside. "Why are you leaving when you just arrived, and so full of promise? We had so much hope. Why? What can I do? I'm helpless."

I don't know where the strength came from to plead again, but it came. How I prayed—prayed for his life, prayed for faith, prayed for understanding, prayed to know what to do! I felt so alone; almost abandoned. In a near final effort of desperation I cried out to heaven: "But you don't understand: he's my son, my only son."

I don't know whether I said those words or just thought them, but as soon as they had begun to leave my mind I felt my whole universe tremble and quake. The world as I knew it started reeling back and forth and it seemed that everything I could touch or see or hear or feel was being torn away and was slipping from my grasp.

In the midst of this incredible turmoil there came a quiet, unexplainable feeling of peace and power that seemed to fill the immensity of space and to hold total control over everything and everyone. Instinctively I listened—listened so intently that for a moment I wondered if I could even continue to exist. I seemed to hear a voice coming from the very depths of eternity, full of the most tender compassion imaginable, saying, "I know; I know." The warmth, the truth, the love that I felt is beyond description. I basked in this heavenly influence, desiring nothing more.

Suddenly I began to realize what I had almost done. I was crushed by the thought that I had presumed to think I knew anything. How could I be so arrogant! How could I possibly think God did not already know my feelings and the feelings of everyone a million times over? How could I, desperate as I was, ask for anything without first expressing my total willingness to submit fully to His will? I fell to the floor pleading for forgiveness. I don't know whether my mouth opened, or just my heart and mind, but I found the thoughts or words flowing freely, willingly: "*He'e ko ho foha—fai pe ho finangalo.*" ("Here. He is thy son. Do as thou wilt.") (It seemed too personal, too sacred to express in English, and as I soon found, there were other reasons why thoughts and words and feelings were more appropriate in Tongan at that time.)

With this heartfelt expression of trust came a quiet, peaceful resignation and a recognition of my nothingness and my inability to understand much. I was shored up and strengthened by the absolute certainty that God's will is *always* best, no matter what.

I wanted to stay immersed in those clouds of peace and quiet forever, but it was not to be. Once again I began to feel the heavy weight of darkness pressing down, down, down, as though more determined than ever to take our little boy right then.

The struggle between resignation and resistance continued. I wondered: Why these conflicting feelings? Wasn't I willing to obey God's will—even if that meant letting him go? Or was I secretly still fighting to keep him? I knew it was right to willingly return that which was a gift from God in the first place, with perfect assurance that God's will is always best. Even though I knew this, it was still one of the most difficult moments of my life. I seemed numb and disassociated from the physical world around me. I felt that I must honestly say a final good-bye to our little boy. As painful as it was, I felt I had to do it and do it willingly. I quietly began: "Thy will be done . . . blessed be thy name . . . thy goodness and wisdom stand forever . . ." But before I could finish I heard something, something very distinct yet very distant; something coming, as it were, from another world. It continued and I could not ignore it.

Was that someone knocking? I sat up. There it was again. Who was it? We had asked to not be disturbed, but I could definitely hear a knocking sound. I found myself slowly returning to the physical surroundings of floors and walls and doors and sounds. I again heard a distinct tapping. It must be the door. I looked at our son. He was very quiet, yet his eyes were open and seemed to be following mine. He was still with us!

Another knock. I quietly opened the door. A large delegation of faithful Saints was standing outside. Their spokesman reverently whispered in Tongan, "The Lord has heard our prayers. Your son will live. The missionaries and members as well as many nonmembers in Tonga and Fiji have been fasting and praying for John Enoch the last two days. Thousands of Saints gathered this very hour in their respective chapels and have just completed their final prayers and broken their fast. The Lord has answered our plea and told us that your son can live. We just thought you would like to know that your son, John Enoch, our Tongan baby, will live. You may need to do other things like getting him to America for specialized care, but he will be fine and we will be here to help. Isn't that wonderful, to know that eventually he will be well? Thanks for all you do as our mission president. Good-bye."

I looked at each person in the delegation. Every face shone with fiery faith and assurance. I saw a twinkle of joy in their eyes. They knew that God had acknowledged their faith and fasting and prayers and would bring full life back to "their Tongan missionary baby."

I didn't know what to say, so I simply said, "*Malo, Malo, Malo.*" ("Thank you. Thank you. Thank you.") I closed the door and turned to look at our son again. Jean was with him now. Had she just come in or had she been there all the time? Was what I had just been through a dream? I wondered. Yet I knew it was much more.

I explained to Jean what the Tongans and Fijians had done and the promise they had received from the Lord. Tears came to her eyes and to mine. We felt the strength of their faith—and oh, how we needed it! I looked at Jean, she looked at me, and together we looked at John Enoch. He seemed about the same—quiet, listless, weak; only there was something slightly different about his eyes. We knew what it was.

We held each other and our baby and offered up as sincere a prayer of gratitude and desire for direction as we could muster. At the end of the prayer I said: "We must call Dr. Tapa again and see if there is something more he can do. I will make arrangements for you and Mom and John Enoch to fly home when the plane comes in two days. Start packing!"

My feelings were not exuberant, but rather more like submerged excitement. I knew I needed more faith but was grateful I could lean on the faith of the Tongans for now. I immediately made reservations for Mom, Jean, the baby, and myself to fly to Fiji. I also requested a flight from Fiji to the United States for Mom and Jean and the baby.

When I explained the medical emergency they informed me the international flight would not take the baby without a doctor's certification that the baby was well enough to fly that far. I suppose they didn't want a sick baby dying on the flight.

They also required a passport and proof of United States citizenship for the baby. Since there was no American consulate in Tonga, the British consulate handled our case. All they could do was issue him a "Certificate of Identity." The American consulate in Fiji said they would accept that and grant him onward passage to the United States.

Next we needed proper medical certificates. When we explained to Dr. Tapa our desire to take John Enoch to America, he said it was critical that he receive intravenous feeding to put fluids back into his dehydrated body or there was no way he could make the long flight. We took him to the hospital with great hope, but found a new complication there. They had no infant-size IV needles, and even if they had one, his little body was so emaciated that the doctors weren't sure they could find a vein that would allow a needle to enter. One doctor said he remembered a procedure he had seen done in Australia. He thought he could do it here and we all agreed he should immediately try.

He proceeded to make an incision at John E's ankle, making what he called a "block" or "cut down." I didn't understand it, but I had faith in him. Soon our little baby was lying on a quilt on the floor with a bottle of glucose water flowing into his body through a tiny tube inserted directly into a vein at his ankle.

After a few hours of this the change in him was amazing. He actually started to move a little. His eyes came closer to the surface. His head took on a more normal shape, and his whole body, while still very frail, seemed to fill out miraculously. As the intravenous feeding procedure appeared to be helping, Dr. Tapa said he would be happy to give us a certificate stating that he felt the baby would be able to make it to the United States alive.

At times the challenges seemed insurmountable, but despite them all, when the plane left for Fiji two days later we were on board. We had come to the airport directly from the hospital, where the doctors

Grandma Groberg and Dr. Tapa at the airport,
with Jean and John Enoch in the car.

waited until the last possible moment to remove the IV tube and stitch up the "cut down" at John Enoch's ankle. Dr. Tapa personally came to the airport to help if needed and to wish us well. How caring everyone was!

When we arrived in Suva we were able to get the necessary papers to enter America, thanks to lots of extra effort and help from the British and American consulates, airline personnel, and several dedicated Church members in Fiji.

Standby arrangements had been made to take the baby to a local hospital at each point along the way if he did not fare well on that leg of the journey. He had done amazingly well from Tonga to Fiji, so we felt good about continuing on to Nadi and deciding there about the international flight to America.

When we arrived in Nadi we had all the necessary papers and tickets in hand. John Enoch still seemed to be doing well, so we decided to have Mom and Jean and the baby proceed on to the United States. It was 2:00 A.M. and very warm in Nadi as we waited for the plane from Australia to set down on its brief stopover in Fiji before proceeding to Honolulu and San Francisco. The sky was cloudless. The moon was down and the stars were as bright as I ever remember seeing them.

Eventually the plane arrived, documentation was checked, and the time for departure came. As they called the flight, I gave my mother a hug and a kiss of love and appreciation. Then I held Jean and John Enoch for as long as I could before kissing them good-bye and watching them board the plane. When would I see them again? When would I hold them in my arms again? All I knew was that we were doing what was right and the end result, whatever it was, would be right. Had not an Apostle of God been given special impressions, had not thousands of faithful Saints been given assurances, and had not many miracles already occurred? Had not life-giving fluid miraculously flowed into a tiny body, and had we not been able to get all the necessary documents and make the necessary arrangements? And above all, was not our baby still alive?

Yet despite all of this I had a rather heavy feeling as I watched those three precious souls board the plane. This feeling stayed with me as I saw the door close and the giant craft leave the terminal, taxi to the end of the runway, and prepare to begin its long flight to Hawaii.

I found a secluded spot where I could see the plane. It was now at the far end of the runway. It was the darkest hour of the night, not long before sunrise. Nearly everyone had left the airport, so I was virtually alone.

I watched the flashing red lights and the powerful white lights of the plane. It was just sitting there, probably waiting for clearance to take off, at least that is what logic told me; but in my heart I felt it was hesitating so as to give us one last opportunity to say a final good-bye. And why not? After all, isn't love the strongest force in the universe? I stood and cried out to the plane, to the sky, and to all eternity, "Oh, fly safely! Do you know what a precious cargo of love, faith, fulfillment, and miracles you carry?" Almost immediately I heard a quiet, loving, even familiar response coming, as it were, from the end of the runway as well as from the depths of eternity: "I know; I know."

I tried to express my love and appreciation to God for His goodness, and for the power of faith and love and understanding and fulfillment. I could not begin to express the smallest portion of what I felt, yet I sensed His understanding and acceptance of my efforts.

I don't know what being translated is like, but if it has something to do with being removed from things physical and placed in a dimension or an understanding of things spiritual, including love, faith, and eternity, then I can relate. All was quiet, very quiet. My heart or soul, or whatever I was made up of then, was throbbing in a synchronized pattern of love and gratitude that came from beyond myself.

The roar of engines broke the spell. I watched that giant machine thunder down the runway. Faster and faster it went until it dipped briefly out of sight, only to reappear above the runway moving upward and onward into the clear Fijian sky. I watched for a long time as it climbed higher and higher then made a wide turn and headed back overhead on its way to Hawaii.

I focused on the blinking lights for as long as I could see them. Finally even they melted into the stars and I could no longer tell which was plane and which was star. As I struggled to distinguish between them, a peaceful realization came over me and I sensed that it didn't matter, for they were in the hands of God.

My heart, mind, and soul resonated to that simple thought. It seemed to fill my very being, and I saw things and felt things that are sacred and true and eternal. I wrote a lot that night but I share only these brief phrases, which are neither prose nor poetry but rather just a rush of feelings imperfectly put on paper.

To Jean

I watched you leave
That starlit eve
Through soft Fijian sky.

You held our son
Our only son
With love and faith to try.

I watched you climb
And take your place
Among the stars above.

Oh help me Jean
Build up my faith
Send me your warmth and love.

I strain to see
But cannot tell
Just where you really are.

Yet God is there
And you are there
A brilliant shining star.

Oh Jean, my love

Please hold my heart
And touch my clouded eye.

Where are you Jean?
I need to know.
Please hear my lonely cry.

I want you here
I hurt so much
I need you by my side.

I search for you
But cannot see
Beyond the arching tide.

Yet what is that
So pure, so clear?
Oh Jean, I see, I see!

What is a star?

It's you and me
And our family
Through all Eternity.

I Know.
I Know.

26

Waiting and Wondering

In the morning I returned to Suva, where I had to wait for my
flight to Tonga. While in Suva, I received a call from Jean in Salt Lake
City. The undersea cable to the United States had a hollow echoing
sound as we spoke, but we could hear each other fairly well. She said
John Enoch seemed to be doing fine, and briefly told me of how kind
everyone had been along the way.

She also told me about meeting a doctor friend we had known in
Idaho Falls who had missed his scheduled flight so he "just happened"
to be on the same flight as Mom and Jean and the baby. After Jean explained the baby's health history, he strongly suggested that they stop
in Salt Lake City and go straight to the Primary Children's Hospital
rather than go to Idaho Falls first. So that is what they did.

John Enoch was admitted at Primary Children's Hospital and immediately put into an isolation room, since he had come from a foreign country with a yet unknown illness. Jean told of her amazement
at seeing how sterile and carefully monitored everything was. The contrast to the humble situation in Tonga was so great that it was a little
frightening to her. Skilled doctors immediately put the baby on intravenous feeding with the most up-to-date equipment that measured
and controlled the flow of fluid in "mini-drops." As she observed this
meticulous care she was overwhelmed with gratitude for the help and
protection given John Enoch just three days earlier in Tonga. There,
she had watched the same life-saving fluid flow rapidly, and largely
unmeasured, directly into the vein at his ankle. Yet it gave him strength
to endure the trip to that haven for infants in need.

She told me that above all she was grateful for the blessings of God and the fasting and prayers of so many faithful, loving people, which in the final analysis made all the difference. Jean explained that many tests were being conducted in an effort to identify John's exact condition and she would let me know when the results came in.

Many questions went unasked. It was so good to hear Jean's voice, I just wanted to listen and absorb the love it carried. I explained how terribly I missed her and John Enoch, but promised her I would take good care of our daughters in Tonga just as I knew she would take care of our son in America. I let her know that the Saints in Fiji had joined and would continue to join the Tongan Saints in fasting and prayers for our son. It was hard to say good-bye, but it was time to go to the airport. We each expressed our love and faith and recommitted ourselves to following God's will.

I left for Tonga feeling buoyed up, knowing they had arrived safely and that John Enoch was in the care of skilled doctors and nurses at the Primary Children's Hospital. I felt the love of a faithful wife uncomplainingly giving her all for our family. I was grateful that Jean had chosen her family as her career. Nothing could be more challenging or more fulfilling. I knew her career was difficult, but because of her love and faith she was blessed with the vision and help to not only succeed but excel. How blessed we were!

To our anxious daughters as well as to friends, members, and missionaries I reported all that had happened. Over the next several days telegrams flew back and forth, and with each new message the smiles on the faces of the crowds of faithful Tongans, who regularly gathered for updated reports, broadened and deepened in satisfaction and gratitude.

In my first weekend back from Fiji there was a district conference in Nuku'alofa. I intended to say a few words of thanks to the members for their fasting and prayers and faith on behalf of John Enoch, then speak on the life-giving mission of the Savior.

As I started to speak, something remarkable happened. A hush came over the congregation that acted like a vacuum and literally pulled thoughts and words and phrases from me. As I spoke of the eternal importance of families I couldn't help but talk of stars and promises, of Jean and John Enoch, of life and faith and love, and of the Savior's central role in all of this. The words flowed in such a beautiful profusion of deep meanings that every eye glistened with emotion and understanding. I knew the words were not mine, I don't know

Tongan that well. The love and faith of these good Saints were literally pulling truth and beauty and understanding from heaven.

When I finished I was so weak that I asked someone to drive me home. I was asleep almost as soon as I got in the car.

I thought that would be all, but the very next weekend at a district conference in Vaini almost the identical thing happened. I had not written down or remembered exactly what I had said before, but as I started to speak the Spirit again took charge. The unbroken stream of Tongan words and phrases could only be put together by angels—and I acknowledged such.

After the meeting, the district president whispered to me that as I spoke he saw Jean at my side holding our baby boy. I told him it was true, as she was always there. What a choice experience!

There are very few occasions in life where the situation is right and the Spirit gives approval to talk of such deep and important things in public. I was grateful that these were such occasions.

In addition to the constant requests for information about the baby from the members and missionaries, we received inquiries from the palace, the Minister of Health, the hospital, the British consulate, and many others. It was humbling to realize how many were sincerely following this extraordinary case. After all, he was their "Tongan Baby Boy." Everyone felt greatly relieved when we received the following telegram: "Baby's problem identified. . . . Serious but repairable. Will explain later."

Soon another telegram arrived explaining that an operation would be needed very soon. It didn't say by whom or where or when, but once again the hand of the Lord became evident and everything fell naturally into place. Our doctor friend from the plane had specialized in the type of surgery John Enoch needed. He had recently moved his practice to Provo, Utah, and Jean's parents had recently moved from California to nearby Orem, Utah. Thus Jean would have a place to stay as well as the needed support during the days of the operation and re-cuperation.

When I read the telegram outlining this proposal by Jean, a warm feeling came over me and I had full confidence it was the right decision. I responded by telegram: "Yes, go ahead with the operation in Provo under the direction of Dr. Hatch. Stay at your parents' home for as long as needed."

There was more fasting and prayer on the day of the operation.

Many exercised great faith that I know helped immensely. All we could do now was wait.

As the time arrived to receive a telegram on the outcome of the operation, people began to gather and just "hang around" the mission home. A feeling of anxious anticipation filled the area. When the telegram finally arrived, I could tell by the grin on the courier's face that it was good news: "First operation successful. Pressure relieved. Immediate concerns lessened. Baby improving." The only thing the local people saw or talked about was the phrase "operation successful." There was gleeful enthusiasm among all who felt part of this Tongan baby miracle.

I remember our daughters squealing for joy as they jumped up and down, pulled on my arms and legs, and excitedly asked:

"When does Mommy come home?"

"When is our baby brother coming back?"

"I get to hold him first!"

"No! I do!"

"No, me!"

"Please, let me!"

I assured them we would work that out when the time arrived.

While I was ecstatic about the good news, something in the back of my mind told me there were other concerns. I couldn't put my finger on just what they were, but I knew they were there. I felt calm but a little apprehensive. Before long I received the sobering telegram: "For medical reasons John Enoch should not return to Tonga."

Now new questions had to be dealt with. There was still over a year left on our mission. Would it be cut short? What should we do? I decided to leave everything in the hands of the Lord, knowing that thus the right thing would be done.

Weeks slipped by. I tried as best I could to keep up my schedule of district and missionary conferences. I went to a conference in Niue, where I had an opportunity to visit with Feki. What strength and support I received from him! As I left, he expressed his love and faith and told me of the fasting and prayers of the Saints on Niue for John E.

The only way to get back to Tonga from Niue was via Samoa. On my stop-over in Samoa I found that one of the teachers at the Church school had a "ham" radio, and he patched me through to Jean at her folks' home. It was the first good talk we had had for a long time. I was elated to hear her voice again and feel her love and her willingness to do whatever was best. She filled me in on the details of John

An outing at Hufangalupe Beach during Jean's absence.

Enoch's progress. He had been born with a congenital defect and, while the initial surgery had removed the immediate danger, an even bigger and more serious operation would be needed to fully correct this problem. The doctors suggested we wait until he was at least two years old for this operation.

She explained our various options: first, she could stay with John Enoch and leave the girls with me in Tonga; second, the girls could join her and John E; or third, we could leave John E with his grandparents and Jean could return to Tonga. Medically there was no anticipated crisis with John E for at least another eighteen months. However, the doctors were firm that he should not return to Tonga, but should stay close to specialized care and modern facilities. As she reviewed the various options, I told her that I felt we should postpone a final decision until we had more time to think and ponder. Jean agreed.

We were leaning toward Jean's returning and leaving John E with his grandparents, but we wanted to be certain that this was the Lord's will. Making this decision called for additional fasting and prayer. I was willing to wait, as I was sure a definite answer would come when the time was right.

27

A Late-Night Caller

When Jean had been gone a little over a month, I woke suddenly one night from a deep sleep. No sound woke me. I was not sick. I had not been bitten. Nobody had touched me, but I was wide awake.

I looked at my watch; it was 3:00 A.M. I thought I should try to go back to sleep; however, I was so wide awake that I didn't know if I could. Rather than just lie there I decided to go to the office and read for a while. I quietly dressed, slipped out the bedroom door, and stepped into the semi-darkness of a moonlit night.

As I crossed the open courtyard I was struck by the beauty of that balmy night. The warm wind rippled gently through the banana leaves and softly caressed the flowers. They responded with a nocturnal sigh that filled the air with a fragrance so delicate and so desirable as to cause me to almost stop in mid-stride. My senses were saturated with the aroma of that beautiful scene. I thought of shepherds in olden days watching their flocks by night. I thought of those who have developed the ability to see and feel and smell things that most of us sleep through. Thus in a way these beautiful nighttime smells and sounds and sights are not really part of our world. I sensed we were the poorer for missing so much.

After a few moments of savoring that wondrous sensation I opened the door to my office, entered, turned on the light, and started reading the scriptures. I was currently reading in Psalms. As I read I almost felt myself transported to those shadowy plains and hills of yore where shepherds watched their flocks by night and saw and heard and understood things of utmost importance.

I had been reading and pondering for just a few minutes when I heard a light tapping on the glass louvers. I wondered who it could be at that hour. When I opened the louvers I saw the solemn face of a member of the branch presidency from Fo'ui.

"President," he said almost apologetically, "my aunt passed away a few hours ago in Fo'ui. The family asked if I would come to town and see if you would speak at her funeral? I walked to town immediately, but when I arrived at the mission home I saw that all the lights were out. I didn't want to disturb you, so I waited for a while. When everything stayed dark I decided to go back to Fo'ui. I hadn't gone very far when I noticed a light go on in your office. I thought maybe it was a sign, so I came back. Can you come?"

"What time is the funeral?" I asked.

"Well, she died just after midnight, so I think around nine or ten in the morning would be fine. At least, she must be buried before noon. When can you come? We'll have the funeral then."

I told him I would be there at nine o'clock.

I sat back down and thought of that good man walking for several hours through the night on the vague hope (or profound faith?) that I might be in town, that I might be awake, and that perhaps I might be able to come. I pictured him walking all the way back to Fo'ui and telling the family he had fulfilled his assignment and I would come. In my mind I could see the extended family, with many friends and neighbors gathered around the body of this faithful woman, spending the night singing hymns of hope and keeping the immediate family company in their hour of need. What love. What faith.

I read and pondered for another hour or two, then returned to the family side of the building to get the children up and ready for the day. After breakfast I took the older children to school before going to Fo'ui for the funeral. In Fo'ui I visited with the family of the deceased woman as well as many other people who had gathered for the funeral. I thought I would talk about David and the Psalms, as prompted by my reading earlier that morning. However, as I visited with the family and the large crowd of mostly nonmembers, a clear impression came to me. I knew exactly what I should use as my text; it was not the Psalms.

The deceased woman was a faithful Church member and the mother of several children. She had died while still relatively young. Because she came from a large family, a big crowd of extended family members and friends was in attendance. Since our little chapel in

Fo'ui could not accommodate the crowd, the services were held outside on the lawn. The branch president conducted. After a few words of welcome and explanation and an opening song and prayer, he turned the time to me. I was the only speaker.

As I stood and looked over that large, attentive gathering, I saw more than a group of Tongans sitting reverently on the ground. I saw a somewhat misty yet beautiful gathering of special souls. I knew very few people there, only the members, yet as I spoke it was as though a veil was taken from my mind. Everyone seemed familiar. Where had I seen them before? I could not tell, but I sensed clearly that I was entrusted with the challenge of speaking the truth and bearing testimony to this remnant of the house of Israel. I saw them not as members or nonmembers but as children of Israel, descendants of the prophets who needed to hear their forebears' testimony of the Savior.

I turned to 2 Nephi chapter 9 and began to read. I know of no single chapter that so clearly cries out with such appropriate explanations as were needed at this funeral. For almost an hour I read and explained and testified of those priceless principles recorded so many centuries ago. They were still as fresh and meaningful as the day they were written.

I was given great fluency, both in the Tongan tongue and in the ability to understand and testify of important truths. The phrases from chapter 9, along with additional explanations, seemed to flow fluidly:

"O how great the goodness of our God!" (v. 10.)
"O how great the plan of our God!" (v. 13.)
"O the greatness and the justice of our God!" (v. 17.)
"O the greatness of the mercy of our God, the Holy One of Israel!" (v. 19.)
"O how great the holiness of our God! For he knoweth all things, and there is not anything save he knows it." (v. 20.)

The Spirit seemed to envelop everyone and direct the whole occasion. Everyone gave me rapt attention, but for some reason my eyes were drawn to one stately man who sat erect in the partial shade of some *kape* plants to my left. His large tattered mat showed his respect for the departed and indicated that he was probably a close relative. He seemed to embody everything that the prophets of yesteryear desired to touch with their testimonies of the Savior and of God's plan for Israel.

At times I was able to read those sacred verses without even looking at them. My testimony on each point seemed to come effortlessly not only from within but also from distances and times and places that are beyond explanation. I knew that earnest desires were being fulfilled.

As I came to the closing verses of that beautiful chapter, I read with shared emotion:

> Come, my brethren, every one that thirsteth, come ye to the waters; and he that hath no money, come buy and eat; yea, come buy wine and milk without money and without price.
>
> Wherefore, do not spend money for that which is of no worth, nor your labor for that which cannot satisfy. Hearken diligently unto me, and remember the words which I have spoken; and come unto the Holy One of Israel, and feast upon that which perisheth not, neither can be corrupted, and let your soul delight in fatness.
>
> Behold, my beloved brethren, remember the words of your God; pray unto him continually by day, and give thanks unto his holy name by night. Let your hearts rejoice. (2 Nephi 9:50–52.)

I looked again at the attentive crowd. No one stirred; all eyes and hearts were focused. I noticed the disheveled hair, the torn mats, the dust and ashes—all undeniable signs of mourning in an Israelitish culture.

Their expectant eyes seemed to pull the next verse from me: "And behold how great the covenants of the Lord, and how great his condescensions unto the children of men" (verse 53).

At that point my eyes focused directly on the man by the *kape* plant. The sun had moved, leaving him no longer in the shade, but he made no effort to shield his eyes or alter his position. He sat cross-legged, looking intently at me. As I returned his gaze I noticed tears starting to trickle down his cheeks. He made no movement; but I felt him saying: "It's true, I know it; something inside tells me it's true."

I could not hold back my own tears as I concluded the balance of that verse: "and because of his greatness, and his grace and mercy, he has promised unto us that our seed shall not utterly be destroyed, according to the flesh, but that he would preserve them; and in future generations they shall become a righteous branch unto the house of Israel" (verse 53).

I paused and looked again at the people sitting in front of the small chapel, filling the lawn and spilling into the nearby garden area.

For a moment I thought I could feel and see serene smiles on ancient faces. I felt weak, yet fulfilled.

I concluded by testifying that familiar voices had been heard and eternal truths had been taught. I explained that if those present would heed God's counsel and obey His laws, families would be united, even over centuries of time. I pleaded with them to listen to the missionaries and follow what they taught. I testified of the Savior, asked the Lord's blessings on everyone, and sat down—or rather, collapsed down, so weak was I.

The branch president had previously announced the closing song and prayer, but the power of the Spirit was so strong that no one moved for several minutes. Finally the same man who had tapped on my office window not many hours before stood and offered a heartfelt benediction. The body of the deceased woman, wrapped in tapa cloth and fine mats, was carried to the waiting grave and reverently deposited into the earth.

The normal crying and wailing were held in abeyance, not by anyone's request but by the power of the Spirit and the wonder of all that had occurred. When my strength came back I visited with family members and others for a while.

When it was time to say good-bye I started walking towards the car, accompanied by several family members. Suddenly I remembered the man sitting by the *kape* plant and asked those with me who he was. They were not sure. I looked back at the crowd to point him out but could not see him. I was sure I would recognize his face, but I could not with certainty locate the man.

I talked to the missionaries and described him as best as I could. I asked them to meet with him immediately, as I was confident he was ready for their message. They could not remember seeing such a man, but they assured me that they were aware of every nonmember present and would visit each of them very soon. They were good missionaries and I had full confidence they would do as they said.

I returned to my office in town and was soon caught up in the press of affairs there. I could not, however, get that occasion nor that particular man out of my mind.

The missionaries from Fo'ui had much success in the ensuing months. But despite my descriptions, they were never able to identify with certainty the man by the *kape* plant. Occasionally I went to church in Fo'ui and looked for him, but I was never sure who it might have been.

I have pondered on this event for many years. It would be so nice to know that he joined the Church and remained active, but to this day I don't know what happened to him.

I have come to understand that the value of following the prompting of the Spirit does not lie in knowing what happened to someone else or in having a nice story to tell, but rather in knowing that you have done what the Lord wanted you to do. In one sense it doesn't really matter how things turn out with someone else. What matters is what we did. Were we obedient to our charge? Did we follow the promptings we were given? The Lord gives the increase. We have the privilege of being instruments in His hand to bring about His purposes. The results or the increase are up to Him. We should never seek an outward sign as verification of our standing before Him, but rather seek the internal assurance that we have done what He wanted us to do.

I suppose one of the tests of our faith is to do what we know is right and not have things turn out the way we thought they would. It takes a lot of faith to know that whatever He makes of our feeble efforts is His business, not ours. I am sure that over time every ounce of obedience on our part is used in the best way possible by an all-seeing, all-knowing, and all-loving God.

When the things we think should happen because of priesthood blessings we have received, or because of strong feelings we have had, do not happen, we sometimes ask, "Why? Was the blessing not inspired, or were our feelings wrong?" Possibly, but not necessarily. Maybe we misinterpreted those feelings or blessings, or maybe there are other factors that only God is aware of. Maybe others used their agency and simply chose another course. Maybe there was an accident or an interference by an outside influence, or maybe the timing was not yet right in God's infinite wisdom. One thing we can always be sure of is that, regardless of how things *seem* to turn out, if we do what we are prompted by His Spirit to do we *know* everything will eventually turn out the way it should. If we remain faithful, someday we'll understand all things, and when we do we will praise His patience and wisdom.

I am sure that someday, somewhere, somehow, I will know what happened to that man by the *kape* plant. Then I will understand more of the significance of that episode in a far-off island of the sea among a beautiful people of faith. Until then, I simply wait.

28

Go Anyway

When the alarm sounded it was still dark. I was a little disoriented, so it took me a while to remember why I needed to get up so early. Then I remembered I had a conference to attend in Ha'apai. It was rainy, windy, and miserable. I knew the ocean would be terrible. I didn't want to go.

Despite these feelings I more or less mechanically got ready, ate a quick breakfast, packed a few things, made sure all was well with the children, and got in the car with the elders. As we drove to the wharf I again had second thoughts about the trip. I suppose I was starting to feel sorry for myself. I rationalized that the children really needed their father, especially while Jean was gone. I was very tired and starting to feel ill.

These feelings grew, and I thought of more reasons why I should not go. Voyages to Ha'apai and Vava'u were always trying. It was not only the rough seas but the smells, the time involved, and the uncomfortableness of it all. I longed for an airplane or a helicopter—or even a larger boat. Everything I thought of seemed to justify cancelling the trip. I decided to tell the elders to turn around and take me back home.

Just as I started to tell the elders to turn around, another feeling came saying that even though I didn't feel like it I really should go anyway. It was not a command or even a forceful feeling, but rather a quiet feeling from somewhere deep inside me. It was enough to stop my words to the elders and start a new round of mental jousting.

I reasoned back and forth, first feeling fully justified in not going and then sensing that I really should go anyway. It was not so much a battle between right and wrong as it was a battle between right and comfort. I don't consider myself a particularly strong person, for when these choices come I sometimes go one way and sometimes the other way. I am convinced that to do what the Lord wants us to do we must be willing to move beyond our comfort zone. I managed to be quiet long enough to arrive at the wharf.

As the perceptive elders put my things on the boat they said, "We weren't sure if you were going or not." I replied that I really didn't want to go but I felt that I should go anyway.

The trip up was worse than usual, and more than once I wondered if I had made the right decision. I was not able to rest at all, being sick most of the fifteen hours it took to get there. The rain and rough seas were gloomy. They fairly accurately mirrored my feelings.

About an hour out of Pangai the captain asked me to come to the back of the boat. When I arrived he pointed to a distant object that I could barely make out. "What is it?" I asked.

"It's a sailboat, and I think it's in trouble. Should we go over that way?" I didn't have to answer, for the rule at sea is that you always help anyone who might be in distress. When we were within shouting distance we saw that it was a boat filled to over-capacity with Church members from the island of Uiha going to our conference. Their sail had torn, and beset by the contrary winds they were floundering and having a difficult time going anywhere. We threw them a long rope, which they tied to their boat. We pulled them for the last hour or so of the voyage to Pangai. All of us were grateful that our paths had crossed.

As we concluded the conference I shuddered to think how close I had come to choosing another course. If I had done so I would have missed the spiritual feast of the conference as well as the joy of helping the boat from Uiha. I was grateful for that little spark that kept saying, "Go anyway."

I have not always made that same choice. At the conclusion of a conference months later I felt so tired that I could hardly keep going. A choice came up, much like the choice of going to Ha'apai or not. This time I said, "I'll do it, but not now." In other words, because I was so tired I chose comfort. It was not a huge issue and I didn't feel any anger from the Lord in that choice, only I knew that I should have given a little more, taken one more step, and gone another mile

despite my tiredness. I have often wondered what would have happened had I done so. I recognize that often these decisions don't affect things eternally, for the Lord is kind and patient and gives us
plenty of chances. Just as I was blessed for going to Ha'apai, perhaps
there would have been blessings in obeying promptings at this other
conference.

Years later I heard President Marion G. Romney tell about a time
when he felt impressed to do something yet didn't do it, and he often
wondered what would have happened had he done it. He went on to
explain that God always gives us more chances. I was comforted to
know that I was not alone in my question.

How good God is to us. He is very patient, encouraging, and helpful. God, like all great coaches, doesn't "drop" us when we "drop the
ball," as we sometimes do. Rather than forgetting us, He regroups and
starts a new set of circumstances in motion that will give us new opportunities to stretch and prove ourselves (see Moroni 6:8). He knows
that when we are ready we will choose correctly. He wants us to
acheive the greatness He knows is in us.

On the other hand Satan tries to catch us when we are tired, ill,
discouraged, lonely, or unprepared. For years I thought this was particularly unfair. I thought Satan should not be allowed to do that, that
when he tempts us we should be at our best strength to fight him off.
But we should realize that Satan is not a fair person. He always takes
advantage of any weakness he can find. That is where the real test
comes in. We must overcome these weaknesses, or plug these holes in
our armor. God is always willing to help us do so, as He wants to help
us counteract Satan's onslaughts.

The Savior was tempted after fasting forty days. He was kept up
all night facing false accusations in illegal hearings. Think of the trials
He faced after He had been abandoned by His friends, beaten for no
cause, berated by traitors, and left alone. Surely He was more tired,
more ill, more alone, and more unfairly treated than any of us could
ever be. Yet He did what He should. He went anyway.

The scriptures beautifully capture these truths: "For behold, I,
God, have suffered these things for all . . . which suffering caused myself, even God, the greatest of all, to tremble because of pain, and to
bleed at every pore, and to suffer both body and spirit—and would
that I might not drink the bitter cup, and shrink—nevertheless, glory
be to the Father, and I partook and finished my preparations unto the
children of men" (D&C 19:18–19).

If we will ask for help and then listen, the Spirit of God will whisper to us and tell us what we should do and give us the strength to do it. Even though the voice of the Spirit is small and comes from deep within us, it has more power than all of the tiredness, illness, or discomfort we can ever feel.

If we do what we should only when we are *not* ill or tired or lonely, where is the test? Where is the growth? Where can blessings come from? I know that God loves all of His children perfectly. No matter how they act, they will one day know that He consistently loved them with all His heart and always had faith and confidence in them.

What a marvelous way to treat people! What a great example of parenthood! I hope I can remember these principles and act as God would, so that my children and grandchildren and others I work with can look back at me from any point in time and be able to say, "One thing we know, you always believed in us and you always loved us."

God loves us, and despite our tiredness or illness or discouragement He will always help us to "go anyway" so that we can experience the joy that comes from doing so.

29

I Need You Here

On my birthday in June I received one of the best gifts imaginable. A letter arrived from Elder Monson informing me that a stake had been authorized for Tonga. He expressed his deep satisfaction with the approval and his testimony that God's hand was clearly manifest in guiding this action.

He asked that I not say anything to anyone until someone was officially assigned to create the stake. He expressed his love and gave some positive comments on our baby, John Enoch. He also explained that in the normal rotation of assignments he would be replaced by Elder Howard W. Hunter as our first contact.

As I read the letter I found my emotions flying all over. First I was ecstatic that the stake had been approved. Then I felt a pang of anguish that Jean wasn't with me to share this joyous news. I was grateful for the good report on our baby but felt the emptiness of not having him and Jean with me. I was saddened that Elder Monson would no longer be our first contact but was happy to be able to work with Elder Hunter.

I wanted to shout to everyone the news about the stake but realized that I would have to restrain myself from saying anything. However, I knew I could express my gratitude to my Father in Heaven and ask for His help on how to proceed. As I did this I received His calming assurance that this was His will, that Jean and the baby were fine, and that He would give them the same spirit of peace so we could all enjoy it together.

All I could do now was work hard and wait—wait for additional information on the stake and wait for word on John Enoch's condition and on Jean's possible return. Some of our biggest challenges come by having to wait for things over which we have little or no control.

Days turned into weeks, and weeks into months. Oh, how I missed Jean! I was always busy during the day with interviews, meetings, playing with the children, and helping them with schoolwork. When evening came, however, and the children were in bed, I seemed shrouded in a feeling of deep melancholy. Each evening, after kissing the children good-night, I walked alone down to a little-used wharf a few blocks from the mission home. I went to the very end of the wharf and stood staring to the Northeast over the vast Pacific Ocean, attempting to reach America. In but a moment I seemed to travel those thousands of miles to the shores of California, then beyond to Utah, where I could visit night after night with my wife and my son. Even though thousands of miles separated us I felt very close to them. I also felt their love and faith and assurance as they returned my projected thoughts and feelings.

I was alone yet with my loved ones on those nightly sojourns to the edge of the endless sea that for so many years had physically separated Jean and me both while I was on my first mission and now.

A Father's Day photo sent to Jean and John Enoch, June 1968.

Occasionally as I walked to and from the wharf someone would ask if there was anything they could do to help. I would just give a slight shake of my head and the person would fade into the night, not wanting to disturb.

I felt I was gaining spiritual strength every day and becoming more and more certain that the outcome of John E's situation would be positive. I felt I could deal pretty well with most anything now. But sometimes when we feel we have "weathered the storm" and can "take on the world" we get new surprises. The Lord has a way of keeping us humble.

One particular night I noticed some large shipping containers that had been left near the end of the wharf. As I went beyond the containers to the very end of the wharf I sensed that someone was close by. For the first time in all those weeks I began to feel a little uneasy.

I decided to leave early. As I started to return home I heard some muffled whispering. Almost immediately a young woman appeared and began talking to me. In effect she offered her services—a little apologetically, I felt. I shook my head and kept walking. "I won't charge," she said, "I just want to help. We've been watching and talking about you." (So there were others!) "I can understand a few weeks, but your wife has been gone almost two months now."

I just shook my head and kept walking, never really looking at her. She kept following, and when we reached the road she spoke again. "Are you sure? I'd like to help. I won't charge and I won't say anything to anyone." I just shook my head again and kept walking.

When she could tell I was leaving she stopped and said quietly, "You must really love your wife."

For the first time since she started talking I stopped, turned, looked at her and replied, "I do love my wife. I love her with all my heart." She stared into space. I saw tears trickle down her face and sensed a slight trembling as she spoke to no one in particular: "*Mani, keu amanaki ki ha me'a pehe.*" ("Oh, that I could even hope for such a thing." Or in our vernacular, "How would it be?")

I felt a sense of sorrow for her. I had felt that such women were motivated by evil forces, but now I wondered how many have been trapped or taught incorrectly, or had other problems we do not understand. My mind flashed to the Savior talking to the woman at the well, to Mary (out of whom seven devils had been cast), and to the woman taken in sin to whom He said, "Neither do I condemn thee: go, and sin no more" (John 8:11).

I wanted to say more—and maybe I should have. Instead I simply said sincerely, "Thanks for understanding," and hurriedly walked the last two blocks to the mission home.

As I knelt in prayer that night I expressed more deeply than usual my thanks to God for extra help and protection. Then, almost without thinking, I found myself asking Him to bless that woman and help her to find a better life and help me to not judge others, yet always hold fast to the right.

For the next several days I stayed away from the wharf. I had become so used to visiting with Jean through the air and over the seas each evening that I felt I had been robbed of something very precious. Still I felt that under the circumstances I should not go again.

A few days later I found the following unsigned note under my door. "Please don't stay away from the wharf. No one will ever bother you again. I promise." I had no idea where it came from, but I felt that whoever wrote it was telling the truth, so I started going to the wharf again. True to whoever's word it was, I was never bothered again.

As a postscript: While I never learned for sure who wrote the note, an incident happened many years later in Hawaii that shed some light on the mystery. After a conference in Honolulu, an older Tongan man came up to me and said: "You don't know me but I know you. Years ago I observed you turn down a proposal at a wharf in Nuku-'alofa. Knowing the situation with your wife being gone so long and a beautiful woman being available for free, I couldn't believe you would just walk away.

"I had been baptized as a youth, but had never really been active. I resolved that evening that there must be something to the Church. It took me several years, as I had many things to overcome, but I want you to know that I am now an active temple-going member and have a son on a mission. Thanks for showing me that we can receive power beyond ourselves."

I didn't ask any questions but encouraged him to remain faithful and true to his covenants.

I am convinced that God uses every right thing anyone does to help someone, somewhere, somehow. I thanked God again for His help and protection on that lonely night those many years ago.

More weeks passed, the days flying by but the nights dragging slowly on. One evening a heart-tugging incident happened during a combined mission presidency and mission council meeting. Our five-year-old, Marilyn, came wandering in saying she had "nothing to do."

I picked her up and gave her a hug and asked her to sit quietly by me until our meeting was over, as we were near the end. She sat quietly for a while but then turned and started looking at the pictures of the missionaries and our family on the wall behind us. In a very small voice, almost talking to herself, she pointed and said: "Oh yes, now I remember. That's my mommy. I had forgotten what she looked like. Hmmm .... so that's my mommy."

I turned and looked at her. Her childlike expression of love and longing hit me with great force. I didn't think anyone else had seen or heard or felt the significance of her words. Yet as I turned back to the other leaders there was hardly a dry eye in the room. These were big men, strong, tough, and full of experience, yet they had been touched to the core by the honest expression of a little girl. We closed our meeting with a special prayer to be guided to know with certainty what Jean and I ought to do.

A few days later, as I was helping the children with their school-work, a very clear impression came to me. I could hardly wait to get to the phone and try to place a call to Jean. Usually the lines from Tonga to the United States would fade or be full of static, so we seldom even tried. But this day heaven seemed to smile on us. The call went straight through and was relatively clear.

How wonderful to hear Jean's voice again! I told her I now felt certain that it would be fine for her to leave the baby there, as the doctors recommended, and have his grandparents care for him. (He ended up staying with Jean's family for three more months, then with my family in Idaho Falls until we returned home from our mission about a year later.)

I could tell Jean was a little torn between wanting to be with our son in Utah and at the same time wanting to be with her husband and her five daughters in Tonga. I finally said: "Jean, I can handle the thousands of Saints here, as we have many good local leaders to help. I can even handle the nearly four hundred missionaries (full-time and district) we have at this time, as they are such well-disciplined young men and women. But I just can't handle these five little girls on my own. I need your help. I need you here."

Jean felt good about the decision and made arrangements to return. Thus, nearly three months after I had watched her and Mom and the baby leave from Fiji I returned to Fiji to meet her. In the wee hours of the morning I watched the same night sky from the same airport trying to see the same star they had left on. Finally I spotted a blinking light that got brighter and brighter and closer and closer until the giant steel bird landed and delivered my beautiful wife back to me.

We both shed tears at not having our son with us, but we knew he was in good hands. God was in charge, and He expected us to move forward. Even though in some respects things hadn't turned out the way we had hoped, we were so grateful for the priceless blessing of life given our son that everything else sank into insignificance.

When we returned to Tonga, Jean was given a reception befitting a returning queen. Everyone, including the reigning queen, wanted a detailed description of all that had transpired. Pictures of a healthy-looking baby boy were passed all over. New assurances were given that he would be fine. I was asked by many to promise to bring him back to Tonga as soon as possible so they could see (and touch) him. For some reason I felt comfortable in making that promise. I knew the Lord had ways of opening doors for those who exercise great faith, as these wonderful people had done.

We felt we should now set that chapter aside and move on with the work of the mission. We knew that the best way to show our gratitude to God and to the faithful Tongans and Fijians and Niueans was to put our hearts even more fully into the work of building His kingdom in that particular part of His vineyard. We knew that as there was no more we could physically do for our son, God would see that what was best for all was done. And it was.

30

O Zion! Dear Zion!

Not long after Jean's return I received an exciting letter stating that Elder Howard W. Hunter and Elder Thomas S. Monson had been assigned to come in September to create the first stake of Zion in Tonga. I was now free to tell others. My natural inclination was to run out and shout the news to everyone. However, as I thought about it, a more subdued feeling came over me. I prayed for guidance as to how to announce this event. The impression came that I should call a special district conference in Nuku'alofa and wait until the afternoon session to announce the stake, and at that time I would be given what to say and how to say it.

I called my counselors and told them about the approval to create the stake and my feelings about a special district conference. They felt the same, so we called a conference to be held in two weeks' time. Because of the curiosity that having a special conference created, we knew everyone would be there.

The conference day arrived. The morning session was wonderful. There was an even bigger attendance at the afternoon session. We had a full slate of speakers. I had asked for only the last twenty minutes. All the talks were very brief, however, and I noticed that we were running out of speakers alarmingly fast. With only forty-five minutes used from our two-hour session, the last of the participants sat down. The conducting officer then announced that the congregation would sing a rest hymn, "O Ye Mountains High," and the balance of the time would be given to President Groberg. I had hoped by now to have some definite feelings on what to say, but my only thought was that it seemed odd to be singing "O Ye Mountains High" there on the small, flat islands of Tonga.

Then as the majestic chorus boomed forth in Tongan: "O Zion! dear Zion! home of the free. . . ." I found myself saying, "O Zion! Dear Zion! Home of the free, home of those freed from sin, home of those made free through faith and obedience, home of the pure in heart, home of the faithful Tongans who have gone before, home of those still here who are striving to purify their hearts. Home of all those who through patience and perseverance will possess their souls in purity, peace, and truth." I was thumbing through the Doctrine and Covenants. Section after section received a paper mark, and I noted down verse after verse. My mind was racing now and I was seeing and hearing and feeling things unfathomable to the mortal mind.

I'm sure they sang other words, but all I heard was "O Zion! dear Zion! home of the free" over and over again, as though it were coming both from above and from those around me. I wasn't sure when the song ended, for as everyone sat down and I moved toward the pulpit I was still hearing, "O Zion! Dear Zion! home of the free—home of the pure in heart—home of all who have overcome the world through Jesus Christ, the Savior of all mankind. In thy temples we'll bend; all thy rights we'll defend; and our home shall be ever with thee—the healer of the penitent and the purifier of all who will come to His Zion and enter into His rest."

For long moments I looked at the audience in silence. I hadn't started talking, yet already I could see tears rolling down the faithful faces of the Saints in front of me. I still didn't know where to start or what to say. The eyes looking at me were filled with hope, love, and anticipation. But there was something else—a longing look that seemed to focus my attention on a different element. I began to sense the presence of others as real as those physically visible. A little embarrassed to wait so long, I felt I should say something. Still, I knew that a great deal of communication was taking place in the profound silence, and it seemed a shame to interrupt that silent sermon, but I now knew what to say.

"Jesus lives and He loves you and me and all people. Think of all that means and all that implies! There is no greater message anyone can give anywhere. I know it to be true. You know it to be true. He has heard and answered your prayers and those of your faithful forebears who have moved on ahead. We are witnesses to and recipients of His love. He has caused life, light, love, and His gospel of faith and repentance to come among you and to be given to you. It is His will that His gospel be lived and renewed and passed down in purity by you through the stream of time. We are all witnesses to this. We all know it to be true." There were humble nods of acknowledgment.

I then spoke about life and birth and light and love and faith; and of Jesus, who is the center of everything. I explained that John Enoch had been born and given life through the light of Christ and that his life had been preserved through their faith and love. I gave a brief report on his well-being. I then explained that in a similar manner the Tongan Mission had been born and given life through the light of Christ. When it was in serious danger, its life had been preserved through faith and love. I explained that through the coming jubilee, life and faith and love would be passed to another generation. Those who had sacrificed so unselfishly and endured so much before would not only be honored but would be active participants in helping to see that the greatest elements in the universe—life, light, and love—would become an ever larger part of our lives and thus help light this whole world. Their sacrifices would also affect the lives of many as we lived, shared, and taught the gospel of Jesus Christ to our children and to others.

I explained that every Tongan and every child of God on either side of the veil has a right to hear the gospel of Jesus Christ and develop a sufficient love for Him to eagerly follow Him and do what is necessary to be forgiven and saved by Him.

I then explained that to do this the Lord Himself had given us the means whereby we could more fully accomplish that mission. He had given us His kingdom—which was The Church of Jesus Christ of Latter-day Saints. I told of our being able to be baptized, hold the priesthood, attend church, serve missions, and go to the temple. A few could even go back to the temple and help their departed loved ones.

I was led to read various scriptures about the vision of Zion—that elusive dream which through the ages has been the desire of all the prophets and Saints. I continued: "For this is Zion—THE PURE IN HEART" (D&C 97:21). Yes, the gospel and all of these precious truths are to help us become pure in heart so that we may become inhabitants of Zion. They are to help us stand firmly in the truth so that our feet may be as the beauty of the feet of those who stand on Mount Zion, who help save others, who declare glad tidings of good, whose hands are clean and whose words and thoughts are not deceitful, and whose hearts are pure."

I explained that there were many types of birth—people, missions, causes, testimonies. Now there was another significant birth that God had ordained to take place soon in Tonga. I paused and looked into those faithful, expectant eyes, then continued: "Purify your hearts by remembering your forebears and by loving and helping them. Through faith and love extend your reach to all your brothers and sisters not only directly but also through the missionaries and through temple and family history activities. Be kind to one another and teach your children properly by raising them in light and truth and honoring the priesthood, which is among you. You have done these things. Now as you continue doing all these things, God has decreed that on September 5, 1968, a stake of Zion will be born in Tonga!"

I had not intended to wait for any kind of dramatic effect, but as the tremendous significance of what had just been said sank in I could say no more. There was profound silence. Even the sobs and the falling tears seemed to be a part of the reverent stillness. For a moment I wondered: What is the difference between a chapel full of faithful Tongan Saints and a gathering of angels? What is the difference between Zion here and Zion there? In a way I knew the answer.

I felt impressed to read all of Doctrine and Covenants section 65. Each verse was beautiful and was understood perfectly. When I came to the fifth verse I read, "When Jesus shall come down in heaven" and we all understood instantly that it meant exactly what it said—not *from* heaven, but *in* heaven, or bringing heaven with Him.

I continued by explaining what a stake is, and I promised that more details would come later. For now, the important element was proper preparation. To prepare properly we all needed to purify our hearts so that there would be a total unity of purpose. I felt impressed to ask every family to gather together that evening and thank God for the blessing of a stake and ask Him to help them become worthy of it.

I bore my testimony again of the Savior and of Zion—dear Zion, land of the free, land of the pure. I expressed my testimony of the Prophet Joseph Smith and of God's present mouthpiece on earth, David O. McKay. Then I sat down.

No one could sing the closing song because of the sobbing and the chills and the self-introspection brought about by the profound desire to purify hearts that overshadowed all present. Finally someone gave the closing prayer. No one stirred for some time after that; then gradually we began to come back to temporal reality in the Matavai

Moʻui chapel in the heart of beautiful Nukuʻalofa—"the abode of love." The messages from heaven had perfectly filled the time allotted, and the conference ended on schedule.

The members were almost ethereal in appearance and demeanor. Their tears were sincere and their hearts were subdued and pure. It was an extraordinarily beautiful day. The breeze was cool, the sky was blue, the clouds were white and clean, the sea serene, and the waves seemed to speak of eternity.

As we returned home, an aura of spiritual light was still hovering over everything. I was able to listen to the children with new ears and see them with new eyes. I felt deep gratitude for each of them and especially for their mother, my God-given helpmate. It was so good to have her back and have her participate in this miracle. We talked about Zion, about our family in Idaho and Utah, about John Enoch and home and grandparents, and about love and unselfishness, helpfulness and faith. We talked about what it would be like when Jesus came again, when Zion, in all its glory, would be fully established.

I looked off into space and calmly observed, "I don't know exactly when or how that Zion will come, but I know it will be familiar to us, for we have just been there." Jean looked at me with understanding and we realized we were still there.

31

Obedience

In Tonga, obedience was understood to be a prerequisite for a mission. As I watched the missionaries I realized that honest obedience is actually the ultimate expression of faithfulness, for you can't have one without the other.

I was in a store one morning when the store owner looked at a large clock over the door and saw it had stopped during the night. He called to his clerk in the back room and said: "Bill, what time is it? The big clock stopped last night and I need to reset it."

I looked at my watch, but before I could give him the time and before his clerk called back, he suddenly said: "Oh, never mind, Bill, it's nine o'clock. I can see the Mormon missionaries leaving their *fale*."

I looked at my watch. It was nine o'clock straight up. I turned to the owner as he was setting the large clock on the wall and asked, "You can set your clock by when the Mormon missionaries leave their house?"

"Of course," he replied. "They always leave at nine o'clock sharp, never a minute before or after. It's one of the things we rely on around here."

I thanked him, completed my business, and then drove a few blocks away to wait for the missionaries to come by. When they arrived I got out of the car, gave them each a big hug, and thanked them for being so obedient. I said: "You may not know it, but this village sets their clocks by your departure time. Thanks for doing what is right."

They looked at me a little puzzled, almost as if to say: "Well, what did you expect? The mission rule is to be out working at nine o'clock, so of course that is exactly when we leave."

As I drove home I wondered how many people set their clocks (both physically and spiritually) by the actions of the missionaries. I have learned from long experience with missionaries all over the world that they will rise or sink to whatever level of obedience we establish for them. This obedience cannot be in words only but must have honest expectations that are met and reinforced.

Once every three or four months on the main island we had a "transfer meeting." All the missionaries laboring on Tongatapu came to Nuku'alofa with all their possessions. Each missionary carried his or her own mat into which they rolled their pillow, sheet, towels, clothes, and personal effects. They also had a hand-woven basket into which they put their scriptures, other teaching supplies, and occasionally a loaf of bread or a green coconut to drink. They seldom wore shoes and they slept on the floor in members' homes, and since they ate with the members they didn't need to carry pots and pans or other bulky items. They normally had about three changes of clothes, which usually lasted them throughout their mission. (They used very little money except for a few bus and boat fares that either we or the members gave them.) Thus from the transfer meeting they were prepared to either return with the same companion to the same location or be assigned to a new area or a new companion or both. There were usually in excess of a hundred young men and women at these meetings.

Beforehand I met with my counselors, the missionary assistants, and others and got their feelings about transfers. After receiving their input I spent most of the day in fasting and prayer, reviewing the missionaries' individual reports and making a list of changes that I felt the Lord approved of. The vast majority of changes I felt should be made were in line with the recommendations I had received. It was a testimony to me that the Spirit gives the self-same message to those who are humble and desire to do what is right.

However, there were inevitably a few changes that I felt should be made which were different from the recommendations I had received. Sometimes I tended to "fight" with the Spirit, as certain impressions I had didn't seem to make any sense.

One such occasion involved a certain Elder Vai, a wonderfully successful zone leader who had only four months left on his mission.

He had joined the Church while attending school at Liahona and was the only member in his family. His father was a preacher in another church and was very unhappy when his son became a Latter-day Saint. The father was confident, however, that his son would come back to "their" church. You can imagine the father's frustration when his son announced that he wanted to go on a mission.

His father told him not to go and said he would not help him in any way, and in fact would do everything possible to stop him from being a "Mormon missionary." But Elder Vai was converted to the truth, and threats could not keep him from doing what he knew was God's will. Even when he was a new missionary his sparkling eyes, happy countenance, and determined spirit told me that he would be a strong missionary.

In our initial interview he mentioned his father's anger and stated that under the circumstances it would probably be best for him not to be assigned to his hometown. Since nearly all of our missionaries were local Tongans, and since Tonga is a fairly small country, basically everyone "knew" everyone else, and close "relatives" were literally everywhere. Still we generally avoided sending young men and women back to the villages they grew up in, this policy being based on the Lord's statement, "A prophet is not without honour, save in his own country, and in his own house" (Matthew 13:57).

During his mission Elder Vai had fulfilled every expectation I had of him, but now, with four months of his mission remaining, I was feeling that he should spend those four months in his hometown! "But that's crazy," I kept saying to myself. I knew he would do whatever I asked of him, but I also knew this would strain his faith almost to the breaking point. What to do? I went to the Lord time and time again desiring a different answer, but each time the only thing I felt good about was to assign him to his home village for his last four months. This was against all reason, against the recommendation of my trusted counselors, against my own thinking, against our policy; but for some reason it seemed to be in accordance with the Lord's will.

I kept struggling all day. Why, I wondered, was there such a conflict in my feelings? If it was right I should just do it. However, I wondered what part common sense and reason should play. It is very difficult to be a leader in Tonga, because whatever you ask the members to do, they do it. You simply must not make a mistake. I finally decided to announce the transfers in a particular order and leave Elder Vai and his companion till near the end, secretly hoping that the Spirit might in the meantime direct things differently.

The meeting began with a power that defies description. No one has heard real missionary singing until they have heard one hundred-plus Tongan missionaries praising the Lord with all their hearts and souls and voices. It brought goose bumps to every person present.

After a wonderful meeting and an appropriate feast provided by the Relief Society, we reassembled for the "transfer" portion of the meeting. Everyone sat with the present companion until his or her new companion was announced; then the junior companion would move and sit with the new senior companion, and so on, until all the changes had been announced.

We went down the list, taking time for each change to be well noted by all and the new companions seated next to each other. As we reached the last ten missionaries and the last five areas yet to be assigned, a hush came over the missionaries. Everyone knew that neither Elder Vai nor his home village had yet been assigned. You could feel the tension. It increased as the unassigned missionaries dropped to eight, then six, and the unassigned areas dropped to four, then three. I announced the next set of missionaries and their area. Now there were only four missionaries and two areas left.

I looked at Elder Vai. He had his head buried in his hands. I looked at the other missionaries. I sensed a strong plea: "Oh, President, please don't. He is such a good elder. Don't do this to him!" The tide of feelings from those gathered missionaries was sweeping over me. I had to make the announcement. What should it be? Should I respond to a clear feeling of preference from the missionaries or should I ask yet again for assurance from God as to His will, which I knew had not changed?

Not wanting to suffer this questioning any longer, I stood and announced the next two missionaries to serve together. This left only Elder Vai and one other elder who would obviously be his companion. Now I needed to announce where the first two would serve. I hesitated as I felt two hundred-plus eyes burning towards me and powerfully beaming the same message—"Please don't, President. Please don't send Elder Vai to his hometown."

I took one more deep breath. I knew what I had to say: "Elder X and Elder Y will serve in Mu'a." This meant that Elder Vai and his companion would be going to the only area left—his home village! Almost immediately there was an incredulous universal gasp.

Tears of joy and sorrow were shed during both the closing song and the prayer, but eventually the missionaries, two by two, gathered their rolled mats and baskets and with their new companions left for their new areas. Elder Vai's new junior companion sat silently, not knowing for sure what to do. Finally, when only the two of them were left, I went over to talk to them. I could see pooled tears in Elder Vai's eyes. His only comment was, "President, just assure me once more that this is God's will."

"It is," I replied. "I know it is."

"Fine, then, we'll be on our way. Pray for me."

"I will, and so will hundreds of others." Since his home village was not too far away, I asked him to come in each Sunday evening and personally report to me how things were going.

They departed, and I was left alone to ponder on what I had done. Or had I done it? It had to be God's will; no one else would do it. I knew He would bless and justify that decision. He had to, I thought. We had been obedient—both Elder Vai and myself—now we needed His *blessings* and His *fulfillment*. Oh, how I pleaded with God for both!

It is hard to know how messages in Tonga get transmitted at times. Even before Elder Vai and his companion arrived at their new area, word had reached his family about his new assignment.

The next day in church Elder Vai's father stood before his congregation and announced what everyone already knew; that his son had disappointed him by becoming a Mormon, had then added insult to injury by becoming a missionary, and now was showing the ultimate disrespect by actually coming to his own town to try and convert his own people to his newfound religion.

"I know these Mormons, though," the father said. "If none of you listen to my son, and if no one lets him in their home or even smiles at him and never helps him in any way, and if you all ask your neighbors to do the same, he will soon be gone, for these missionaries want 'results.'"

The people did as he asked. The first week went by and Elder Vai reported that they had not gotten into a single nonmember home nor given a single standard discussion. We knelt in prayer and asked for the Lord's guidance. At the end of the prayer we felt they should continue trying for another week.

The father, in the meantime, congratulated his congregation on their fine work and assured them that while his boy might come back for another week he surely would not stay long if they continued to snub him.

The next weekly report was equally as dismal, but after prayer Elder Vai and his companion returned again. The father assured his congregation that the end had come or was very near, but the next morning sharply at 9:00 A.M. Elder Vai and his companion began their fruitless effort to find someone to teach. There was another small village close by which was in their area and where they made a few contacts, but most of them quickly faded away.

At the end of the third week I could sense that Elder Vai's spirits were starting to drag. He had been so used to success that this situation gave him a new and uncomfortable feeling. We talked a lot and he assured me how determined his father was. I asked him if he was still willing to do whatever the Lord willed. He said he was, and after prayer I gave him a big hug and said, "Elder, I don't know why, but I feel you should go back to your area." He and his companion returned without looking back.

The fourth Sunday the father was less vehement in his denunciation of his son, but still congratulated the people on their shunning him and assured them this whole chapter was now over. When the fourth Monday dawned, however, and Elder Vai and his companion started tracting, there were a lot of raised eyebrows and whispered questions. But still there was no change in the policy of "no contact."

On the fifth Sunday, after four full weeks of basically nothing, Elder Vai and his companion were very discouraged. I have to admit that I was beginning to wonder myself. What if I had made a mistake?

We visited for a long time, and as we did I found myself saying, "Elders, let's pray together, and then whatever you feel is what we will do." We knelt in prayer. I prayed first, then asked Elder Vai to pray. There were long pauses and lots of emotional struggles, but when the final "amen" was said, we embraced each other. With a fire of faith that only comes from humility, Elder Vai quietly said, "I'm going back to my area."

Unbeknown to Elder Vai, this was the first Sunday his father had not said a word to his congregation about his son. His silence on the subject was noted by all. They wondered if a transfer had already been made and the battle was over. But Monday morning promptly at nine o'clock, Elder Vai and his companion emerged from their home and began walking down the street looking for someone to teach.

As they turned the corner they saw a man waving at them and motioning for them to come to his house. Elder Vai couldn't believe his eyes. That was his house! That was his father!

The two missionaries went over to the house. The father wanted to know what gave his son the determination to keep coming back even though he was rejected on every side. His son assured him that truth always prevails and, since he knew he had the truth, time was on his side. He explained: "As long as I know I am doing the Lord's will, other problems don't really bother me much."

Intense discussions followed, and within a short time Elder Vai's mother and father and some other family members were ready for baptism.

On the appointed day Elder Vai suggested that they wait until evening and then quietly slip unnoticed to the beach. It was now the father's turn to teach his son. "Son, I thank you for bringing me and your mother and our family the truth. I know it is true and I am not ashamed of it. Your mother and I will dress in white clothes in our home and promptly at noon tomorrow we will walk the entire length of the village to the seashore, where we would be pleased to meet you dressed in white to baptize us. We want the whole village to see."

That of course is what happened, except that Elder Vai, rather than meeting them at the seashore, came to their home and walked along with them.

Elder Vai finished his mission in his hometown, and before he left, more than forty souls had joined the Church. In an exit interview I asked him how he felt.

"President, when we are obedient the Lord blesses us, and when we continue to be obedient despite all obstacles, He fulfills all of His promises. I know it is so. I hope I can remember it my whole life."

"I hope I can, too," I replied.

32

A Stake in Tonga

Elder and Sister Hunter and Elder and Sister Monson arrived to a welcome of large banners waving, a band playing, and school-children cheering. This was probably the first time two Apostles had been in Tonga at the same time. The anticipation and expectation of the Tongans was very high. They didn't know quite what to expect, but whatever it was they knew it would be special.

The Hunters and the Monsons were taken to a *saliote* (horse-drawn two-wheeled cart) that had been covered with tapa cloth and decorated with mats and flowers. I shall never forget the smiles and laughter of our honored guests as they climbed into this "Tongan limousine" and graciously enjoyed the bumpy ride to the prime minister's nearby summer home. There we transferred to cars for the trip into town.

The Brethren were on a tight schedule, so Elder Hunter wanted to begin interviewing, teaching, and holding meetings right away. This conflicted somewhat with the Tongans' desires to have feasts, dances, a kava ceremony, orations, and all the things that to them were part of hosting important dignitaries. (We had more feasts than the Brethren expected, although less than the Tongans wanted.)

Elder Hunter asked me to give him some background on our local leaders. He was amazed that I knew so much detail about each person and their extended family back several generations. He asked how I had learned so much about their families. I really couldn't answer, except to say that I just knew it, as all Tongans did. As we talked more, I began to realize, probably for the first time, how different the Tongan

The children rode on this decorated saliote *as part of the festivities.*

emphasis on families is from the Western emphasis. In Tonga you don't *study* genealogy or family relationships, you just grow up with it and know it because it is so pervasive in all that is done. It is as natural to know about your own and other people's family history as it is to know what color their hair is or how tall or how old they are.

I was not familiar with the procedure used in organizing a new stake and thus had not said much about it to the local leaders. There were many mistakes made, but they were all honest and mostly came from lack of experience. For example, hardly any of the leaders being interviewed spoke English, so I was asked to translate for the two Apostles. When the Brethren asked the leaders who they thought the stake president should be, they nearly all said, "President Groberg, of course." The Brethren then asked me to explain the difference between a stake and a mission and tell them they needed to think of someone besides the mission president. As I explained this to each one there was genuine consternation on their faces. How could they have another leader besides the mission president? Such a thing had never occurred to them. It took a lot of extra time, but the Brethren wanted everyone to have an opportunity to express their individual feelings and then receive individual instruction.

Despite the different attitudes and approaches, we finished the interviewing and soon had a full stake organization ready, including a

stake presidency, a stake patriarch, a full high council, complete bish-
oprics, and fully staffed auxiliaries on both the stake and ward levels.
We scheduled a special conference for that evening at the Liahona
High School gymnasium for those units involved in the stake creation.
Because of capacity problems we asked others not to come, but this
was a futile effort, since everyone was curious and excited and full of
anticipation. The members would not be kept away, as they knew the
congregation would hear testimony from special witnesses and be part
of something unusual and special. They were not disappointed.

I had talked to the members about the spiritual aspects of a stake
but very little about the physical aspects. Thus the members were full
of interesting questions. They wondered just what would happen.
Would angels come and bring a certificate saying we were now part of
Zion? Would the Apostles give special blessings? How did the missionaries fit in? What was the difference between the units invited to be
part of the stake and those not invited? Were some less worthy? What
did they need to do to be part of a stake? Just exactly what was a stake
anyway? Was there a special mark to distinguish members of the
stake? The questions and speculations I heard were both comical and
humbling.

Despite all the dancing and singing and "merrymaking" that had
gone on before, when we entered the fully packed gymnasium that
Thursday evening the reverence (and the awe) was unbelievable.
Tongans are good that way—outgoing and bombastic one moment,
quiet and reverent the next. Sometimes we think we should be all one
way or the other, but God gave us both and expects us to appropriately use each. The scriptural expressions to "praise God with song
and dance" and "keep silence before the Lord" seem to be written for
the Tongans.

When the appointed hour arrived, the attendance was way over
100 percent of the "stake" membership. We welcomed everyone and
began the meeting with some enthusiastic singing that came as close
to "raising the roof" as it is possible for singing to do.

The Brethren asked that I do all of the translating for them to
make sure all the terms were conveyed properly. As they presented the
proposal to form a stake and to give it a name and to sustain a stake
presidency, everyone accepted and supported and sustained without
reservation. I noticed that while they were very quiet and very obser-
vant, they seemed to be waiting for something else.

The Brethren next explained the office of patriarch. They said that a stake needed a patriarch in order to be complete. They also explained that patriarchs were chosen only by the Apostles and that God had revealed to them who the patriarch should be. As I translated this, an unusual hush came over the audience. It was clear to me that to them this was a most important step. This is what they had been waiting for. They had had presidents before, they had had counselors and other officers before, but a patriarch—this came only with a stake; this came only through Apostles, and God had sent two of them to accomplish this!

When the name of the patriarch was given for a sustaining vote there was an audible gasp of joy, wonderment, and support that far exceeded the quiet raising of hands. Tears began to fall as Brother Cahoon, a former mission president from decades ago who now lived in Tonga, slowly stood to be acknowledged by all. The Tongans knew they now had a true stake of Zion.

The meeting continued, but I'm not sure that any of it exceeded the moment the first patriarch for Tonga was announced.

As Elder Monson spoke he was very moved. He had gone through much to see that this stake was formed. As he concluded his talk he referred to his visit with little John Enoch at his grandparents' just before coming to Tonga. He told of how healthy and happy the little boy was and what a major contribution the faith and fasting and prayers of the Tongans had been in John Enoch's ability to survive and live and grow. There were literally thousands of reverent nods of understanding and tens of thousands of tears freely flowing in gratitude and goodness. The Spirit of the Lord comforted everyone.

As Elder Hunter concluded the meeting he bore solemn testimony of the rightness of the action taken that evening. Everyone knew that he spoke the truth and acted with divine authority.

Knowing how important this event was to our members, some of our friends in the government had suggested that we might wish to record the meeting and then broadcast it later over the national radio so that members on the faraway islands could participate. I thought this was an excellent idea, and asked the visiting Brethren if we could do this. They both agreed. With their approval, I asked the king if we could air the entire meeting over the national radio the next night. He said that would be fine. I was thrilled when the entire proceeding was aired as agreed with no editing or censoring done. Every word and every testimony came across loud and clear. What a remarkable thing to have the witness of two Apostles heard by an entire nation. There was only one radio station in Tonga then and everyone listened to it.

After the closing song and prayer the Brethren asked me to assist them in setting apart the newly called officers. I was happy to do so, but I was concerned because I knew how anxious the members were to visit with the Brethren. I was also anxious to talk to Jean, as I had noticed that during much of the meeting she had been softly crying. I knew she missed having our baby boy with her, he being the first of the children she had not been able to hold closely and love and nurse for many months. I wondered, however, if her tears might have been occasioned by something else.

As the Brethren requested, we closed the drapes on the stage and set a few people apart, including the patriarch. Then almost miraculously to me, as I had said nothing about it, the Brethren, sensing something, indicated that there were many people who would like to visit and ask questions. Since we had all day Friday to hold training meetings, they suggested that we stop for now and continue setting apart leaders the next day.

As the curtains opened, we were taken aback to see that hardly anyone from the vast audience had moved. Now, nearly the entire congregation pressed forward. They were full of smiles, questions, hand-shakes, and embraces. There were hundreds of people asking thousands of questions. They just wanted to be a part of this momentous event in any way they could. The newly called patriarch, Brother Cahoon, was like a magnet to many. Since he could speak both Tongan and English, and thus interpret for the Brethren, I asked them if I could be excused for a few minutes.

A smiling Elder Howard W. Hunter (at far right) riding on a saliote.

I immediately took Jean's hand and found a small alcove away from the press of the crowd where we could be alone. I gathered Jean into my arms and held her tightly, trying to reassure her and me that everything was all right. I gazed into her beautiful brown eyes, made even more beautiful by the shimmering pools of tears through which they shone.

"What's wrong?" I asked, and then before waiting for an answer (a common fault I have) I continued on: "I know you miss John Enoch terribly, as I do, but he is in good hands and is doing well. You heard Elder Monson."

Then, as only a spiritually sensitive woman could, she looked at me and replied: "I know he is fine. That's not the reason for my tears. Don't you remember when we were first married you told me: 'One day there will be a stake in Tonga. Then I will take you there and have you meet my beloved people.' Oh, John, we're here, we've participated in the creation of a stake in Tonga. It's done. We're part of it. Thanks for keeping your promise."

I was humbled. I had experienced some very deep and majestic feelings about Zion and about stakes and about purity of heart and purpose, yet I had not remembered this promise. That was left to Jean's more sensitive spirit.

I wondered, "What other promises will I only remember through her?" I thought of Mother Eve and other great women who had also remembered things promised, made connections to things necessary, and reminded others of things eternal. I felt that just as breath is needed for life, the love of a faithful wife is needed for life to be eternal.

For a brief moment a bit of heavenly Zion descended and enveloped us and allowed us to company with others unseen and unheard but not unknown or unfelt.

We had an overwhelming desire to do better, to be one with the unending universe and all the light and life and truth therein. We literally felt Zion. I sensed that it is immaterial what language we speak, or whether we be with Tongans or Americans or anyone from any age or group, from either here or there. The only thing of importance is to be pure in heart—to be part of Zion.

We remembered covenants made and were determined to build our own Zion and help others flee Babylon and come to Zion where joy abounds, and where God will "wipe away all tears." Zion is much more than a concept, or a place, or a stake, or an organization; it is a state, with all of the vast implications of that word. No one is more pure in heart than God, therefore Zion goes with God and can go with us if we will. As we feel Zion, the world and its glory pales into oblivion. Only Zion is real. Only purity of heart lasts forever.

Once we have tasted the sweet fruit of Zion we are never satisfied with anything less and never fully at home in the alien environment of this world. We were meant for Zion. We were born to come to Zion—to purify our hearts and escape from Babylon and rejoice in Zion. How important it is that we do so!

33

The Anniversary Ring

The day after the conference Elder Monson and I visited the king. We reported to him on the formation of the stake, invited him to listen to the radio broadcast of the conference, and reminded him of the upcoming jubilee. He had a few questions and then wanted to talk about other things. I was so full of the spirit of the marvelous happenings of the previous days that I felt impelled to say: "Yes, we can talk about other things in a while, but first I must explain again what a great event has just taken place in your kingdom. Apostles of the Lord Jesus Christ have come here. With authority from God they have established a stake of Zion in Tonga. This means that there is a heaven-recognized part of God's kingdom in Tonga. This stake will be a refuge from the storms of evil that will increasingly fill the earth. All the pure in heart are invited to come unto it and partake of its beauty, participate in its joy, and receive of its protection.

"We are all children of our Father in Heaven, who loves us. He loves you and your family and all of the people of Tonga. So do I. With all my heart I invite you to learn His truths, be baptized into His kingdom, and bring your whole family with you. I invite you to lead not only your family but also all of your people who are willing to that greatest of all destinations—Zion. It is the abode of the pure in heart, the only sure refuge from the storms of evil which are gathering momentum for the final battle between good and evil, in which the forces of God will prevail."

He listened respectfully but said he wasn't ready to change. I replied that he might not be ready now, but when he eventually saw things as they really are I didn't ever want him or any of the people of Tonga to be able to say that I hadn't testified and invited them to come and participate in God's kingdom.

He said that was fine, but he now wanted to talk about other things. So we did.

That evening, at the hotel, we held a special banquet for the new stake officers and their spouses. As we concluded the meal the Brethren asked me to give a few remarks. I said: "Today is our eleventh wedding anniversary. I have something I would like to give to Jean, if you will allow me." Everyone agreed.

During the time when Jean had been in America with the baby, I had a conference in Fiji. On my way to a meeting in downtown Suva I passed a jewelry store, and something seemed to pull me back to it. A diamond ring in the window caught my eye so strongly that I could not ignore it. I went into the store and asked the jeweler if he could put that particular ring aside until I came back from my meeting. He was more than happy to do so.

I thought that during the meeting I would probably forget about the ring, but when the meeting was over I found myself running back to the store and anxiously asking to see the ring. The attraction now was even stronger. The ring seemed to cry out: "Buy me. Buy me for Jean. You know you should."

It was well overdue, of course. At the time of our wedding we had no money for a diamond, so we bought simple matching wedding bands. I had planned to get Jean a diamond on our tenth anniversary, but that idea had been buried in the hectic pace of the mission the year before. Now it had been suddenly resurrected.

I wanted to buy that ring. But how? Where could I get the money? All at once I remembered something that had happened two years earlier, just as we left Idaho Falls.

We had sold nearly everything except our house and paid off all our debts. We had rented our home out so we could keep up the mortgage payments. The day before we left I received a call from our broker saying that after finalizing the transactions there were still three thousand dollars left. He wondered what he should do with it. My mind by then was far from business ventures, so I replied, "What do you suggest?"

He suggested either buying some stocks or putting the money in a savings account. Both sounded fine to me, so I said, "Buy something with half and put the other half in savings." He then suggested that

with the portion for stocks I invest in a company named SONY that
looked like it had a bright future. Although I had never heard of it, I
told him to go ahead and buy it.

Now, standing in the jewelry store in Suva, I thought: "The money
put into SONY might be lost, but the savings account should be OK."
I sent a cable asking for all the money in my savings account to be
wired to me. With the accumulated interest it came to almost exactly
the amount I needed for the ring. The next day I returned to Tonga
with the ring in my pocket. I had thought I would give it to Jean on
our next anniversary, September 6, and hoped she would be back
from America by then.

I had not planned it this way but it was now September 6, so in
front of that auspicious group I gave Jean the anniversary ring and
briefly explained what she meant to me, and what she had recently
been through with our son. I didn't say much, but I could tell that
those present understood.

After the dinner Jean and I walked the few blocks from the hotel
to the mission home. It was a balmy, star-filled evening, and we felt almost as though we were in a dream world. How could things be more
beautiful? How could feelings be more all-encompassing, more fulfilling—more eternal? Maybe they could be, but as we arrived home and
saw our five daughters quietly sleeping and knew our son was being
well cared for and tried to comprehend all that had happened, we
were satisfied.

The next morning we took the two Apostles and their wives to the
airport. As I watched their plane fly away I thought of all that had
happened while they were in Tonga: a stake created, a patriarch ordained, a testimony borne to a king and to a nation, temple vows remembered, love refreshed, an understanding of Zion firmly put in
place. Who could desire more?

34

"Come Home, Felila"

In one of the villages on the western end of Tongatapu an infant girl was born to a faithful family. They named her Felila. There was happiness and joy as this grateful spirit made her debut into mortal life, but the parents could tell there were problems. Her head was abnormally large. The doctors diagnosed it as hydrocephalus. The question of brain damage or other problems raised its haunting specter.

After much fasting and prayer, the elders quorum president approached the branch president, who in turn talked with the district president, who, after adequate checking, came to me as the mission president to see if there was some outside help available.

The medical authorities were consulted and it was determined that there was little, if anything, they could do locally. Letters were written, information was sent back and forth, x-rays were taken and analyzed. There were many questions to be answered, and many pieces to fit together. Finally, after long delays, things began to fall into place. A family in Salt Lake City agreed to accept full responsibility for the infant—even if it meant years of out-patient care. The doctors agreed on the possibility of her eventual recovery. The Primary Children's Hospital accepted the case on a service basis. Funds were raised for her airfare. Some people returning to Utah agreed to take her to the hospital. Now we had to obtain a visa, a health certificate, a reservation, and a passport. This would take time and effort.

All during those trying days the family and the elders quorum, and even the whole branch, continued to fast and pray for her welfare.

One morning, amidst many pressing matters, I had the strong impression that I must take the time *now* and put forth the extra effort required to get everything done so Felila could go without further delay. The consulate in Fiji finally agreed to issue a visa, the airlines made the reservations, the passport people agreed to waive the normal regulations, others gave extra effort and cooperation, and soon all was in order. Normally I would have sent someone to bring the family in to sign the final papers, but I felt impressed that I should personally go and see the branch president.

I located him in the early afternoon near the school where he was teaching. He was standing alone outside, as though he was waiting for me. Excitedly, I ran up to him. "Guess what? It's all set. Miraculously everything has worked out, and Felila can leave tomorrow. Please get word to the family immediately."

His calm penetrating gaze quelled my exuberance. "It's true," I said. "I know it's been long and there have been many disappointments; but she really is going now. What's the matter?"

His steady gaze seemed to penetrate my very soul. Then softly, in his liquid native tongue, he informed me that when all the preparations had been made, when the hearts of so many had been stretched in service, when the goal of unity and selflessness had been achieved in those many hearts, when all concerned had made the final commitment of others above self—at the height of all this activity, that very morning little Felila had quietly and unobtrusively slipped away, gone to that better world where she would be free from pain and suffering.

Gone? This morning? It can't be! All that work, all that time, all that fasting and prayer and those strong feelings! Gone? No!

Without once shifting his gaze he, having more faith than I, offered a few words of truth and encouragement and then quietly turned and rejoined his class. And I was left alone, or so it seemed.

I moved slowly and heavily down that dusty trail. Why? Why? After all that work and the faith of so many and those strong impressions, why? I sensed the brightness of the sun and felt the warmth of the breeze as it lazily tossed the palm leaves and slowly shifted the silent clouds against the clear blue sky. A feeling came over me; I realized that the earth was beautiful, that life went on and was eternal. It was as though one took me by the hand and led me to a high place and stood by me and said, "Look"; and I looked and beheld such beauty and magnificence as man cannot conceive; and I heard a voice, such a tender, compassionate voice, yet so unmistakably powerful that all nature stood still and listened and obeyed: "Come home, Felila, my daughter. Come home to the care your loved ones have sought for you. I have heard their prayers and have known their fasting and love for you, and I answer in my way. Come home, my daughter. You have finished your mission in life. Hearts have been softened, souls have been stretched, faith has been increased. Come home now, Felila."

He knew her! He knew her name. He knew all about her and about all those others. How perfect our Father's love! He had heard and answered prayers. He had done what was best. He knew everything about the whole situation. In some marvelous way that is beyond our mortal comprehension, He knows and understands all things.

My questions as to why, as to justice and reasons, were all at that moment completely swept away. They were so irrelevant, my questioning so totally out of place, like someone trying to dig the Grand Canyon with a teaspoon.

I thought of Jacob's words:

> Behold, great and marvelous are the works of the Lord. How unsearchable are the depths of the mysteries of him; and it is impossible that man should find out all his ways. And no man knoweth of his ways save it be revealed unto him; wherefore, brethren, despise not the revelations of God. . . .
>
> . . . Seek not to counsel the Lord, but to take counsel from his hand. For behold, ye yourselves know that he counseleth in wisdom, and in justice, and in great mercy, over all his works. (Jacob 4:8, 10.)

I know that there is total and complete justice in eternity. God's dealings with man have no tinge of partiality, favoritism, capriciousness, or anything less than complete consistency, balance, and perfectness. As we begin to comprehend eternity we gain a whole new catalogue of values. Caring is all-important—the intensity, the duration, the amount, the quality, the extent—for in God's wisdom, caring creates faith.

"Oh," I thought, "may we all have a little Felila in our lives. There are so many: the mentally impaired, the infirm, those needing special help (both spiritually and physically), the aged, the infants. All these soften our hearts in love, stretch our souls in tenderness, confirm our worth in caring for others, and above all strengthen our faith in Him who knows all. Even He who in caring totally gave His all, and in giving His all lives forever, and in living forever rules eternally, and in ruling eternally cares omnipotently."

35

A Feast from Fasting

The level of excitement and enthusiasm for the jubilee rose daily. Everyone sensed that something big was happening and they hardly talked about anything else. Tongans love a celebration, and this was something extra special. I felt good about all the arrangements being made. However, as I sat through meeting after meeting, heard numerous reports, and noted with satisfaction the progress on a long list of activities, deep inside I felt as though something was unfulfilled.

I applauded the plans for a spectacular dance festival involving thousands of youth. I had a good feeling about the huge feast planned for five thousand invitees. I felt wonderful about plans for the Saints to come from the outer islands and be cared for by members on this island. I was enthused about the commemoration service to be held with the king and queen and many other government and religious leaders in attendance. I was confident that the history being prepared under the direction of Brother Ermel Morton would add beauty and dignity to the whole event. Why then did I feel this persistent sense of discomfort as though something more needed to be done?

Early in our planning we decided that the jubilee celebration would be oriented toward missionary work. I began to wonder if we were emphasizing feasts, dances, and activities too much. Yet I felt good about them because they were such a big part of Tongan culture and such a traditional way of commemorating the great work of those who had gone before us.

I wondered if more needed to be done with the missionaries. I called the missionary leaders in for a special meeting to discuss missionary work in connection with the planned jubilee events. The reports of the zone leaders were great and I felt very good about their plans. They reported a substantial increase in baptisms. They felt that by November they would be baptizing nearly a hundred a month, which was double the number of the year before even though we presently had a few less missionaries. Who wouldn't be thrilled with such a report? The uneasy feeling I had been experiencing slipped farther into the background but never quite left.

Finally, one of the young elders said: "Why don't we call a mission-wide fast and have all the missionaries on Tongatapu come to a special meeting in Nuku'alofa? The missionaries on other islands could join in the fast and hold a similar meeting at the same time. We could break our fast together and thus be united in doing the Lord's will for the jubilee.".

It was a great idea. On the appointed day all the missionaries fasted, prayed, and met together on their various islands. I met with the missionaries in Nuku'alofa. What a wonderful group of young men and women! How handsome, beautiful, and faithful! What more could possibly be expected of them? Their spirituality and performance had been rising each month. I had never felt good about setting outside goals in terms of numbers but had always tried to help the missionaries set their own goals in terms of individual performance and excellence. I knew that if each missionary performed better—through more diligent study, more sincere prayer, and harder work—everything would improve, and it certainly had.

The meeting was wonderful and the reports were exceptional. I was sure these young "Warriors of Christ" could and would do anything they were asked to. This assurance seemed to envelop me with great force as the meeting neared its conclusion and I found myself in a spirit of deep contemplation.

Suddenly all was quiet, and from my somewhat distant state of reverie I was told it was my turn to speak and conclude the meeting. I thought I would assure the missionaries of their greatness, commend them for their wonderful work, and encourage them to continue moving forward.

I didn't feel like speaking quite yet, however, so I asked everyone to stand and sing a beautiful Tongan hymn about the Savior. The sincerity of those voices and the power of the spirit they generated all but lifted me off my feet. I felt that I was in another element, a place apart from walls and roofs and floors. The sweet yet powerful spirit brought on by the combination of beautiful voices, youthful vigor in a righteous cause, and faithful fasting with pure intent was so beautiful that I never wanted it to end.

Eventually, however, the last verse was sung, the beautiful echoes faded away, and a hush came over everything and everyone. I knew it was my responsibility to give the final blessing to this marvelous meeting. I stood and faced scores of beautiful faces bright with faith and goodness. Their eyes shone in anticipation of something wonderful to come, some powerful manifestation of God's will befitting the unusual strength of spirit generated by the meeting thus far.

I still wasn't sure what to say. I began by expressing my deep love for the missionaries and for their faithfulness. I bore my testimony and told of my undying love for our Lord and Savior Jesus Christ. I reminded them that they were true representatives of the Savior and assured them that they could do anything He wanted them to do—anything.

Suddenly the words began to flow so fluidly and so powerfully that I found myself saying things I had never even thought of before. In a special rush of inspiration I heard myself saying:

"The Lord is behind the Golden Jubilee celebration in November. It will be a missionary jubilee, and He has prepared five hundred souls to be baptized into His kingdom in November. He is giving you the choice privilege of being the instruments in His hands to accomplish this. You will fulfill and justify the faith of that small group of Saints who fifty years ago put their lives on the line and who in faith looked forward to this day."

There was an audible gasp and a brief glancing at one another as though to say: "Did you hear that? Five hundred baptisms in one month! How can that be? Yet the President said five hundred, so that must be the Lord's will, and since we are His agents, we must do it; but how?"

I began to realize the enormous significance of what I had just said. I had never before set a numerical goal, as I didn't believe in them. I had spent my effort teaching correct principles and then trusted missionaries to do what was right, which they had done and had made great progress thereby. Why, then, had I given a specific number? I wondered if I should modify what I had said, but when I looked into the trusting faces of those faithful missionaries and saw the fiery determination of faith flashing from their tear-filled eyes, I could do nothing but let my tears flow. I knew I must trust the missionaries. I must trust the Lord and the specific inspiration of His Spirit.

I concluded my remarks by saying; "We will dispense with the closing song and all of us will kneel in prayer, and as your mission president I will officially break our fast and offer the gratitude of our collective hearts for the choice opportunity of being here and being witnesses of the power of His Spirit."

As the prayer concluded we all felt the presence of others and did not want to stand or leave or even open our eyes. This was something beyond a normal experience. This was something to savor forever. Finally there was a stir here, a slight movement there, a hushed sob somewhere; and slowly, one by one, those faithful missionaries rose from their knees and sat down on the benches in full anticipation of hearing more.

The meeting was over, but no one would leave. I didn't know what to do. Then suddenly a direction came to me that both impelled and inspired me to stand at the pulpit again and say: "The Lord has prepared these five hundred souls to be baptized in the jubilee month of November, but you are not to hold anyone back until November or rush anyone forward to November. When they are ready, baptize them. One other thing, every one of you is to go back to all the former investigators you have ever had or ever heard of. Concentrate on them as well as on part-member families. If you are faithful, God will guide you and you will accomplish His purposes. There is something more special than any of us can imagine about this jubilee in November. It is not our jubilee, but God's. You know that the power to accomplish all He wants done comes from Him, so our duty is to humble ourselves sufficiently and work and pray and study hard enough to receive that divine power and influence in our lives so this jubilee will fulfill its divine purpose."

Only the softest of voices could be heard as that marvelous assemblage of faithful youth glided out to fill the islands and fulfill the mission set for them. I was so full of gratitude and confidence and wonder that I virtually floated home that evening.

Before long, however, mortal reality put questions in my heart and mind. "Five hundred in one month! Why did you say that? The missionaries have barely reached ninety a month. In all of 1966 we baptized only 604 people. In 1967 it was 833. Now I am asking for five hundred in one month! That's crazy!" Then the spiritual reality of faith came again and answered the questions by saying: "You asked nothing. The promise came from God, not man. Trust God and all will be well."

No one talked much about the meeting. All the missionaries from Tongatapu were in the meeting, but only the zone leaders from the outer islands had come to Nuku'alofa. Thus they needed to take the message to their missionaries, who had been fasting on their respective islands. I wondered how the Spirit would be conveyed in a "second-hand" sort of way. I should not have worried, for the reports I received from the distant islands were that the missionaries there were equal participants in the same rich outpouring of the Spirit. The missionaries on the outlying islands received with calmness and faith the charge given them. All the missionaries were united. God's Spirit had been felt and His will would be done.

The missionaries were wonderful and never questioned (at least not to me) the challenge they had received. They knew it came from God, so they worked harder and with more devotion and obedience than ever before. The spirit of confidence was so strong that I was swept along with it. Once or twice in the first few weeks I allowed little shades of doubt to cloud my vision. But as I met with the missionaries and heard them sing and bear their testimonies, my faith was always renewed. The missionaries by their words and actions constantly re-assured me that the challenge truly came from God (and not me). Therefore I tried to put doubts and questions aside and moved forward with those fearless, faithful missionaries.

36

Countdown

Everyone was working feverishly to see that every event and aspect of the jubilee was planned and prepared properly. It was a fast-paced but good time. We sensed we were doing eternally valuable things that had the Lord's approbation.

In October the stake leaders returned from general conference. They had met with the First Presidency and with Elders Hunter, Monson, Young, and others. They gave glowing reports of Elder Monson's talk in conference in which he spoke about Tonga, the stake, and John Enoch. By mid-October visitors from various Church departments began coming to Tonga to train the newly called stake priesthood and auxiliary leaders.

As the time before the jubilee got shorter, the list of things to do grew longer. Late in October I received notification that Jean and I were to attend a mission presidents seminar in New Caledonia the first week of November. I also learned that Elder Henry D. Taylor would be touring our mission the week after the seminar. Another letter came which informed me that the first quarterly conference for the new stake would be the following weekend, and that I would need to be there to translate. The charter airline we worked with also informed me that the date for the 1968 temple excursion was set for November 30. In addition, President N. Eldon Tanner of the First Presidency wrote that he would be the official Church representative at the jubilee celebration, and would arrive on November 27.

There was already more to do than seemed possible. Now these new things were added. I could see November slipping away from me.

I was worried. Quickly and quietly, however, a peaceful feeling came that said to me: "All of these requests are from the Lord's servants, therefore they are from God. The jubilee is from God. He will see that everything gets done properly. Assign more things to others. Go where you have been asked to go and do what you have been asked to do and everything will be as it should be."

I called a special meeting of the mission council. Without apologizing, I explained what I had been asked to do and indicated that this meant each of them would have to take additional assignments. There was not a flinch from anyone.

Within a few days Jean and I left for Suva, where we met Elder and Sister Hunter. We then flew with them to New Caledonia, where we met the Taylors and the other mission presidents and their wives. We had a wonderful seminar.

While I was away I worried about the zone leaders who had so much responsibility in trying to achieve the all-but-impossible goal we had jointly set. As I prayed for them I felt a deep calm, and I knew the Lord would expand their ability and increase their capacity so that all they had planned to do, plus all they had been newly assigned to do because of my absence, would be accomplished. This was the Lord's work, these were the Lord's assignments, and these young men were the Lord's agents.

Upon our return to Tonga we "toured" the mission with Elder Taylor. Elder Taylor also presided at the stake conference. He was kind and gracious and helpful. At the final session of the stake conference he asked me to speak. My heart was very full as I realized that that day, November 17, marked both the fourteenth anniversary of my first arrival in Tonga and the eight-month anniversary of John Enoch's birth. The memories of these events flooded back and I testified to the Saints of the goodness of God.

When Elder Taylor left, November 20, there were less than five days left before the jubilee officially started. Everyone had done well with their assignments, but there were still many concerns to be resolved.

One of my main concerns was the missionaries and how they were coming on the inspired goal we had been given. My mind wanted to rationalize that since they had been left on their own so much during this critical month, and since they had been asked to do so many extra things to prepare for the jubilee, I could not really expect them to reach that goal. Yet I felt the whisperings in my heart: "Be faithful; have confidence; express encouragement; trust them, trust me."

I asked the assistants how things were going and what our meeting schedule was. They answered that everything was going well, but they thought that we should not meet until the week after the jubilee, as everyone was so busy teaching and baptizing that they didn't have time before then.

I wanted to give all the strength and encouragement I could to the missionaries. But how? Sensing the spirit of urgency among them, I decided the best thing to do was to leave them alone and trust them to follow the Spirit, which was working strongly among them.

I learned that after we are sure people understand what is expected of them, often our best help is to just leave them alone. At times we tend to be over-protective and feel that only with lots of help from us can others succeed, when in fact excessive overseeing often hurts rather than helps. If we "hover" too close to those we have given responsibility to, how can they grow on their own? God sent us to this earth partly so we could be on our own and learn therefrom. He is always near, but usually He waits for us to ask Him for help rather than interfering, even when we do things wrong. We learn by our own experience.

Another big concern was the booklet containing the brief history of the Tongan Mission that Brother Morton had written. A printing company in Fiji had agreed to print several hundred copies in English and several thousand copies in Tongan. The booklets had not yet arrived when Elder Taylor left. I called the printers and received evasive excuses. I immediately asked one of my counselors to take the final payment to Fiji and not return without the booklets. The plane left in forty-five minutes, but he made it. When he arrived at the printers they had just started to take our job off the press to make way for a larger order. He was able to convince them to keep their commitment and complete our order. He paid them and returned to Tonga with our booklets.

Since no one in the area had the proper equipment to print the pictures or the golden covers, I had written my parents in Idaho for help. They not only had them printed and mailed, but paid for them as well. How wonderful to have supportive parents!

The package from Idaho had been mailed weeks before but had not yet arrived. I sent a cablegram to my parents, who contacted the postmaster, who found the package was stuck in Honolulu. He got it "unstuck" and it arrived in Tonga on Saturday, November 23, about noon. Now we needed thousands of covers stapled to thousands of booklets before Monday morning. As I was discussing this concern with my staff, one of the men from the Liahona High School happened to be in the office. He told us to leave it to him. Within an hour nearly all of the teachers were there, with their own heavy-duty staplers. They had the job finished shortly before midnight Saturday.

Another major concern was how to house and feed the thousands of members and nonmembers who were coming from the outlying islands to participate in the jubilee. We had decided to have each district on Tongatapu house and feed a "sister" district from the outlying islands. However, while I was away those left in charge changed plans and secured several acres of land across from the Liahona High School and built four long *fales* (Tongan houses). This required the Saints to cut enough trees, weave enough *polas,* dig enough holes, and construct enough latrines to accommodate thousands of people. I don't know how I would have reacted to such a plan, but fortunately it was not only decided but also completed by the time I returned. I still don't know how they did it in such a short time, but it turned out to be the best solution.

Having done all we could to prepare, we still needed near perfect weather for all the Saints and others from the outlying islands to arrive safely and on time. It had been stormy, but to our delight, just as the Saints started coming, the storms ceased, the seas became calm, the wind remained brisk, the skies cleared. Boatload after boatload arrived safely and were taken to the makeshift village.

The many miracles that happened are too numerous to recount here. Suffice it to say that, despite all odds, when the time arrived everything was in order for the greatest week in the history of the Tongan Mission—at least to that point.

Monday dawned bright and beautiful. With His help, we were ready for the Lord's jubilee in Tonga!

37

Jubilee

What a week this would be! We started with two days of sporting events. There were competitions in rugby, basketball, softball, tug-of-war, and other games. The enthusiasm occasionally got a little rambunctious, as not only players but also spectators joined in the action. Yet sportsmanship and good feelings prevailed. It was great fun for everyone.

The Relief Society sisters celebrated by holding a mission-wide bazaar. They displayed row after row of the most beautiful handiwork imaginable: beautiful quilts, carefully crocheted tablecloths, ingeniously woven mats and baskets, smart-looking clothes often sewn all by hand, and on and on. Presentations of the best handiwork were made to the honored guests.

The queen graciously attended this event and addressed the sisters. She reminded them of their important role as women. She expressed gratitude for their faith and contributions to their families, their church, and their country. Her wonderful talk was later published in the *Relief Society Magazine* of the Church.

A grand ball was held one evening at Liahona. After a brief welcome and opening prayer the formal dancing began with a massive grand march. The costumes and routines were beautiful. Many government officials and Tongan nobility were present. There was Tongan as well as American or European dancing. The weather was perfect, the crowd was huge (several thousand) but orderly, the electricity stayed on, and even the sound system worked without a hitch. I don't know how the evening could have gone better.

President and Sister Tanner arrived in Tonga to a royal welcome with banners, bands, singing, and dancing. They seemed to feel right at home and added so much to the celebrations. They participated warmly in the events and were sincerely appreciative and moved by all they saw and experienced.

One day we took the Tanners to see the sights and hear the sounds of Tonga. We witnessed the blow-holes on the southern coast line, the "flying foxes" (fruit bats), and a demonstration of *tapa* making. After a tour of the Liahona School campus I took President Tanner across the street to the long *fales* where the outer island Saints were staying. We saw dozens of *umus* (earth ovens) being prepared, pigs on spits being roasted, and coconuts being husked and shredded. Children were playing, mothers were nursing infants, and life was in full swing. President Tanner was amazed. He asked about the cost, safety, legal permits, and so forth. I was happy to tell him it cost no money, there were no legal regulations, and there had been no accidents. As we left he asked, "Do the Brethren know about this?"

"No. I didn't know we needed to tell anyone. What do you think?"

He smiled broadly and said, "I think it is great!"

We held a special meeting for the youth. President Tanner testified

The long fale *village where Saints from the outer islands stayed during the jubilee celebration.*

Members roasted pigs on spits for the feast.

to them that, regardless of what else they accomplished in life, nothing would be of more importance to them or to the kingdom of God than the family they would rear. He asked them to be clean and pure and always pray for God's help. If they did this, God would guide them to the right person to be their eternal companion.

President Tanner asked all the young men and young women to stand. The men were sitting on one side of the room and the women on the other. About two hundred young men and two hundred young women stood and rather naturally turned toward each other. He promised them that if they would be prayerful and sincerely seek to do God's will by making marriage and family top priority, God would bless them in ways they could hardly conceive of now. For a moment my mind went soaring as I thought of the possibility of hundreds of new families, strong in the Church, creating homes and worlds of love here and hereafter.

The day set for the commemoration service, Friday, 29 November 1968, had arrived! How much planning and praying and fasting had gone into this day? I suppose much more and from more places than we could imagine. When we arrived with the Tanners at the gymnasium it was already full. Thousands of Tongans were sitting outside looking through the open glass louvers that lined both sides of the

*The king stepped from his Cadillac onto decorated tapa cloth
as he arrived for the commemoration service.*

building. Everything was bright and fresh and orderly. Well-disciplined Boy Scouts served as ushers.

The top government officials and nobility arrived according to protocol, then promptly at 9:55 A.M. the king's huge black Cadillac rolled up. Jean and I escorted the king and queen down a path of beautiful new *tapa* cloth that led up the stairs to the stage, and presented the Tanners to their majesties. At 10:00 A.M. the service began.

Every moment of the next two hours was a fulfillment of dreams—not only the dreams of those present who had worked so hard for this day, but also the dreams of the early Saints and missionaries in Tonga who had played such a big part in making this meeting a reality. Having the king and queen, the Royal Methodist Choir, and the Tongan nobility and government leaders in the Liahona gymnasium, honoring the jubilee of the Church's permanent establishment in that country, was a watershed event in Tongan history.

I couldn't help but think of the dramatic contrast to the harsh times experienced by the Church when it first started in Tonga. Early Church members and missionaries, like the pioneers, had through deep faith overcome great trials from antagonists, natural disasters, and the calamitous diseases. We were now enjoying the benefits of the firm foundation they had laid.

We sang "The Spirit of God Like a Fire is Burning." And was it ever burning brightly! During the song the queen caught my attention and showed me the flyleaf of her hymnal. The inscription read, "To Prince Tungi and Princess Mata'aho. Thanks for your help. Ofa Atu, Elder Groberg, May 1957 Pangai, Ha'apai." She had kept it all those years and brought it on that special day and sang every word of every song.

Sovea Kioa, a member of our mission council and a high ranking *matapule* (talking chief) gave a wonderful talk. As the first speaker he used all the proper respect phrases and said things only a person in his station could say. In traditional Tongan culture only certain Tongans are allowed to talk directly to the king. As a *matapule,* Sovea officially spoke to the king and the nobility on behalf of his fellow Church members.

I spoke next. Since nearly half the audience were not members of the Church I explained that we are all children of our Father in Heaven, who loves us. He wants us to return to His presence and has a plan and a church with proper authority to accomplish this. He is no respecter of persons, and the gospel is free for all to hear and obey. I explained the purpose of the Church in Tonga and outlined the Lord's guiding hand over the last fifty years. I testified that Tongans are descendants of the house of Israel through Joseph, who was sold into Egypt, and that they all had a right and a responsibility to become members of His kingdom. I read Moroni chapter seven, bore my testimony, and sat down. I knew God had confirmed the truth to many.

President Tanner then read a letter from President David O. McKay expressing his appreciation for the king's kindness and wishing him a long and prosperous reign. President Tanner quoted from the twelfth article of faith and explained that we sustain and honor the law. He spoke about the organization of the Church in Christ's day and our having the same organization today. He bore solemn testimony of Joseph Smith. He said the Prophet Joseph was a descendant of Joseph who was sold into Egypt. He testified of the reality of the First Vision, the truthfulness of the Book of Mormon, and the divinity of Christ.

The king was the concluding speaker. He had told me he would only take ten minutes, but he spoke for more than half an hour. He admonished the people on the need for personal faith, not just public faith. He explained that in his experience many people outwardly professed to believe something but inwardly did not practice what they claimed to believe. He said people should be free to join whatever church they felt changed their lives for the better. He expressed appreciation for the good things the Church had done in Tonga and for those people who practiced privately what they professed publicly.

Outside the Liahona school gymnasium, signs announced
the jubilee celebration.

After the king's speech, I thanked everyone for all they had done
and we finished shortly before noon.

The meeting had been like a perfect precious jewel. The past with
its depth of sacrifice, commitment, and faith, and the future with its
endless promise and hope, had come together in one brilliant now.

After the spiritual feast, it was time for another type of feast. The
rugby field had been turned into a feasting field. The king and queen,
President and Sister Tanner, and Jean and I sat at the head *pola* (a *pola*
is made of beautifully woven coconut fronds filled to overflowing with
food). I was proud of how beautifully and wonderfully everything was
prepared. The mountains of pineapple, *talo, ufi, lupulu,* bread, roast
pig, yams, pudding, fish, chicken, lobsters, watermelon, crab, Indian
apples, and on and on, were unbelievable. More than two thousand
roast pigs were served that day.

We had prepared food for about five thousand but in fact over
sixty-five hundred people came. This caused some anxious moments.
The spirit of cooperation and goodness prevailed, however, and we
simply asked many active Church members to give their places to
others. They did so without hesitation.

As we ate, the various districts put on their well-prepared *lakalakas*
and other Tongan dances. A *lakalaka* is a Tongan dance involving up to
hundreds of performers. They normally form into double or triple-

*President Groberg (at far left) seated next to the
king and queen at the head pola.*

tiered rows, the first row sitting cross-legged, the middle row kneeling
and the back row standing. The men are on the right and the women
on the left. A large "choir" stands behind them. They sing and chant in
beautiful harmony. The body movements add a fascinating rhythmic
element. The men are more active, while the women's actions are
softer and their movements more refined. Each side moves their
hands, feet, heads, even their whole bodies, in perfect unison. The
beauty that comes from this harmonious blend of poetry, dance, song,
and action, is unforgettable.

Each dance that day told a story about the restoration of the
gospel, or about an event in the fifty-year history of the Church in
Tonga, or about a basic belief of the Church. All the parts were choreo-
graphed, sung, and performed so well and with such deep emotion
that their messages were clearly understood. I looked around and noticed how attentive the king and queen were, as well as everyone else.
That afternoon many government officials heard, saw, and felt great
truths presented in the best poetic and artistic Tongan way possible.

I looked over the large crowds of people quietly eating, watching,
and listening; everyone was well behaved, there was no arguing or any
other problems, only peace. The weather was perfect. I felt the Spirit
of the Lord hovering over everything. I knew He was smiling His approval.

A dance from the Vava'u district entertained guests at the feast.

Then, something beckoned me to look beyond the dancers and the crowds. I looked past them and out across the campus. The sparkling, cream-colored school buildings seemed to glow in the afternoon sunlight, but my eyes were inexorably drawn to something else. What was it? I looked carefully. Then I saw a shimmering new building of learning standing as if in the air. It was different from the others—more ethereal, more luminescent, more lovely, and more important. It was a temple.

A feeling of peace came over me and I knew that, through the goodness of God, the fire of faith had been successfully passed from one generation to another; and through that same goodness, this generation would successfully pass it to the next generation. Soon they would be blessed with one of the greatest of all the blessings of Zion, a House of the Lord. I knew a temple of God would one day stand in Tonga. I kept this in my heart and said nothing to anyone about it until it was fulfilled.[1] I knew the spirit of this jubilee would ripple throughout eternity.

---

1. Fifteen years later the Tonga Temple would be dedicated by President Gordon B. Hinckley on a site immediately next to the Liahona School campus.

Friday night was the final event of the jubilee. The youth had organized and prepared a dance festival to be held in Nuku'alofa on the grounds adjacent to the palace. As we arrived at the royal parade grounds we were met by a wondrous sight. More than eleven thousand people were jammed everywhere. A large police force was there in anticipation of some rowdiness, but there was no need. There was no vulgarity, no displeasing levity, and no drunkenness. The police were amazed. What a beautiful evening it was! The light, beauty, and spirit of the occasion cheered the hearts of all present. Many government leaders attended and were very impressed. They expressed their delight at the order and precision of the events. They asked me how we did it with only young people in charge. I replied that young people with the Spirit of the Lord are more capable than experienced people without it.

The dances were spectacular. At one time we had eight hundred square-dancers doing some of the most beautiful and fun dances I have ever witnessed. The costumes were outstanding and the overall effect was breathtaking. The standing crowds of Tongans couldn't hold back their glee, and they clapped and swayed with the music. The formal ballroom dancers brought oohs and ahs from everyone.

At the conclusion of the last number, the premier spoke to the crowd. He, like everyone else, was visibly moved by the occasion. He reminisced on the wonderful spirit he had felt in the Tabernacle when he had visited Salt Lake City some years previously, and he said he felt that same spirit again this evening. He wished us as much success in the next fifty years as we had had in the past fifty. Then he turned to President Tanner and asked him to take a message of love and support to President McKay, and to tell him that while the rest of the world might be in turmoil, Tonga was at peace.

As he spoke I heard the muffled breaking of waves along the shore and looked at the silk-laced leaves of the toa trees. A soft breeze sent a quiet murmur through them on its way to the dark blue ocean beyond. I observed the large crowds of patient, awestruck Tongans and remembered the brilliance of the costumes and the smiles and the order of the whole evening. I felt I was more in a part of heaven than a place on earth. Yes, I thought, there may be wars, civil unrest, political walls and curtains in other parts of the world, but Tonga is truly at peace.

When the premier concluded I asked President Tanner if he would like to say anything. He answered: "I have only one request. With this

Hundreds of dancers in elaborate costumes participated in the celebration activities.

beautiful feeling in this peaceful place, with all these wonderful people, I would like you to give the closing prayer." I was surprised but not totally unprepared. When I started to pray, words were put into my mouth: gratitude for peace, for unity, for love, for harmony, for the hearing and answering of prayers. I expressed gratitude for the Lord's church, which was now firmly established in the kingdom of Tonga, and for the jubilee of that establishment which we were celebrating. I thanked Him that darkness had been forced to stay away, forced out by the light of the Spirit and the fire of faith that burned so brightly in the hearts of so many wonderful people. I concluded with a plea for continued peace and for a continued rolling forth of the truth of the gospel in Tonga and throughout the world.

As I sat down I was filled with wonder as I contemplated what had just happened. More than eleven thousand people in the open air, on the royal courtyard in Tonga, quietly and reverently pausing late at night to join in a heartfelt and heaven-sent prayer of thanksgiving.

After taking the Tanners to the hotel and Jean and the children home, my counselors and I returned to the *mala‘e* (parade ground). We wanted to continue to be part of the peace we felt there and also to help with the cleanup. The committee was so well organized and so many had such a strong desire to help that there was very little for us to do except express thanks, visit with everyone, and bask in the aura of goodness that surrounded everything. Eventually the last chairs were loaded, and one by one the lights were turned off. Even as the brilliance of the powerful man-made lights faded away, a deeper and more powerful light seemed to quietly descend from the heavens above.

I could still see every movement, every person, every feature clearly and distinctly. I should have been surprised, but I wasn't. The evening was soft and still. A bright moon and millions of sparkling stars filled the sky, but there was more. It was almost as though each star was a smile from heaven, filling everything and everyone with light and love.

I didn't want to leave; neither did anyone else. Tonga is warm in November, but this evening was perfect in every way. Many lingered. Everyone wanted to talk about the wonder of the events of the jubilee. We desired to express gratitude to God, and appreciation to all who had worked so hard. It was a marvelous feeling to know, with no reservations, that God was pleased with what had been done.

I didn't know how late it was and I didn't really care. I had long since given up being concerned about time. That beautiful evening now belonged to us Tongans. We could have stayed and visited all night, but someone reminded us that there were still many people waiting at the mission office to be interviewed for their temple recommends, as the charter flight to New Zealand was to leave in the morning.

As we quietly and with reluctance left that peaceful *mala'e* for the mission office a thought came to me: "There is always a jubilee somewhere. The very essence of a jubilee is forgiveness and freedom. We can always have the jubilee spirit as we forgive and release and in turn are forgiven and released."

The spirit of jubilee is eternal. "And ye shall hallow the fiftieth year, and proclaim liberty throughout all the land unto all the inhabitants thereof: it shall be a jubilee unto you; and ye shall return every man unto his possession, and ye shall return every man unto his family" (Leviticus 25:10).

38

Angels

All during the night after the dance festival my counselors and I held temple recommend interviews. The people came and came and came. No one worried about the hour, only about getting the right things done—the right papers signed, and above all the right understandings and attitudes solidified. To the Tongans, the middle of the night was as good as the middle of the day, maybe even a little better, as it was cooler then. We completed the last interviews just as the sun began to lighten the eastern sky.

The day was beautiful, with a light breeze blowing and a few clouds tucked here and there to give accent to the brilliant blue sky and trace interesting patterns across the brown earth and green vegetation.

The temple group's charter flight to New Zealand was to leave that morning, half an hour before the Tanners' flight home. As I arrived at the airport with the Tanners I found a scene and a feeling that was a continuation of the spirit from the evening before.

The small check-in area and waiting room were filled with the well-dressed members of the temple excursion group. They were quiet and helpful—but more than that, they seemed to shine with purity. There was a literal glow about them. When they finished the check-in process they moved to another area and waited patiently for the plane to arrive. They had no signs, no band playing, no policemen or guards protecting them, but there was such an aura of light and power surrounding them that it set them apart as surely as any renowned diplomat or important political figure could ever be.

Even the crowds of foreigners who spoke no Tongan could tell the difference. It seemed that the feeling was contagious. Everyone was more patient, more subdued and more helpful. The normal turbulence of large airport crowds was simply nonexistent.

I noticed a few from a foreign tour group who started to laugh and talk loud, and even pull out some cigarettes. Suddenly, with no words being spoken, they quieted down. The few who had cigarettes left for the outside. It was just too uncomfortable for them to be in the intense light that emanated from the spiritual strength of the temple group. There were no physical signs saying No Smoking but there were spiritual signs of much greater persuasion that radiated from the temple group. Even though the temple group said nothing, they were everything. The power of goodness was stronger and more effective than signs or threats or explanations could ever be.

How much of this was the goodness of the temple group and how much was a protective shield cast around them by the thousands of ancestors whose names they were carrying to the temple? It was undoubtedly some of both. I felt a link and a unity between the heavens above and the heavens below, and realized that the firmaments, separated those ages ago, were, at least for a few hours and among a few people, back together again.

The chartered plane arrived. As the first charter to Tonga, it caused quite a sensation. After the paperwork was done, the temple group began boarding the plane in a quiet and orderly manner. It seemed to me that even the baggage was put on reverently.

The captain and crew asked me to verify the passengers, help get everyone seated, and give the needed instructions in Tongan. As the group took their assigned seats, there were no problems or complaints or demands. Everyone just obediently did as they were asked. In much less time than the crew had anticipated, everyone was ready for departure.

As I started to leave the plane the head steward asked me: "What kind of power do you have over these people? I have done charters to other islands and I don't really look forward to them. There is usually a lot of drunkenness, yelling, and shoving. But these people, they were like angels in comparison. I am amazed. How do you do it?"

I told him that his use of the word *angels* was closer to the truth than he thought. I explained that if he knew where they were going and the preparation and sacrifice they had gone through to be ready, he wouldn't wonder any more. All he could do was shake his head in amazement. I said a final good-bye to the group, asked them to remember who they were and who they represented, left my blessings with them, and quietly descended.

This was the first group Jean and I had not accompanied to the temple. There was a little tug in my heart as I watched that plane taxi down the runway and gently lift into the clear blue sky with its precious load of Tongan "angels." I looked up and breathed, "Watch over them; protect them; help them; bless them." I seemed to see the heavens smile and hear the soft wind respond, "We will. We will."

I returned to the waiting area, where President and Sister Tanner were seated. He asked me to take a chair next to him and then said, "That was special, wasn't it? As fine a temple group as I have been around. There was a special glow of goodness about them. Thanks for helping prepare them." I nodded. He continued, "Yes, very special. The whole thing, not just today, not just last night—the whole jubilee. God's Spirit has been in rich abundance through this entire event." I already knew that, but it was wonderful to hear a member of the First Presidency confirm it.

President and Sister Tanner (seated in front) with President Groberg
and his counselors at the Nuku'alofa airport.

As we visited, I felt at ease and loved and trusted. I suppose that was the essence of President Tanner's true greatness—to have those he worked with feel at ease and loved and trusted. I was sure he had learned how to do that from following the one perfect example.

Sister Tanner went for a little walk. When she had moved beyond earshot President Tanner turned to me and said, "Have you ever seen such a beautiful seventy-year-old woman? She's an angel!" He continued telling me of Sister Tanner's wonderful attributes. I observed him reverently watching her, heard his sincere praises, saw the look of love in his eyes, and heard the sound of admiration in his voice. He himself had an angelic look. I knew President Tanner loved the Lord with all his heart, loved his wife with all his heart, and loved others with all his heart. He showed it in his words and actions. At that moment a thought came powerfully to my soul. "Greatness is sincerely loving others with all your heart."

President Tanner taught me a great lesson that day. He helped me recognize eternal beauty. Eternal beauty is ageless. Only mortal beauty fades. If all we see is mortal beauty, we really see nothing. However, if in mortality we can learn to see eternal beauty—the beauty of purity of character, the beauty of love, trust, and obedience to truth—then we see beauty that does not fade. Such beauty is not diminished with time, for where that beauty is, time is no more. I determined to love my wife as sincerely, purely, and openly at seventy, eighty, or whatever age, as President Tanner loved his wife.

As the Tanners boarded their plane I realized the jubilee had officially come to an end. The aura of peace and love and goodness that had pervaded everything about the jubilee was still in its beautiful afterglow phase. The last few days had been a veritable feast in the broadest and deepest sense. Prayers were answered, honor paid, lessons learned, and a heritage of faith preserved and passed to another generation. I had confirmed in my heart that this jubilee was planned in heaven and carried out under its direction.

As the Tanners' plane took off I sensed that the sky was full of angels—the Tanners, the temple group, and all those ancestors who this day would become more than angels.

Years later we received from the Church Public Affairs department a video of the jubilee events. As our family watched it early one evening, we had the impression to call Sister Tanner (President Tanner had previously passed away) to see if there was some time in the next few weeks she would like us to come and show the video to her.

To our surprise, she immediately responded, "Yes, there is a time. Could you come over tonight? Here is my address. . . . I'll have someone meet you at the gate."

We took some of the children and went to visit her. She seemed pleased to see us, and after briefly chatting she asked that we show the jubilee video to her. As she watched it she became very excited. She laughed at times, and cried at others. "Oh, look at Eldon," was the phrase she used most often. All evening she talked lovingly of her "Eldon." It was almost a mirror image of his words to me about her, so many years previously.

Later Sister Tanner's health deteriorated and she was confined to a nursing home near where we lived. We took some of our children and visited her. She did not recognize us. Each time I returned it was always the same—no apparent recognition. I would hold her hand and talk to her about our time in Tonga with her and her Eldon. I never felt that she understood what was being said, but I always had a warm feeling when I said it. Even in less than ideal circumstances, Sara Tanner carried a quiet dignity about her. To me she was always beautiful, just as President Tanner said.

Sister Tanner passed away while I was on a distant assignment. When I heard the news I sat down to ponder and remember. I saw Sister Tanner walking somewhere. Then I saw President Tanner smile and say to me, "Isn't she beautiful?" I nodded. Then I saw Sister Tanner looking at President Tanner. She turned and looked at me and said, "See, he is the best, the most handsome, the most wonderful man. You see what I mean?" I nodded again.

I didn't see or hear more, but my heart was full. I could feel the joy, the fulfillment, the jubilee celebration experienced by them and by all who live with love for God and for one another. I knew the Tanners understood the meaning of love and were happy therein. They were indeed angels full of love, just as they had been in mortality. I marveled, and I wondered why so many of us wait so long to learn this simple truth.

I hoped I could do better. I hoped everyone could do better and be able to see their spouse as the most handsome, or the most beautiful, for then it would always be true.

39

Promises Fulfilled

It was now December, and the time allotted to fulfill the missionaries' goal had expired. With all the extra assignments they were given for the jubilee I wondered whether it was even possible for them to accomplish their goal. Yet everything about the jubilee was a miracle clothed in hard work and dedication. Why not a miracle for the missionaries also? This was a season of miracles. That evening I met with the zone leaders and thanked them for their efforts and their faithfulness. They reported that everyone had worked their hardest, but they would not have all the reports in for another week or two.

They reminded me that there were nearly forty missionaries to be released and almost that many new missionaries to start work in December. Accordingly we decided to hold a special missionary meeting in two weeks. It would be our regular transfer meeting but also a special day of fasting and prayer to express our gratitude to the Lord for His blessings to us.

On the scheduled date I entered the chapel and found it filled to overflowing. There were not only full-time missionaries but also district missionaries and many priesthood leaders who had come on their own. So intertwined with the missionaries had their lives become that they were not going to be denied this opportunity to fast and pray and give gratitude to God for His manifold blessings.

There was not a boisterous or jubilant attitude among those nearly two hundred missionaries, but rather one of reverence, gratitude, and anticipation. The singing was magnificent. The zone leaders' reports were marvelous. Although each mentioned the number of baptisms in his area, it was almost an incidental part of his report. As I listened to these young men, I knew I was sitting among true greatness.

After the last zone report had been given, I stood and spoke. I recalled the feelings of two and a half months earlier when the number of five hundred converts had been given. I reviewed the request for total faith on everyone's part so that goal could be achieved.

I told them how pleased I was with their efforts. They had not held back, but had put every ounce of effort and faith they could muster, including their very lives, on the line. I explained how pleased the Lord was and how wonderfully He had blessed them. I expressed my love for and confidence in the zone and other leaders who had carried the load while I had been away to seminars and conferences and involved in the many elements of the jubilee celebration. I told them that as long as we lived (and that would be forever) our being part of this great event would be one of the high points of our existence. All eyes were focused and all ears were listening to every word. These were servants of God and His Spirit was with them.

One of the assistants, who had been recording the number of baptisms from each zone, handed me a slip containing the total. I looked at it, then said: "True to His promise that He had five hundred souls prepared, the total number of people baptized in the mission during the month of November is 507."

As those words were spoken you could have heard the proverbial pin drop. There was no explosion of sound, no clapping, no yelling, no cheering, just a roomful of intent eyes welling over with tears of gratitude.

I could say nothing. As I looked at that marvelous group of young men and women with tears quietly streaming down their faces my understanding was quickened and I sensed angels standing above them nodding their approbation. I was aware of the majesty and power of the Master of the universe encircling that little battalion of "Warriors of Christ" in a divine embrace that can only be felt, not explained.

The missionaries, while happy, were very calm. They had never doubted the outcome. What faith! What work! What majesty! What goodness and what power I saw before me. I thought of the sons of Helaman and said to myself: "You are of the same class. You have fought a good fight and come off victorious. Many of you do not have mothers or fathers in the Church, but you have developed faith and leadership and goodness and power that knows little equal. Indeed you are worthy to be called my sons and daughters, but am I worthy to be called your father? I hope so."

I don't know how long I stood there saying nothing physically, but feeling everything spiritually. I sensed that this was not the last time I would be with that special group. We all felt the same. Spirit-to-spirit communication is marvelous. When two hundred people can all instantaneously know what each other is thinking and feeling, one's understanding of prayer and the answering thereof takes on a whole new dimension.

Eventually we sang a song. It was reverent yet powerful, quiet yet beautiful, simple yet majestic. After the song I announced the new zone leaders and the transfers.

It is an amazing phenomenon to watch the process of missionaries becoming zone leaders. One moment you see ordinary faces in a sea of missionaries; then as they rise and come to the front of the room, something changes. Right before your eyes they become new men, new zone leaders in God's kingdom, trusted, responsible men full of faith and power and vision and knowledge. An actual change comes over them. It is marvelous.

After the new callings were given, the releases extended, the new missionaries welcomed, and the transfers announced, it was time to close. No one wanted this time to come, but as life teaches, the appointed hour to move from one place to another eventually arrives. With only a slight rustle of mats and clothing, everyone reverently slipped to their knees.

As mouth for the group, I was overcome by the realization that what was once a seemingly impossible goal was now a reality. How could I express the love, faith, and gratitude of so many wonderful, dedicated Tongan missionaries? It was overpowering. I tried to begin, but had difficulty. My heart and mind and soul were so full that there was little room or energy left for mere words.

Soon the flood of feelings became words. The words, heartthrobs, soul stirrings, or whatever you chose to call them filled the room and every heart therein. It was a prayer from everyone and everywhere—for all were of one heart and one mind and were one with God. We all understood better the scripture, "and they did not multiply many words, for it was given unto them what they should pray, and they were filled with desire" (3 Nephi 19:24).

There is no greater feeling than uttering a prayer and expressing gratitude to God and knowing that the thoughts and feelings and words are coming from Him. It is worth every effort to achieve such an assurance. When we come closer to God our prayers become very simple: basically a desire to more adequately express our appreciation, a desire for deeper understanding of God's will, and a desire for more strength to do His will forever.

How do you end a spiritual feast? I suppose the answer is, you don't. You simply put it in a chamber of your heart, rise from your knees, and go about the assignments God has given you. So that is what we did.

Those being released were invited to the hotel for a special farewell dinner. The rest were invited to a magnificent Tongan feast prepared by the wards. The hotel gave us lower prices, a private room, and plenty of time. They too felt a part of the spirit these powerful servants of God carried with them. To many, this was the first meal they had ever eaten at a hotel; to some, it would be their last as well. But that didn't matter. They had already experienced the most exquisite of all feasts and they knew it.

I thought of feasts. In physical feasts there is a great variation among men: those with wealth, power, and influence enjoy them often; those who lack money or connections seldom do. Spiritual feasts are open at anytime to anyone, whether rich or poor. Spiritual feasts are a matter of desire, and of paying the spiritual price, which is affordable to all—especially the meek and the humble.

As we finished the day I thought much about promises. How often do we make promises? How often do we fulfill those promises? How often do we receive promises? How often are those promises fulfilled? What a glorious thing to receive a promise from God. When we do our part, it is always fulfilled. How marvelous, how eternal, how satisfying: Promises Fulfilled.

40

Have Miracles Ceased?

Following our missionary meeting I spent the next several days interviewing and releasing the forty missionaries whose time was finished, as well as interviewing and setting apart nearly an equal number of newly called missionaries who were just beginning their service. What a spiritually exhilarating yet physically tiring time this was!

As each one came and went I had this overwhelming feeling: "Little does the world know what is going on here; all this work, all this organization, all this effort, for what? To try to save people. This is the most important work going on in the world. If only they could understand. Wars and contentions and other worldly problems are in some ways immaterial, but this work—what these young men and women, and these couples are doing—this is the reason for our existence, this is the reason why the earth still stands. As long as the Lord calls missionaries there is yet hope, even promise. Some people, somewhere, through the efforts and faith of these missionaries, will see the light, accept the truth, live the laws of God, and come to Zion."

I tried my best to explain this glorious concept, and to have each missionary feel the importance of his or her personal calling as an ambassador of Christ. I knew that to be successful, each one needed to feel deeply their personal responsibility and their great opportunity to help Him in the process of saving the world and preparing it for His second coming. I stressed the importance of their living pure lives so they could receive revelation and be guided and protected by Him. I explained the vital importance of their studying and praying and working hard so they could receive His help.

I assured them that as leaders we would do all we could to help them, but that for the most part they would be on their own. Often they would be on small islands for many months with little contact with headquarters. I testified from personal experience that God knew who they were and where they were and what their concerns were, and He would find them, bless them, protect them, and guide them, if they would only listen and obey.

They believed, and they accepted these charges and left with a smile and a warm glow about them that caused me to exclaim: "Jesus, as the life and light of the world, has truly entrusted His eternal message to these ambassadors of His, and as a sign of the same He has transferred some of that light to them. If they keep it burning brightly the world will recognize that glow and accept it!"

I spent considerable time with each missionary being released. I mainly wanted to encourage them and have them share some of the great spiritual experience from their mission. This large group seemed to be particularly strong in their knowledge of the guidance of the Spirit.

They shared many examples of faith and courage and guidance from the Lord during November 1968. Here are some examples:

While the Ha'apai Saints were preparing their songs and dances for the jubilee, very unexpectedly the town's best *punaki* (combined poet and choreographer), who was not a member of the Church, asked if he could help them prepare their *lakalaka*. "Sure," they said, thrilled with the prospects of getting the best talent available to help in their preparations. "Our theme is: The Nauvoo period, the martyrdom of Joseph and Hyrum, and the trek across the plains."

"Well, you will have to change that, as I know nothing about Church history," he said. To make a long story short, the Saints said they wouldn't change and sent books on the Nauvoo period for the poet to study. Incensed, the poet turned his back on the group. Then, not knowing why, he asked to see the books. Soon he was engrossed, and before long he had composed a poetic story to be danced and sung, telling of those important events of Church history. Week in and week out they practiced. The poet's minister became alarmed at the sudden interest the poet was showing in our church. But the practices went on. "Don't worry," the poet told the minister, "as soon as the conference is over I'll be back. We're determined to have the group from our village win first place."

But the message of the truth touched his heart. As the poet stood with his group on the night they won first place, tears filled his eyes. The inspired group acted out in dance and song those moving episodes of Church history. When they drew the parallels with the early history of the Church in Tonga, he could take no more. Soberly he acknowledged the hand of the Lord in bringing light to his mind. After receiving the missionary lessons, made easy by an open heart, he and his whole family were baptized at the conference.

Elder Paula and his companion couldn't understand what had happened. Mrs. Hopoate had committed to be baptized, but now she wasn't home. They inquired and found that her husband had suddenly been taken ill and the couple had made an emergency trip to the hospital on another island. How the elders had counted on her being baptized! But Elder Paula was transferred the next day, so that was that.

Weeks later Elder Paula was so busy teaching and baptizing people in his new area that he had all but forgotten about Mrs. Hopoate. Then came November 30. Oh how he, like all the missionaries, wanted five hundred baptisms! Elder Paula worked hard all day and into the evening.

As he and his new companion returned to the home of the Church members with whom they lived, he was surprised to find Mrs. Hopoate waiting for him. "Oh, Elder Paula," she exclaimed, "I've been looking all over for you. My husband has been ill and we didn't know whether he would live or not. Finally, just this evening the doctors told us that he would be OK. We are so happy. I have been by his bedside ever since I left our island. I told him that I wanted to show the Lord, in the best way possible, our appreciation for his getting well. We talked about the missionaries, and suddenly the most burning desire to be baptized filled my heart. I told my husband I must go and find the elders and be baptized. That is how we are to show our appreciation to the Lord.

"My husband said, 'Then go, if you believe it that strongly. I'll probably be baptized soon. Go find the elders. After they baptize you, bring them to me.' I was so excited when I found out you were in this town and I didn't have to go back to my island. I have been waiting so long, I can't wait any longer. Please baptize me now."

One set of missionaries had a baptismal date set with an eighteen-year-old girl, who had permission from her parents to be baptized.

When the missionaries went to check with her, she had suddenly and unexplainably changed her mind. Her parents were still agreeable, but for some reason she just didn't want to be baptized.

Understandably, the missionaries were shaken. As they left the home discouraged, they remembered their mission president's challenge to be sure and check back with their old contacts, even those who had said no before. Suddenly another eighteen-year-old girl came to their mind. But that was silly, they thought. Her father was bitter and had consistently refused to give permission for her to be baptized. The last time they had gone there, the father threatened to take a machete (bush knife) to them if they ever came back. Still they felt impressed to go to that house again. "We're all ready to baptize someone now," they thought. "Why not her? Let's go see."

At that moment this second girl felt impressed to ask her father again for permission to be baptized. He became violent and struck her several times, knocking her down. "Now will you ever ask again?" he said, glaring down at her.

"Yes Father, I will continue to ask until you give permission, for I know the Church is true!"

"Ha," said the father, "I've chased the missionaries away from here so many times they will never come back. But I'll give you a test to see if your church is true. If the next person that walks through our gate is a Mormon missionary and asks me again to let you be baptized, then you can be baptized. And if not, then the Church isn't true and I will never give my permission for you to be baptized."

As the young girl prayed, the missionaries, fearing and trembling but prompted by the Spirit, approached the house. Overcoming their fear, they boldly opened the gate and in the full force of spiritually guided strength announced, "Mr. Aholelei, we have come to ask that you allow your daughter to be baptized, for she knows the Church is true, just as we do."

It was now the father who fell quaking to the floor. The young girl rose, and looking down in compassion she explained: "You see, Father, it is true. I'll change now for my baptism. Will you come along?"

In a choking voice the father managed to say: "Go quickly. I am an evil man. Maybe the Lord will bless me and have mercy on me through you. Quickly, go and be baptized."

As soon as that baptism was over, the first girl came running over. "Please let me be baptized. I really wanted to all the time. I believe the

Church is true. I can't figure out why I said what I did. Will you forgive me and let me be baptized?"

The missionaries were quiet, but after the second baptism and witnessing the joy on those two faces they knew what had happened.

Here is a sample letter from a typical missionary during this period.

"I feel very humble because of the numerous blessings the Lord has bestowed upon my companion and me. Our plan for this week was to baptize four people, and I am happy to report that we accomplished it and even more. In fact, this week has been a landmark for us because we had three baptisms by Tuesday; then on Wednesday we had another baptism, one more on Thursday, with three more on Friday and another one this morning, which makes a total of nine baptisms for the week. I'm writing this letter in the morning and so we still have the rest of the afternoon in which to work and I think that before the sun sets tonight we'll have another one or two baptisms. One of the best things about the fifteen people we've baptized during the past two weeks is that they are all about twenty years old or over, and I think they will be good Church members. Most of them are young men.

"Next week we will work with our investigators and plan to baptize four of them. I'm certain that through our fasting and praying we'll be able to achieve our goal, and I know that only through the help of the Lord will our work be effective. My companion and I love the work and really feel the spirit of the work. We're at a point now where we don't feel like eating and find it difficult to sleep, just because we're continually thinking of the work and ways to make it progress. When I wake up in the morning I have a warm feeling in my heart and a great desire to preach the gospel and testify of Jesus Christ to the people. I truly love the work and the people and continually thank the Lord for the choice opportunity I've had in being a missionary in Tonga.

"P.S. We have been able to baptize three more (Saturday evening), which gives us a total of twelve for the week."

The missionaries' deep devotion, firm faith, and hard work allowed the Lord to work miracles through them.

As I thought of the work and faith of these great young men and

women and these couples, I couldn't help but feel that many of their
Book of Mormon ancestors were smiling upon them. I re-read the seventh chapter of Moroni and was humbled thereby. "Have miracles
ceased? Behold I say unto you, Nay; neither have angels ceased to
minister unto the children of men." (Moroni 7:29.)

"And Christ hath said: If ye will have faith in me ye shall have
power to do whatsoever thing is expedient in me" (Moroni 7:33).

41

Pleading Eyes

One of the strong branches in the mission was in a small village in the Eastern district. The branch president, Kelepi, was a convert of not many years. His wife and children were stalwart examples. His parents had been very angry when he joined the Church, and threatened to disinherit him. Over the years, however, he proved to be a good son, and they allowed him limited farming privileges on their family land.

Kelepi was a strong leader who worked hard on his farm as well as with the members of his branch. His vibrant testimony, easy manner, and willingness to share were major factors in helping branch members to return to activity and investigators to be baptized. Under his leadership the branch prospered in numbers and spiritual strength. I visited there as often as possible; it was refreshing to feel such a good spirit with so few problems.

One afternoon, a member from this branch came rushing into my office. He asked if I could quickly go with him to the hospital because there had been a terrible accident. The branch president was in serious condition and desperately needed a blessing.

We hurried to the hospital. When we found his room we were met by a most pathetic sight. The branch president lay there, his body contorted, his neck obviously broken. He could not move or speak, but his eyes seemed to plead: "Please help me! I have so much to do. Please help me—bless me—ask God to bless me. Don't leave me like this."

We gave him a priesthood blessing. As I sealed that sacred ordinance, the words I wanted so desperately to say just would not come. I felt helpless, yet knew that God's will was different than mine. I had to submit my will to His.

When I had finished, I looked again into the eyes of our wonderful branch president. They seemed subtly different. They were still alive with desire and were trying to make me understand something. I tried to understand his message but didn't fully succeed. I felt he understood me as I expressed my love for him and his family and as I assured him that we would watch over him and his family no matter what happened. I told him again that he was in the hands of God, that he had been given a proper priesthood blessing so we knew that God's will would be done. For some reason I felt there was another message he was trying to get through to me. Why couldn't I understand him?

The doctor entered and gave him another heavy shot of morphine for the pain. After this shot, he seemed to relax somewhat and eventually closed his eyes. I felt bad that despite all his struggling I had been incapable of fully understanding his message or satisfying his desires.

The doctor told us that while he most likely would be paralyzed from the neck down, he would probably live. He also said they would have to keep him on pretty heavy medication. This meant there would be little chance of communication for several days.

I left the hospital that evening with a heavy heart. Why had this happened—of all people, why him and why now? Why couldn't I promise him the blessings I thought he needed and deserved? And why hadn't I understood the message he had tried so hard to get through to me?

As we left I asked some of the family members to come to the mission home with me to get some much-needed food and to explain what had happened. They told me the branch president had started out on his horse early that morning to work in his garden. Usually he worked several hours, had a small meal in the bush, and then returned home in the early afternoon when it was too hot to get much done. This day, when he was still not home long after noon, his wife had felt a pang of concern, especially since it was a very hot day.

She asked some neighbors to go and check. When they got to the garden area they quickly spotted his horse faithfully standing over its fallen master. It appeared that some time during the morning he had fallen off the horse and hit his head in such a way that it broke his neck. He was thus unable to move or yell or get anyone's attention. He must have lain for several hours in the broiling heat, suffering excruciating pain.

As I heard this explanation I shuddered to think of the pain and the heat and the frustration. Why hadn't someone felt a prompting to go earlier—or more important, why had it happened at all? Why—why—why?

By prior schedule we were to leave early the next morning for district conferences in Ha'apai and Vava'u. Now I didn't want to go. I called my counselors over and we had a decision-making meeting. As we counseled together we agreed that it would be best to sail in the morning as planned and leave the branch president and his family in the loving hands of the Lord. After prayer we were assured this was the right course.

That night I went again to the hospital but found that the medication had rendered the branch president incapable of even eye communication. I assured his wife that we loved her and her husband and their family. She assured me that they were ready to accept God's will. I told her about our scheduled conference trip, and before I had a chance to say more she immediately encouraged me to go and not disappoint the people in Ha'apai and Vava'u.

Early the next morning we left, even though my heart was still torn. We had such a wonderful outpouring of the Spirit at our conference in Ha'apai that I felt better. The stricken branch president was remembered in all of the prayers.

In those days the main method of getting news from island to island was by the national radio station, which went on the air for two hours each morning, another hour at noon, and about two more hours in the evening. That day we faithfully listened to each broadcast but there was no news about our branch president in the personal announcements, so we assumed things were going along about as the doctors had said they would.

As we left the protected harbor after the Ha'apai conference, the seas proved much rougher than we had anticipated. I knew the Lord was pleased with the conference we had just completed and that He would protect us as we sailed to our next conference in Vava'u. Still, I felt an uneasiness that was hard to explain. My discomfort wasn't so much due to the heavy seas as it was to my mind seeing the branch president in unspeakable pain lying for hours in the merciless sun with his faithful horse just looking at him. I kept asking why? why? and shuddering in sympathy for an event that was past.

I looked at that little group of Tongan leaders on that small boat that fearful night and thought, "How faithful they are and how much they have committed to the Lord—just like the branch president." I shuddered again and wondered what lay ahead for him and his family and for these leaders. The seas were rough, but the Tongan leaders didn't seem to be worried. Even though our little boat was constantly being pummelled by an angry sea, they were not complaining or questioning. I felt they knew things I didn't know. How I admired them.

Finally the time arrived for the evening broadcast. We turned our portable radio on and listened to the crackling and whistling of strange sounds as though coming from an alien shore. It is hard to describe the feeling of being on a storm-tossed sea at night with a group of twenty or so humble Tongan leaders faithfully holding to one another. In some respects their only link with the solid world was that small portable radio. At the proper moment, as though by magic, the radio obediently reached into the sky and captured music and words and phrases and squeezed them through wires and cones and brought them forth in a way that all on the boat could hear them. "This is ZCO the Voice of Tonga with the evening broadcast."

Everyone was glued to the radio to hear what announcements would be made. Even above the howling of the wind and the crashing of the waves, silence seemed to reign as the time for personal announcements arrived. My heart almost stopped and I sensed a quick rush of half gasps as we all heard the mournful sound of the funeral dirge that was always played before announcing a death. The music ended, and even before the somber words rolled forth over those dark tempestuous seas, I knew.

There was silence as the announcer intoned: "We regret to inform you that Kelepi passed away early this evening. The family wishes those involved in the conference to continue their meetings and not return for the funeral." There was more, but I didn't hear it. All the pent up emotions of the last several days seemed to burst in a gush of tears and questions. Why? Why? Why? He was so faithful. Things were going so well—but now, a widow with eight children and the rights to her husband's lands not fully settled. Why now? And why in that painful way?

There were hushed whispers and inquiring eyes. The captain looked my way. I said nothing, trying to comprehend what was happening. I was stunned into near immobility. Finally I gave a slight hand signal pointing to Vavaʻu. I knew we should go on. The captain briefly nodded and everyone settled back for the long night at sea. I moved to the front of the boat. The others respectfully stayed behind as they sensed I wanted to be left alone.

For hours during that tumultuous night I poured out my heart— my grief—my questions—my lack of understanding—my emotions. I hurled them defiantly at the shrieking wind and they came flying back as stinging salt spray and crashing seas. Where was peace? Where were answers? The poor widow and those innocent children. Why so much suffering?

The moon was bright, the wind was strong, and the seas were heavy. A few clouds flew by, but the sky was mostly clear. I prayed for understanding and for relief—not so much for physical as spiritual relief. Through that seemingly endless night the boat, like my emotions, went up and down, up and down, at times riding clear and free then crashing into the depths, covered by the cold ocean of fear.

My torment seemed to increase when I half heard the sound of the Tongan national anthem marking the end of the broadcast. Now we were totally alone. Even that thin thread of radio contact had faded away. My heart seemed to cry out, "Oh, don't leave me—don't leave me alone—don't leave me without answers—without some understanding." How I wanted some comfort, but none seemed to come.

Eventually, for some reason the words of a familiar hymn came to my mind:

"When upon life's billows you are tempest tossed,

When you are discouraged, thinking all is lost,

Count your many blessings. . . ."

"Blessings," I thought, "what blessings? I need answers. I need comfort. I need understanding."

Softer now, but still nudging: "Count them. Name them. Think of them—all your many blessings!"

Where were these words and thoughts coming from? Hesitantly I started to think of blessings. "Yes, the branch president died firm in the faith—that is a blessing."

"Yes, now you are thinking better. And his family—are they faithful?"

"Yes. Yes they are. That is a blessing."

"And—"

"And we have had a wonderfully spiritual conference."

"And—"

"We are safe and have families and callings and opportunities to teach the truth and bear testimony of Jesus."

"And—"

Slowly a small spirit of peace began to make its first tentative overtures to my soul. I began to realize that the radio waves were not our only contact with others. There was something more—something more real, more sure, and oh, so much more important and desirable.

In my mind's eye I began to see the pleading eyes of the branch president again, only now I saw something a little different. I studied them with an intensity that was so deep that it hurt. What is it? Concentrate. Yes, yes, that's it. Now I understand. No longer were those eyes pleading in vain. No longer were those lips mumbling incoherent sounds. Now I heard; I saw; I understood. The message I had been unable to receive before was received clearly now and there was no static, no fading.

As my humbled soul and subdued spirit embraced those precious feelings I realized the message was very simple. I listened intently, and as I did my mind comprehended: "I'm just fine. Don't worry about me. You know I have not yet been to the temple. I was worthy but had no means. Please see that my wife and I and our children are sealed. Don't forget."

I had been greatly confused, but now I understood perfectly. The message of those pleading eyes was clear. I knew exactly what I must do. I made a vow that, come what may, I would see that his request was fulfilled. How relieved I was. I no longer felt the heavy seas or the whistling wind or the stinging spray. I was at peace.

I stayed in the front of the boat for some time, and as the night wore on I had many more feelings and understandings. All centered on things that are eternally important—priesthood authority, covenants, promises, temples, families, love, communications, sealings, commitments, sacrifice; and at the center of everything, the Savior of mankind.

I had spent time worrying about the branch president's pain and the seeming injustice of the whole situation. Now I knew that he was not concerned in the slightest about any suffering he had been through or the physical manner in which he departed this earth life. That was temporal, immaterial; it didn't matter. What he was concerned about was his family and the temple and the sealing ordinances performed only there. These were important. These were eternal.

I had asked over and over again why he should depart now when we all needed him so much. I had almost demanded an answer. Now I knew that we must not try to demand anything from above, but rather seek humbly to know what *we* should do—and do it. In one flash I had a slight feeling that maybe even some over there might occasionally ask, "Why? Why is he allowed to stay there when we need him so badly here?" And the answer is the same: "Seek humbly to know what *you* should do and do it."

I realized that at times we may look forward with fear and trepidation to the trials and pain we may suffer in the process of being released from this tabernacle of clay. But in reality this mortal life—let alone that brief part of it we call death—is such a tiny split second in eternity that we ought not to spend time or effort worrying about it. I am sure that as we look back from eternity, the only thing we will be concerned about (and thus the only thing we should be concerned about now) is whether we left mortality gracefully—faithfully, uncomplainingly—having taken upon ourselves the requisite covenants and ordinances and faithfully observed them to the end. Our concern will be whether we left doing good and praising His name up to our last breath. This can only be done as we have true faith in the Lord Jesus Christ; but with that faith it *can* be done, and that is what is important.

As that long night started to yield to the first hues of light from the east, my heart was at peace. I had learned much of importance. I returned in silence to the dozing groups who motioned to a place on the protected side of the deck that they had prepared and held in reserve for me all night. As I drifted off to sleep I felt a deep peace in my soul. What a contrast to the tumultuous feelings that had filled so much of the night!

Our conference went well in Vava'u. The Saints attended in great numbers and the heaven-sent theme of the importance of preparing for the blessings of the temple, of putting everything else aside to achieve those eternal goals, came easily and with certainty to a subdued and faithful group of Saints. Many hearts were touched and softened. Personal and family commitments involving the temple were made that eventually resulted in much good to many people both here and beyond.

After conference we returned safely to Nuku'alofa. My wife had attended the branch president's funeral. She gave me a beautiful account of the services. I was sure things would work out well eventually. We soon found, however, that additional tests awaited this faithful widow and her family.

Our commitment to support her and her family were tested almost immediately. It started with land issues. The in-laws threatened to evict the widow and her family from her house and disinherit her and her children from the needed land unless she renounced "Mormonism" and returned to their fold. She remained firm and faithful, however. Eventually right and reason prevailed, reconciliation was made, and good feelings—even wonderful conversions—followed.

Over the years many people were blessed by being able to help the branch president's family. Finally the entire family was sealed in the New Zealand Temple. I will leave to your imagination what happened as that family knelt at the sacred altar. Suffice it to say that there was peace and fulfillment and gratitude on both sides of the veil.

All of the branch president's children grew up in the Lord, served missions, got their education, married in the temple, and in every way fulfilled their father's and mother's and God's expectation of them. The branch became a ward, and one of the sons became the bishop. Everywhere the members of that family went they proved to be a strength to the Church. As the last child came of age and left home, this wonderful widow became a worker in the Tonga Temple.

I often think of this family and the trials they have been through. As I do, the words of Isaiah seem to hum in my mind, "For, behold, I have refined thee, I have chosen thee in the furnace of affliction" (1 Nephi 20:10). All I can say is, "Yes, it is so. Tempered and true."

Like most people, I have had enough experience to know that things don't always turn out as they did for this family. The fires of trial can consume as well as refine, but the choice is ours. Not the choice of what tests or trials will be thrust on us, but the choice of how we will react to them—the bright fire of faith or the darkness of despair. I hope we can react with faith in the Lord and follow His commands no matter what the trials, or how long they last, and thus reap the blessings available, as this faithful Tongan family has.

42

Kau Tau 'a Kalaisi
"Warriors of Christ"

I was enthralled with the high quality of leadership among the local members and missionaries. At times I felt insignificant compared to their towering spirituality. Their understanding of the scriptures was so deep and so clear that I was often left spiritually breathless by their insights.

I quickly learned that the key to success among the missionaries was to have good—even great—zone leaders. I often referred to the zone leaders as "mini-mission presidents." I expected them to run their zones like a small mission and take care of the problems, training, motivation, and health needs that arose there. I did my best to interview the missionaries, but with over two hundred of them scattered over forty separate islands the main burden of training and shaping missionaries fell on the zone leaders. They did such a superb job of training that we always had a ready supply of wonderful missionary leaders.

I felt a deep personal responsibility to teach the gospel to them. As their testimonies became stronger through a deeper understanding of the scriptures and knowledge of the basic principles of the gospel, they automatically improved their skills and methods in carrying out their duties.

Once the zone leaders understood how much I expected of them, how much I trusted them, and how much I relied on them, they not only rose to those expectations but exceeded them.

Once a month I met with the zone leaders. Occasionally I met with individual zones, but normally I left those meetings to the zone leaders. I wanted them to feel the full responsibility for their zone. The ideas and plans and methods they came up with were absolutely spectacular. Often they were so simple and effective that I was left wondering, "Why didn't I think of that?"

Our monthly zone leaders training meetings were held Sunday afternoon after the regular branch meetings were over. Few meetings were more full of the Spirit. At first they lasted about two hours, then three, then four or more, as guided by the Spirit. Each zone leader gave a report, followed by a selected zone leader teaching us a basic principle. I then taught in depth one basic principle such as faith, repentance, baptism, the Atonement, revelation, and so forth. We concluded with testimonies.

One Sunday afternoon when the zone leaders began gathering, one of our daughters came running to my office and said, "Daddy, I smell a meeting!" And what a meeting it turned out to be! They had come prepared to discuss the book of Mosiah and tell how they had used it to increase the faith and effectiveness of the missionaries in their zones.

I cannot forget that meeting, and even today count it as one of the truly "great" spiritual meetings I have attended. The zone leaders rose one by one and quoted from Mosiah and explained how they had used this idea or that comment in improving missionary work in their zone. Each one seemed to be better than the previous one. I almost felt sorry for those whose turn was later, as I couldn't see how anything could be better—but it was.

More than once I reminded them that we were limiting this discussion to the book of Mosiah. They then turned to a specific chapter or verse and read it in such a way or with such an interpretation that I marveled and was sorry I had said anything. They were always right. I thought: "This is their book. This is written to them by their progenitors and the way they understand it is every bit as valid as mine, if not more so."

The Spirit was so strong that no one noticed that over two and a half hours had slipped by until a couple of our daughters hesitantly stepped in and asked if we wanted something to eat or drink. We took a refreshment break, but the zone leaders were quickly back in their places anxious to continue the meeting.

We continued for another three and a half hours. I was again filled with amazement at the depth of understanding these wonderful young men had. Over and over they explained principles in such simple yet powerful ways that I sat in awe of the majesty I saw before me. They literally shone.

As I listened to them I said to myself, "These truly are children of the prophets." As that thought took root I was caught up in an understanding of relationships that was marvelous. I knew there was a direct connection between the group that surrounded me that evening and the ancient Book of Mormon peoples and prophets. As I listened to the discourses being given by those powerful missionaries on that distant "isle of the sea," I was sure that Nephi, Alma, Ammon, Moroni, and many others were pleased.

I was shaken out of my contemplation by a little tug and a whisper. "The zone leaders are finished. It's your turn to make any corrections or say anything you would like."

I stood almost trance-like, and could do nothing but say: "You are wonderful. In fact, you are the greatest. The Spirit of God has been with us in rich abundance and He has allowed other good and noble influences to attend as well. All that you have said and done this evening has my total blessing and the approbation of our Father in Heaven and of the Savior and others who they have charged to help you. God bless you all. Continue in the spirit of humility and prayer and study and hard work. Bear your testimonies constantly with conviction and even greater blessings await you and your missionaries and your investigators and your people. I know whereof I speak." I bore solemn testimony and sat down.

It was close to midnight when we had the closing song and prayer through many sob-filled pauses. No one wanted to leave. It was warm and late, so that little band of "Warriors of Christ" slept right there on our living room floor.

I went to my bedroom and lay there in some of the deepest contemplation and purest distilling of understanding possible. I must have eventually fallen asleep, for in the morning I was gently awakened by Jean and asked if I wanted some breakfast. I arose and went to the living room. Everyone was gone. The room was spotless. Nothing out of place. I shook my head in reverent remembrance. The room was somehow sanctified and hallowed and even had a glow about it.

What wonderful zone leaders God provided!

Several of that group would soon be released. My heart was swollen with gratitude and love for them. I knew they would be hard to replace, but someway the Lord would provide new leaders and those being released would go on to other important things and would always be a strength to the kingdom wherever they were. They had been touched by the Spirit of God; they had tasted the sweetest of all fruits, felt the greatest of all power, experienced pure revelation, and received firm, unshakable testimonies.

From those dedicated "Warriors of Christ" have come a whole generation of bishops, stake presidencies, Regional Representatives, mission presidents and temple presidents—not only for Tonga but for other countries also. The Lord knows how to prepare His leaders.

A group of Tongan missionaries.

43

When Things Are
As They Should Be

As 1969 began, the spiritual overflow from the jubilee continued to permeate everything. Sacrament meetings, missionary meetings, leadership meetings, and district conferences all increased in spiritual depth and strength. Faith, repentance, and other basic principles were taught from the point of view of a true participant rather than as a principle only. Even though there were many problems to solve, the answers seemed clearer and simpler. They centered mostly on being more obedient, having more faith, and thinking of and serving others with more desire. In many ways these months were some of the best for building the Lord's kingdom in Tonga.

I was grateful for the many chapels being built and dedicated to help house the rapidly growing membership. Each dedication was a huge event involving feasting, dancing, singing, praying, preaching, and more feasting, often for several days. I kept worrying about the chapel at Niuatoputapu. It had been finished for a long time, but permission to dedicate it had not yet come through. I knew something should be done, but what? (See chapter 1.)

One excellent bishop in Nuku'alofa, who had formerly been a member of the mission council, asked if we could assign more missionaries to his ward. He and his ward were very missionary oriented. I felt good about his request. We doubled the number of missionaries, sending him some of the strongest ones we had. Within a few months his ward increased from 250 to 400 members. He was ecstatic and asked for even more missionaries. We sent more.

Within another few months his ward doubled to 800 members. He asked to visit with me again. I thought he would ask for more missionaries. Instead he explained that the solid base of experienced leaders in his ward was limited and he had come to realize that even with all their desire and the help of the missionaries, many of the new converts were not receiving the needed fellowshipping to keep them active while they were gaining a firm foundation. He felt it was best to reduce the number of missionaries in his ward to a level consistent with the ability of the members to properly fellowship the new converts.

I admired his honesty. He understood clearly that numbers without substance or strength was not what the Lord wanted. He quoted extensively from Jacob in the Book of Mormon about keeping the roots and the tops in balance (see Jacob 5).

We prayed together and felt good about transferring most of the missionaries in his ward to other areas. The balance now seemed right. His ward continued to be one of the strongest and was soon divided into two wards.

The missionaries everywhere worked closely with the members in fellowshipping new converts, and seldom did we see any slip in activity rates. However, I was now aware that such a thing was possible. The very thought of new converts not being properly fellowshipped and possibly slipping into inactivity concerned me deeply.

A little later a different bishop asked me to come to his ward's conference. As the meeting was about to begin someone handed him a note. He frowned a little. I asked him if there was a problem. He replied that there were 274 members in his ward and there were only 271 in attendance. "But I can account for the other three. One is in the hospital, one is in Ha'apai helping a married daughter with a new baby, and one is overseas on business. He tried to get back but one of his flights was canceled and he can't make it." I told him I was glad he could account for them all and felt the Lord was pleased with his efforts. He smiled broadly and we proceeded with the meeting. I was again grateful for good, caring bishops who do their duty with all their heart.

I often found myself thinking deeply about the many miracles associated with the jubilee. Miracles are things that happen that we cannot readily explain but which are nonetheless real. We are daily surrounded by miracles that we do not recognize as such because of the constancy of their occurrence. The sun comes up each morning, a baby grows to be an adult, a friend reaches out to a lonely soul—all that is involved in those processes is a miracle, yet they seem normal to us.

Everything connected with the process of baptizing people into the kingdom of God is to me a miracle. November 1968 was a miracle of miracles. The impression that the Lord had five hundred souls ready for baptism; the faith and work of the missionaries to accomplish this goal; the faith, repentance, and willingness of hundreds of investigators to be baptized, often against great pressure—what greater assurance could there be that the Lord was guiding?

I reflected on how smoothly everything had proceeded: more than 100 baptisms in September, more than 250 in October, then the 507 in November, and another nearly 200 in December. While the November phenomenon was a God-given "special," the number of baptisms never did fall back to their pre-jubilee level. Each month they continued at about twice the number for that month of the previous year. What a season of harvest! 1968 had over twice the number of baptisms of the year before, which itself was 30 percent higher than the previous year, and 1969 exceeded 1968! We knew the Lord was pouring out His Spirit upon the faithful people of Tonga.

Despite these figures I didn't feel then and still don't feel today any particular pride in numbers. I realize how relative numbers are, and that what to one mission or missionary or under one set of circumstances may appear spectacular, to another mission or missionary, or under another set of circumstances, may be very ordinary or even small. Those who chase numbers end up being frustrated. The only eternal satisfaction in life comes from understanding God's goals for us and then with His help relentlessly and tirelessly pursuing and achieving those goals. When we do, great blessings follow. Think of the account of Nephi in the book of Helaman, chapters 7 through 10. The people rejected him and turned very wicked, but he still achieved the inward goal, which the Lord acknowledged.

> And it came to pass as he was thus pondering—being much cast down because of the wickedness of the people of the Nephites, their secret works of darkness, and their murderings, and their plunderings, and all manner of iniquities—and it came to pass as he was thus pondering in his heart, behold, a voice came unto him saying:
>
> Blessed art thou, Nephi, for those things which thou hast done; for I have beheld how thou hast with unwearyingness declared the word, which I have given unto thee, unto this people. And thou hast not feared them, and hast not sought thine own life, but hast sought my will, and to keep my commandments.

And now, because thou hast done this with such unwearyingness, behold, I will bless thee forever; and I will make thee mighty in word and in deed, in faith and in works; yea, even that all things shall be done unto thee according to thy word, for thou shalt not ask that which is contrary to my will. (Helaman 10:3–5.)

Spiritual success is an inward thing. It is knowing God's will and doing all we can to achieve it. It is knowing that the Lord will do the rest when we have done our best. It is sincerity of purpose and honesty of effort that counts. That is what God responds to. God measured the faith and sacrifice of thousands of Tongans over many years. During 1968 He meted out miracle after miracle to them.

As we came to the last few weeks of our mission I kept thinking about the jubilee and other miraculous events of 1968. Our current success was really a continuation of the spirit of the jubilee.

Sometimes events that at the time seem important tend to shrink in size or importance with the passing of time or the observer's gaining of more maturity. On the other hand, some events loom even larger and more significant with the passing of time and the gaining of more experience. The year 1968 in Tonga was such an event. As I contemplated the multiple manifestation of God's love and guidance—and reviewed His marvelous blessings sent in response to trusting faith, humble prayer, hard work, and obedience—everything about the jubilee and 1968 continued to increase in importance and wonder. I saw then (and see even more clearly now) the guiding hand of the Lord in accomplishing what under normal circumstances would not have been possible.

The events of that year were guided by the Lord and carried out by faithful workers full of love and devotion. There was no complaining, no questioning, no slacking, just diligent effort by everyone as the fire of their faith consumed any obstacle that got in the way of accomplishing the Lord's goals. O that we could ever do thus!

After years of experience I look back and, Camelot-like, say in calmness: "There was a time—there was a place—there was a people of one heart and one mind."

They did walk after the commandments which they had received from their Lord . . . continuing in fasting and prayer, and in meeting together oft both to pray and to hear the word of the Lord. . . . there was no contention . . . there were mighty miracles. . . . the love of God . . . did dwell in the hearts of the people. . . . there were no envyings, no strifes, nor tumults . . . there could not be a happier people. . . . they were in one . . . children of Christ . . . heirs to the kingdom. . . . And how blessed were they! For the Lord did bless them in all their doings. (4 Nephi 1:12–18.)

Yes, I am convinced that when things are as they should be they will be much like they were in Tonga in 1968.

44

Jesus, Savior, Pilot Me

How do you prepare to leave a place and a people that you have loved with all your heart? In a way, you don't—you just keep working and loving and helping in every way possible, and when the plane arrives you get on and go. I suppose it is a little like leaving this life. You love and work and help as much as you can for as long as you can and then you leave. President Kimball used to say that as long as we have breath we should keep trying. That is how we felt during those last few months in Tonga.

Time was evaporating too rapidly. We wished we could stay longer, but we had to face reality. The rounds of "final" feasts and conferences and interviews and meetings seemed to go on forever, as nearly everyone and every group came up with a reason for another feast or meeting or both.

The queen asked me to come to visit in a non-official setting. She wanted to express her love and appreciation for all that had happened over the last few years and be brought up to date on each of the children, especially John Enoch. As she expressed her interest in and love for John Enoch, as a sort of "godmother" to him, it suddenly struck me that she had also participated in the fasting and praying for him when he was so sick. I didn't ask her, but I could tell. What a marvelous way the Lord has of turning what might to some appear to be a tragedy, or at least a serious problem, into a great blessing. We talked a lot about the gospel and I left feeling grateful for this wonderful woman, as well as the rest of her family.

I had an official farewell meeting with the king and the queen and bade them good-bye. I mentioned how much I would like to say farewell to everyone, but would not be able to because of the lack of time. They asked, "Why don't you give a farewell talk on the national radio, then you could talk to everyone."

I was delighted! I had just written a message to the Church members and the missionaries and had given a copy to our friends in the government, as well as the king and queen. It was entitled "Jesus Lives Today." I could think of nothing more important for people to know than that, so I gave that message in a thirty-minute nationwide broadcast.

We had now arrived at our last weekend as mission president, with its final missionary conference on Saturday and final district conference on Sunday. The spiritual power at our missionary conference was beyond description. It literally shone from their eyes. The fire of faith and power of purity coming from these young men and women were incredible. I could easily see how "so great was the fear of the enemies of the people of God, that they fled and stood afar off" (Moses 7:14).

I felt that they were among the choicest young men and women in the world. I marveled at how the Lord had blessed and protected them and prospered their efforts. He would continue to do so as they continued faithful. To me, nothing in all the world is more wonderful than missionary work, and no missionary work anywhere was more inspirational than right then and there. I felt that when the final histories of missionary work are written, the missionaries in Tonga in 1966–69 will have one of the finest of all chapters.

I looked at my counselors and the other leaders who had worked with them so diligently and helped them achieve this high level of devotion, commitment, and hard work. I realized what a high price in time and effort they had paid, and my eyes clouded over. I whispered: "I'll see you all in heaven, if I make it. I know you will. Please pray for me that I might have just a little of the faith you so richly possess. How I need it!"

The next day we held our final district conference. As we began the meeting the building was overflowing with as loving and as faithful an assemblage of Saints as have ever met anywhere. I had developed a fairly serious cold and cough and wasn't sure I could speak at all. Jean spoke beautifully and had the hearts of everyone right in the palm of her hand. When I spoke, I started very quietly, expressing my feelings of love and testimony. I could feel the warmth of their love, and in that element the Lord gave me courage and strengthened my voice and allowed me to continue.

I challenged the members to seek and find God. I went on to list all of our seemingly small responsibilities that have such an eternal impact. I asked them to pray for faith, endure in love to the end, and always continue to add charity to every other Christlike quality, and through Him move on to eventual perfection. "Yes," I concluded with a power that was not my own, "if you do all these things, you shall have eternal life" (see 2 Nephi 31:20). There was total silence as every heart acknowledged the importance of obtaining this goal and helping others do likewise. We all knew that nothing else really mattered.

As we climbed the steps to the plane a few days later, we were all in tears. The plane lifted into the air and circled once just for us. As I saw those friends below, waving from the beautiful land of Tonga, I knew that the Lord would continue to shower His Spirit and blessings upon them—that the fire of faith within these wonderful people could not be denied or quenched.

The trip home was long and tiring. The past three years had evaporated so quickly that I wondered if they were made of something other than time (and maybe they were). On the other hand, the sheer volume of heart-wrenching, soul-searching experiences over those same three years made them seem in some ways like an eternity.

I thought of our son. It had been a year and three months since I had seen him. What would he be like? Would he remember us? We were anxious to see him and hold him and have him physically part of our family again.

As I thought of him I thought of several close calls we had been through as a family. I remembered many terrifying storms, both physical and emotional, and felt a deep sense of gratitude to God for protecting us and seeing us safely through our mission—or more correctly through His mission, which He had allowed us to be part of.

In a way I was grateful it was over, but in another way I found myself longing for the difficult challenges of a mission and the closeness to heaven they bring. I felt good about the way things had turned out. I did not know what the future held for us but I knew it would be fine because God would be there. What a blessing it is to know that God is guiding our lives regardless of how tough things sometimes seem to be!

From this deep contemplation I heard the captain announce that we were beginning our descent into San Francisco and would soon be landing. It was a clear afternoon, and as we came in low over the ocean I looked down and saw several sailboats with the wind tugging at their billowing sails.

The scene brought back vivid memories. I felt the thrill of a strong wind at my back, filling canvas sails and powering our boat through deep blue waters, sending plumes of lacy spray dancing in the wind. I smiled as for a moment I actually heard the sounds, saw the beauty, and felt the joy of those wondrous days of closeness to God as we traveled upon His vast ocean.

Then I remembered many rough voyages. I felt the rolling motion of small ships at sea. I began to experience motion sickness and was assailed by unpleasant smells and fearsome sounds associated with ocean travel. I recoiled from them and felt grateful for the large airplane that had brought us smoothly over thousands of miles of open ocean in such a few hours.

Yet while I was grateful for the smooth flight, I wondered if anyone could truly enjoy such smoothness without having first experienced roughness. I became a little uneasy as I sensed the danger of actively seeking smoothness rather than letting it come in its own natural cycle.

I was still trying to sort out these conflicting feelings when I heard a voice, as it were, in my mind saying: "The time will come when you will be asked to put your whole family in a small sailboat and head out into uncharted waters. Are you willing to do it?"

I was surprised, even amazed, at this. I closed my eyes, but the boats and the ocean and the wind and the sails and the sounds and the smells were still there. I knew it was not just my imagination but that a real decision had to be made, for someone was waiting for an answer.

The deeply conflicting emotions of discomfort and danger, as well as joy and peace went through my heart, mind, and soul. I struggled with them and found myself becoming very weak. The terror of terrible storms passed through my very being and I grasped for the security of a firm rail and a solid footing. As I did, I caught hold of the rod of God's goodness and power and held on with all my heart. I felt secure. Then receiving a sudden surge of strength I unhesitatingly said: "I will. Of course I will. If that is what is needed, I will. How could I not? Yes. I will. I will."

As that strong commitment ascended from the depths of my heart and flowed into eternity, I heard the comforting words of a hymn: "Jesus, Savior, pilot me over life's tempestuous sea; unknown waves before me roll, hiding rock and treach'rous shoal. Chart and compass came from thee: Jesus, Savior, pilot me."

Instinctively I found myself saying: "I need help. Oh, how I need help, but yes, I will go and take my family. I know chart and compass come from thee. Yes, yes, a thousand times yes, but oh, please, please Jesus, Savior, pilot me!"

The whole experience could not have taken long, for almost immediately I felt the plane touch down and taxi to the terminal. I looked out the window and found myself with tears in my eyes and a determination in my heart that almost caused me to burst with anxiety. "We're back in America," I thought, "but there will be more voyages. I hope I can feel as sure about them then as I do now."

We gathered the children and our carry-ons and left the plane. I decided not to say anything to anyone about the experience, not even Jean. I was confident that sometime, somewhere, somehow our family would get into another small boat and head out into the vast uncharted sea—alone, yet not alone. When that time came we would talk about it.

Although this experience made a deep and lasting impression on me, I was not sure what to expect. I did expect something unusual to happen sometime. Life, however, continued on in what seemed like a normal pattern.

Years rolled by and I was never asked to take my family in any boat or leave for any uncharted sea, at least not that I was aware of. As the years turned to decades, the memory of that experience became dimmer. Occasionally something happened to remind me of it, but when nothing materialized I was left wondering what those deep feelings were all about.

Years later we were living in Hong Kong when our last daughter graduated from seminary and high school and left for college. Now, for the first time in thirty-eight years, Jean and I found ourselves without children at home. I knew we would adjust to our new situation, but it was certainly an adjustment.

My first assignment after our daughter left was to conduct a conference in Indonesia. The people, the climate, and the scenery all reminded me so much of Tonga that my feelings became very tender and nostalgic. As I flew back to Hong Kong I basked in the warmth of the love of those faithful Indonesian Saints. Beautiful memories of past years seemed to cover me as if with a soft blanket of goodness and joy. In a way I longed for things as they used to be.

I thought of Jean waiting at home for my return, only now for the first time there were no children to keep her company. What would it be like to come home with no children waiting? I wondered how many hundreds of farewells and returns there had been (and would continue to be), yet never a complaint from Jean. How I thanked God for a faithful and supportive wife! My feelings of love and gratitude for her knew no bounds. As I thought of her faithfulness and sacrifices over so many years, I felt a strong desire to spend more time just talking with her and being more helpful to her.

Somewhere in this reverie I heard the announcement that we were starting our descent into Hong Kong. This seemed to awaken some distant memory that started to stir and move to a more focused position in my mind. As the plane began its final approach I looked down and saw hundreds of boats filling the harbor. The picture seemed hauntingly familiar. Then my eyes were drawn to some Chinese junks moving quietly by themselves at one end of the bay, their picturesque sails clearly outlined against the darkening sky.

I gazed intently at the scene as though drawn into it by some mystical force. A sensation of warmth covered me and my eyes began to cloud. Then I seemed to hear in my mind a beautiful voice coming as it were from the depths of eternity saying, "Yes, chart and compass are in me. I indeed have piloted thee."

As though by command I looked again at the boats below. As I focused on them, they moved into some sort of a multi-dimensional pattern that seemed to encompass all eternity. This time I saw not only Chinese junks and large freighters but also Tongan sailboats, square rigged galleons, sleek clipper ships, and indeed every type of seagoing vessel ever used by man throughout all ages. As I looked I could tell that each of them was being inexorably guided to some heavenly destination by patient, loving hands.

A spirit of sweetness encircled me and I felt a soft voice saying: "There is farther to go, but know that I have been guiding you and the boat your family has been sailing in."

It was as peaceful and soul-comforting a feeling as anyone could experience. I saw our family not only in Tonga but in Idaho, Indiana, Hawaii, Utah, Argentina, and Hong Kong. I saw our children graduating

from five different high schools on four separate continents, learning
several new languages and making many sets of new friends in various
countries.

An almost instantaneous review flashed through my mind. I saw
our family being guided through many tight situations and scary
predicaments. With every dimension of my being I felt God's goodness, kindness, and love. As a flower opens its beauty only after long
and patient nurturing, I could now see the fruition of these feelings
and promises of years ago.

Even though they had been fulfilled in a way far different than I
had anticipated, I realized it was in a way far better than I had anticipated. A fleeting thought shot through my mind and I sensed that
even this was but the beginning of fulfillment. At that moment I knew
with certainty that all of God's promises are always fulfilled in ways far
deeper and far better than we can even begin to imagine. How vital
that with full purpose of heart we do all He asks!

I cried out within my soul: "Oh, Jesus, Savior, how can I thank
thee? Thou hast guided me over life's tempestuous sea, through hidden
rock and treacherous shoal. Chart and compass have come from thee. I
know there is farther to go. Oh, Jesus, Savior, continue to pilot me."

Everyone's voyage through life is filled with calmness and joy as
well as with stormy seas hiding rock and shoal. If we recognize that
the only viable chart and compass are in Jesus, He as our Savior will
safely pilot us home. Every individual and every family is special to
Him, and their voyage through life is of utmost concern to Him.

This overwhelming feeling made as deep an impression on me as
its counterpart had years earlier. I did not want it to end, but once
again the plane hit the runway and taxied to the terminal. Reluctantly
I returned from this special odyssey, made my way down stairs and
halls, past Immigration and Customs officials, into a van, up an eleva-
tor and into the arms of my Jean.

I started to tell her I knew that no matter what we were asked to
do, if we would just say yes and willingly go into any small boat given
us and sail over any uncharted sea, we would be guided and protected
and in the end we would see that Jesus had been our Pilot, our Friend,
our Helper, our Savior. I say I started to say that, but I could tell she
already knew it better than I did, so I just held her, kept my peace,
looked into her eyes, and marveled at the beauty of true faith.

45

Home Again

During one of our stops on the way back to Idaho Falls we watched on television as Neil Armstrong took that historic "giant step for mankind." We felt we were also taking some new steps in our family history.

As we stepped off the plane at the Idaho Falls airport, my parents were holding up a big, healthy boy. Even though we had followed his growth and progress through letters and pictures from his grandparents, it was hard to realize that this was the tiny infant we had entrusted to others' care. What a joy for us to be reunited with our son, John Enoch. However, he didn't seem to feel the same way. It had been over a year since he had seen Jean and even longer since he had seen the rest of us. There were tears in all of our eyes as he clung to his grandparents, unsure about these strangers who claimed to be his parents and wanted to take him away.

Still it was a dream come true as we held him in our arms and could see that he was healthy and happy. We felt it best to have him continue to stay with his grandparents for a short while until he got used to us. They brought him to our home for a few hours each day until he finally felt comfortable enough to stay with us. I thought of what a marvelous service his two sets of grandparents had rendered in caring for him. They and the doctors and the other folks at the hospitals were a significant part of the answer to the fasting and faith and prayers in his behalf by the faithful people in the Tonga Mission. Prayers are often, if not usually, answered through the help, work, and love of others. Such was the case with our son.

The Groberg family reunited at the Idaho Falls airport,
August 1969.

Shortly after returning, I was called as a Regional Representative. I was excited to learn that my region included Samoa, Tonga, Fiji, and Tahiti. This calling required that I be away from home for several weeks at a time, several times a year. While I enjoyed my continued association with the islands, it was difficult to juggle my role as a father, my Church calling, and my business.

That first winter back in Idaho Falls was especially hard on us. We were not used to the cold, and the change in climate brought some illness. But perhaps the greatest challenge we discovered after our return was that the business we had left behind had basically disappeared. It was a time of recession and no one was building much. We had a place to work, but not much work to do. Sometimes people feel the Lord will bless them financially while they are serving Him. We found, however, that while the Lord blessed us greatly in many ways, we had to struggle substantially just to buy food and pay our bills.

It was soon apparent that we needed an additional source of income. I started teaching a few classes at Ricks College. This helped but still did not fully bridge the gap. Our savings were nearly gone, and we got to a point deep in the winter when every physical thing, including bills, seemed to be dark, cold, and ominous. For a long time we were probably as careful in turning off lights, darning old socks, saving all leftovers, and never throwing anything away as we had ever been. Despite all of this, things just seemed to get worse.

One morning, just a week or so before leaving for another trip to the islands, I woke up and realized we really needed some extra-special help. I went again to the Lord and explained that we had eight mouths to feed and bills to pay. I explained that I was going again to the islands on His errand and leaving Jean with six little ones to care for and I didn't want to burden her more by her having to worry about money to buy food or to pay other necessary bills. I also mentioned that we faced a major operation for John Enoch that coming summer, and while we knew it had to be performed we were wondering how to pay for it.

After the prayer I felt good. What a comfort it was to know of God's love. I felt grateful for our blessings, such as our beautiful children, our testimonies and callings, the opportunity to serve, and the great help of our family and friends. However, despite all my pleading I still did not feel inspired to turn in any new direction. I believed I had worked as hard as I knew how, but I guessed I would just have to work harder.

I tried to put in longer hours, but all that seemed to accomplish was to make me more tired. Finally, I decided to review everything we had to see what we might sell that was not absolutely necessary. As I began that review I remembered the small amount of extra money that had come up just as we were leaving for our mission. I had used about $1500 of that money to buy stock in a relatively new and unknown electronics company called SONY. Maybe there was something there we could use.

Early the next morning I called the broker who had helped me before, and asked about the stock. "I was wondering when you would call," he responded. "What has happened is unbelievable. The stock has gone up more than almost anything I have seen."

We learned that there was enough value in that small investment to pay all of our current bills and give Jean sufficient money for food and clothing while I was gone. In fact, we sold a little of that stock each month for nearly a year, and it was sufficient to take up the slack until the real estate business improved. In a way it was like the meal and the cruse of oil. When we finally turned the corner financially there was still a little left. I have kept that small remainder for sentimental reasons, but also as a reminder of how good the Lord is to us when we try with all our heart and then try even a little harder.

Considering all of my travels during this time, it often seemed that my time at home was even more limited than our budget. Nevertheless I tried my hardest to spend adequate time with Jean and each of the children. I also learned to appreciate more fully whatever time we did have together, regardless of the hour or the circumstances.

In the middle of one particular night we had two children in diapers who both needed attention at the same time. As fate would have it, right then one of the other children got sick and threw up all over her bed. After cleaning the three little ones and getting them settled down again, Jean and I went into the bathroom to tackle the job of cleaning up the smelly mess. (In those days we used cloth diapers.) We kept twin sinks, a toilet, and a bath tub all in full and constant use as we scrubbed and washed and rinsed and flushed the goo and the smell away.

After the worst was taken care of we found ourselves down to the last two diapers, each of us cleaning one in a separate sink. It was late. We were tired. The whole thing had been rather distasteful. Suddenly, for no particular reason the situation struck me as being very funny. Maybe it was the lateness of the hour or something else, but I burst out laughing. I looked at Jean and said: "We're really having fun, aren't we? This is the happiness of a family. This is the joy of children. This is the stuff that memories are made of. Aren't families wonderful?"

I was not being sarcastic and Jean could tell it. She smiled, then also began laughing, "How could we ever have more fun?" she said. "This is life. This is a family. Yes, it's wonderful."

I'll never forget that night and the laughter and good feelings that helped dispel what otherwise could have been an onerous task. I have often thought about that incident and reflected that maybe we need to laugh more. Of course, we need to do our duty, but we can also have fun doing it. I am convinced that the Lord has a sense of humor. It was wonderful to feel a little of it that night.

In my efforts to spend individual time with my children I occasionally took one or two of them with me on my trips. On one trip I fulfilled my promise to the Tongans to return with John Enoch. To see

*John Enoch, age two, visited with the queen
during a trip to Tonga.*

the crowds, watch the eyes, and hear the murmuring as I walked off
the plane in Tonga with a healthy, husky two-year-old-boy, you would
have thought the king himself was arriving. It is a miracle that he sur-
vived the next few days of hugging, embracing, pinching, swinging,
holding, talking, and staring. They were actually seeing for the first
time the fulfillment of their faith, fasting, and prayers of two years before. It was easy to tell who had made that investment. Watching those
joyful people for those few days, I witnessed firsthand how loving,
fasting, and praying for others blesses the giver as much as, if not
more than, the receiver.

    During all my travels, I knew that the Lord was watching over and
blessing my family in my absence. On these assignments I learned
great lessons and returned with inspirational experiences to share with
my wife and children. Some of the greatest lessons I learned, however,
were from my family. They never once complained about my assignments, even those that came without warning.

    As an example, at work one day I received a call from President
Kimball. As all who knew him can attest, he was very kind but also
very direct. "Brother Groberg," he said, "how quickly can you get to
Tonga?" I responded that if all the connections went right it would
take about twenty-four hours. In a very matter-of-fact manner he said,

"Well, we could give you a little more time than that. Could you be there in forty-eight hours?"

I gulped and said, "I will check with the airlines and see if seats are available."

"Good. Get there as soon as possible, hopefully within forty-eight hours."

"Fine," I responded. "And what should I do when I get there?"

"When you get there I want you to give me a call and I will give you further instructions."

I could tell he was about ready to hang up, so I quickly queried, "How long do you think I'll be gone? I probably should give my wife some indication of that."

Almost as an afterthought he said: "Oh, I don't think you'll be gone too long, but if you need a time frame, tell your wife you won't be gone more than six months. I doubt it will take any longer than that."

I was silent, almost expecting a chuckle or some other comment, but there was nothing except, "That will be all. Thank you. God bless you. Give me a call soon."

"I'll do so," I responded as I heard the phone go "click." As I started to think about the assignment, all sorts of concerns came to my mind. In my business we had several construction projects under way that I felt needed my personal attention. There were also many things I knew I should do to help Jean and the family. In some way all of those concerns were covered over by the assurance that when we do the bidding of a prophet, the Lord blesses, protects, and helps us in every necessary way.

I called the airlines and was able to get an almost perfect connection leaving early the next morning. I then went home to tell Jean. She was very busy preparing meals, changing diapers, washing clothes, rubbing bumped heads, settling clashes, applying bandages, answering the phone, and doing the myriad other things a busy mother does. How I admired and loved her. I waited until there was a slight lull in activity and then informed her of President Kimball's call. Her immediate response was: "Go and do what the prophet asks. We'll be fine. Only hurry back as fast as you can—we'll miss you."

From the islands I had several phone conversations with President Kimball. The Brethren had decided it was time to call the first local mission president to serve in Tonga. I was thrilled at this recognition of ability and confidence in the local leaders. After much fasting and

Tongan stake president and former counselor to President Groberg,
Tonga Toutai Paletuʻa (at far right, holding John Enoch),
with the Groberg family at their home in Idaho Falls.

prayer, I gave my recommendation to President Kimball. He accepted
the recommendation and the historic change was made. What a marvelous fulfillment of promises for the Tongan Saints!

When all was completed and I was told that I could return home
it turned out that I was only gone for six weeks rather than six
months. Still it was a happy reunion when I did return, made happier
by the fact that everything had worked out so well with both of our
assignments—mine in Tonga and Jean's more daunting one with the
family.

There is universal appeal in the concept of "going home." We an-
ticipate the joy of returning to our heavenly home largely because of
the love we inwardly remember from there. We can feel the same way
about returning to our earthly home if we always return with love in
our heart. The best way to have love in our home is to bring it with us
when we return home. My efforts to do this were made easier by the
constant love I felt from Jean and the children. How blessed I was to
always be able to return to a home filled with love.

46

Keeping Commitments

I promised Jean that I would do everything humanly possible to be with her at the birth of each of our children. One of my early assignments to the islands seriously tested this promise.

Soon after I was called as a Regional Representative I learned that my predecessor had already scheduled a series of regional meetings in the islands for the month of November. I was alarmed when I received the pre-set itinerary and saw that the return flight would not get me home until late on the night of November 25, Jean's due date for our seventh child. I didn't quite know what to do.

I knew it was my duty to attend those meetings. I also knew that since they had been set for some time and nearly twenty auxiliary board members and their spouses had already made arrangements to attend, I could not change the meeting dates. However, I was also preoccupied with concern for Jean and I wanted to keep my promise to her.

When I expressed my concerns to Jean, she encouraged me to fulfill the assignment and follow the set meeting schedule. After reviewing the flight plans, however, she further suggested that I might be able to find an earlier flight from Hawaii on the way home that would eliminate a lengthy layover. After thanking her for her insight, I quickly called the travel agency and was able to arrange for connecting flights that would get me home on the night of November 24.

All of our meetings went well, and we made it back to Hawaii just in time for me to catch my early flight home. After I had boarded the plane, they announced that there would be an indefinite delay. I only had one hour in Los Angeles to catch my flight to Idaho Falls. When we finally left Hawaii an hour late, my heart sank as I realized that the connecting time was gone and there was not another flight to Idaho Falls until the next day.

As we flew toward Los Angeles I explained my connection problem to the stewardess. She said that we had a moderate tailwind and might make up some time. As the hours dragged on I prayed and wondered how I could keep my promise to Jean. I asked God for just a little extra tailwind. I felt it was for a good reason.

As we got closer I asked the stewardess again if I might make the connection. She was very nice, but said we had only made up a few minutes and there was little chance. She asked why I was so concerned, and I told her about my promise to my wife. I was surprised to then hear myself say: "I must catch that plane to Idaho Falls. I must be there for the birth of our daughter Susan." (Ultrasounds were not routine in those days, and until that moment I had not known the baby would be a girl.)

The stewardess became a little emotional and left with a strange look on her face. As we began our descent into Los Angeles she returned and said: "I believe you. The captain has radioed ahead; and while they can't hold the flight to Idaho Falls for more than a few minutes, we can try to get you there as fast as possible. Follow me." She took me from the very last seat in the huge 747 to the very first seat nearest the door.

We touched down and taxied to our gate. As the door opened another stewardess said, "Hurry down the steps and get into that little Jeep with the yellow light flashing. Sue said it is very important that you catch the flight to Idaho Falls. Good luck." (That was the first time I had heard the other stewardess's name.)

"Thanks," I replied, "and tell Sue thanks also."

The driver rushed as fast as he could to the plane that was ready to leave for Idaho Falls. Just as we rounded the last corner we could see them starting to pull the stairs away from the plane. The driver grabbed his "bull horn" and yelled, "Western Flight 65! I have one more passenger for you. Could you keep the stair there for one more minute?"

The startled man at the top of the stairs signaled for those below not to move the stairs. The door opened, and as I started up the stairs the driver smiled broadly, gave a "thumbs up," and said, "I'll tell Sue you made it. She'll be happy."

I gave the man at the top of the stairs my ticket and entered the plane. As the door closed a good-natured stewardess smiled and said: "Boy, that was close. I asked them to wait as long as they could. We knew you were coming."

"Thanks, Sue." I said. "And thank the pilots and others for waiting."

She looked at me rather strangely and said: "Do you know me? How did you know my name?"

"Just a lucky guess," I replied. "Our daughter Susan has been on my mind."

I landed in Idaho Falls not much before midnight. After we arrived home and kissed each of the sleeping children, Jean suggested that we probably should call my parents and see if they could come and stay with the children while we went to the hospital. A few hours later (and long before the next flight from Los Angeles would land in Idaho Falls) our beautiful dark-eyed Susan made her earthly debut.

As I looked at Susan and Jean and thought of their sacrifice and love and potential, I seemed to see my great-grandmother, Susan Burnett Brunt, and a whole series of other Sues I had met, especially two stewardesses. I had the feeling: "Susan, you have a great heritage. You too will be blessed with faith and courage and will go out of your way to help others. That is what really counts." I felt at peace and was glad I was there.

During the next few years two more children were added to our family. John Enoch got a little brother, Thomas Sabin in 1971. Precious Jennie Marie, named after both her grandmothers, came two years later. Although I did not have to overcome as much to keep my promise to be with Jean on those occasions, I was still overcome with the same joy, hope, and gratitude. I was humbled by the goodness of God in allowing Jean and me to raise such wonderful children.

Through the Lord's goodness I have been able to be with Jean at the birth of each of our children. I know that if we make and honestly try to keep proper commitments, God will help us do so. Experiencing heavenly joy depends more on keeping righteous commitments than we might suppose.

47

Feki Moves On

My assignments to the islands for conferences and other meetings usually lasted between two and three weeks at a time and were always tightly scheduled. For some reason I never had an assignment that took me to Niue Island, where Feki lived. I had not seen Feki for nearly four years, so I was surprised one Tuesday evening in late March of 1972 to receive a call from Feki's sister saying he was very ill and in the hospital in Salt Lake City.

She explained that he had developed cancer in his jawbone and was in serious condition. He had asked about me, and she wondered if I could come down and visit him. I told her I was scheduled to come to Salt Lake City Thursday evening for Regional Representatives meetings and general conference. I asked if it would be all right if I left Thursday morning and visited him Thursday afternoon. She said that would be fine, as he would probably last that long. As she said that I had a twinge of feeling that I should just drop everything and go right then. However, much to my regret I didn't follow that feeling.

Feki passed away Wednesday evening. When they informed me of his death I felt terrible. Why had I not heeded that prompting? When I expressed this regret to his family they said to forget about it. Feki knew he was going, but he also knew I was coming, so just before he died he told his family to give his love to me and tell me not to feel bad about not seeing him before he left. With his ever-present sense of humor he told them that he looked a mess anyway, so it was probably better for me to meet him when he had his "proper body" back. He asked them to tell me that he was going on ahead and we would meet again before long.

I still felt guilty, but as they told me these final words I said: "Just like Feki. Always concerned about the feelings of others. What a Saint! I hope I live worthy to meet him where he has gone."

Upon inquiry, I learned that Feki had developed a problem with his jaw in Niue and had been operated on there. His condition worsened, so he was sent to New Zealand, where they operated again, cutting away a large part of his face. Because he continued to get worse he was sent to Salt Lake City, where he passed away. I could only imagine the pain and suffering he experienced through all of this. His family said he never complained. I knew he wouldn't.

Feki had requested that I speak at his funeral, so I immediately started thinking and praying about what I should say.

Over the next few days I found my mind wandering as I saw Feki's smiling face, felt his kindly demeanor, and basked in the strength of his love, faith, and testimony. What a loyal companion. I often had to wipe tears from my eyes, being so deeply affected by the feelings of love for and from this great man. All my meetings were colored by the deep feelings I had for the goodness of Feki. I realized that in a way that is what the Church is all about—to help develop good men and women. I knew Feki had accomplished that.

When the time for his funeral service arrived there was a wonderful group of family and friends in attendance, gathered around his casket. The morticians had done the best they could, but it was still hard for me to recognize Feki. I knew that what I saw was not the real Feki and I cried out in my heart: "Oh, Feki, Feki, true and faithful to the end. Always setting an example for me to follow. How I miss your sparkling eyes and contagious smile. Thanks for your love, faith, and enthusiasm. Good-bye for a while."

As I talked to his family and felt their longing, I had a hard time reconciling what had happened. Why, of all people, had he been taken so early in life? I knew of no better person or greater leader in the islands than Feki, and now he was gone. I thought of his wife and their small children. I thought of his help to me and of his kindness, obedience, and firmness in the right. What a magnificent person. The music, the feelings, the tears, the love—all combined to put me in a deep state of wonderment.

Suddenly it was my turn to speak. The congregation was about half Tongan and half non-Tongan. I arose rather numbly and spoke first in English. I had prepared some scriptures and gave what I felt was a good message and testimony. Then I told the audience I would give basically the same message in Tongan.

As I started through the scriptures in Tongan, something changed. I was no longer in a chapel in Salt Lake City but on a small island listening to a faithful servant of God preach the truths of the everlasting gospel. This servant preached in such a powerful and convincing way that those listening could not disbelieve. I thought of Enoch and Nephi and realized that Feki was like unto them. I tried to explain this, but found that I could not.

I began speaking about the plan of salvation. It was almost like giving a missionary discussion, only I understood and saw much more. God lives. He bears sway in the affairs of man. He guides His Church on both sides of the veil. In some respects there is more "going on" over there than over here. All of it revolves around being honest, developing purity of purpose in all we do, and putting forth great effort to love and serve the Lord and our fellowmen with perfectly pure motives. The Savior is central to everything—here and there and everywhere. Our greatest need is to develop love and willing obedience to Him and His ways. With this love there is life and light and eternity; without it there is nothing.

As I concluded I felt as though I was wrapped in the bonds of a deep smile from beyond. I knew that Feki was happy and that he had achieved a wonderful status. I knew that he was continuing to work hard in declaring the truths of the gospel. I knew he was helping his family and friends. I knew he would be in the forefront when the kingdom of heaven comes to earth. I knew Feki, and others, were pleased with the services. I felt that even though I had not gone to Salt Lake City on Tuesday as I should have done, somehow the Lord (maybe through the pleading of Feki) saw fit to give me comfort, revelation, and understanding. These feelings will always be a guiding star to me as I reflect again and again on the life and love and service of a great man, my first missionary companion, Feki Po'uha, a true servant of God.

48

The Missing Light

I was often asked to go with others on assignments to the islands. Each time was a joy to me. I not only got better acquainted with these Brethren but also learned much from them. As an example, I was once asked to go with Elder Boyd K. Packer to visit some stakes in Samoa and create a new stake on the island of Upolu. We had a marvelous experience in calling the new stake president. Since there were units coming from other stakes we agreed to let him have a couple of days to decide on counselors. In the meantime we flew to Savai'i and held a mid-week conference there.

Our plan was to fly over one afternoon, hold meetings that evening, then fly back to Upolu the next day. Everything went according to plan—until the weather intervened. By the time we were ready to leave, a storm had arisen that was so intense that the small plane could not land in Savai'i.

The meetings on Upolu were already scheduled and there was no way to get word to them about any change of plan. I was impressed with how calmly Elder Packer took everything. We hoped for a break in the weather, but as the light began to fade from the sky we knew that no plane would be coming that day.

The only feasible alternative was to take a boat back to Upolu. However, as we went to the main port and inquired about boats everyone laughed at us, pointed at the turbulent sea and the darkening sky, and said no one would be crazy enough to go. Finally a counselor in the stake presidency was able to arrange for us to rent a boat for a charter trip to Malifanua (the closest point on Upolu). It was well after dark when we finally left. The flight to Upolu would have taken less than a half hour, and under normal conditions the boat journey would have taken just a few hours. Conditions were far from normal, however. The boat went up and down and rolled and jerked and pitched all over that angry ocean for many more hours than usual.

We lay on our backs on boards covering the motor to keep from getting tossed about too much. Most everyone got sick. One of the men working for the Church Educational System was lying between Elder Packer and myself. He must have passed out, for suddenly, on one of the extra violent pitches of the boat, his limp body flew forward towards the railing at the edge of the deck. The railing was not very high, and he would have gone sailing over it into that boiling ocean had it not been for a post that "just happened" to be right in the middle of the path of his uncontrolled body. He smashed against this pole and fell to the side in a heap. Fortunately this gave us time to jump up and grab his unconscious body before it slipped under the railing and into the jaws of that monster sea. It was a miracle, and was acknowledged as such by all aboard.

We held on to each other more tightly as we torturously jerked through that terrible night. Finally we arrived close to Malifanua. The captain now told us we had another problem. There was only a small opening in the reef and we had to negotiate it perfectly to keep from getting torn to pieces on the sharp coral on either side. Tonight it was especially important to hit the opening just right because of the extra large waves and the unusually powerful ocean currents.

Normally there are two lights for night entry—one at the wharf and another up the hill a way. When you line those two up you know you are entering the opening properly. Unfortunately the only light on that night was the one on the wharf. The one up the hill was not on, so we could not tell accurately where to enter the opening. We later found that the two men who were supposed to turn on the light on the hill had said to each other: "It's a terrible stormy night and no one would be crazy enough to try to come from Savai'i. Let's just stay home tonight and not go out in such a storm for no reason."

This experience helped us better understand what the Savior intended when he talked about letting our light shine and not putting it under a bushel (or not turning it on when it is inconvenient to do so). If we have an assignment to help others find their way to safety, we had better let our lights shine so that others can see and be guided; we must never assume that our light doesn't matter or that no one will be watching us. Often people need to see our light the most when we least feel like lighting it or when we feel no one will be looking for it. This Malifanua experience, then, was a great lesson to all of us.

Without the second light on the hill, the captain simply did not dare try to navigate the boat through the narrow opening on such a stormy night. Again I was impressed with the calmness and faith Elder Packer exhibited. His simple question to the captain was, "What can we do now?" The captain replied that we had two alternatives. We could return to Savai'i or we could continue along the dangerous coast of Upolu all the way to Apia, where the harbor was much larger and better lit. We told him to proceed to Apia. That took the rest of the night. The sea was worse than terrible—it was horrible.

Just as the sky was beginning to grow light, we came into Apia. There was no one at the main wharf, so we had to tie up alongside other small boats and jump over several startled sleeping sailors to make our way to shore.

We were able to get to our Church school in Apia and to find some members who let us shower and clean up in their homes. We then met the new stake president, got his choice of counselors, interviewed them, and drove out to the meeting. We arrived on time at the place where a crowd of well over a thousand Saints was gathered waiting for an Apostle of the Lord to organize them into a new stake of Zion.

As we were singing the opening song, Elder Packer turned to me and said: "What do you notice different about us than any of the other thousand-plus people here?" I thought for a moment and replied that we were the only ones sitting on chairs. (They had brought a few chairs for us but everyone else was sitting on the floor, as was customary.) "No," he replied. "I have been looking and we are the only two people wearing shoes."

I thought how wonderful it was for him to still have a sense of humor and notice a detail like that after the night we had just been through. As he stood and organized that stake of Zion I said to myself, "Little do these people—or other people, for that matter—know of the pain and the sacrifices the Brethren make to carry out the work of blessing the people." As his powerful testimony filled that room, I asked myself, "Do I know what is different? Yes, I know that we have an Apostle of the Lord present today who has overcome whatever obstacles were placed in his path in order to fulfill his errand from the Lord."

As I looked at the reverent, attentive faces and saw the tears of gratitude streaming down many cheeks, I sensed that those faithful Saints in Samoa also knew.

49

A Sacred Grove

From my youth I have felt a closeness to and a love for the Prophet Joseph. The only non-English-speaking area Joseph Smith personally assigned missionaries to was the Pacific Islands. As I traveled among the islands, I felt the influence of the Prophet Joseph Smith. I wanted to learn more about him. I decided to take a book on the life of Joseph Smith and read it on the long flights.

As I boarded the plane from Idaho Falls bound for Los Angeles I sat next to a man who was an inactive member of the Church. I visited with him, so I had no time to read. But by the time we arrived in Los Angeles he had made some very important commitments that later changed his life. A similar thing happened on the flight from Los Angeles to Honolulu, only this time it was a nonmember who was interested in talking about the Church. The next flight was an "all-nighter," on which there was no opportunity to read.

Upon arriving in the islands I became fully immersed in meetings, and before I knew it three weeks had disappeared. There was only one day left before returning home. A meeting was scheduled for that evening, but the day was free. I decided to stay in my room and read. It was my only chance.

No sooner had I opened the book than there was a knock at the door. Some local leaders had come with a fairly serious problem that needed to be resolved before our meeting that evening. It became quite complicated and occupied the whole day before a good resolution was reached.

As I went to the meeting that evening I thought: "This isn't fair. I have a righteous desire to read a book about the Prophet Joseph Smith and I haven't had the opportunity to get past page two." Since the members could not all fit in the chapel, the meeting was being held on the concrete tennis court outside the Pouono chapel in Vava'u.

I had prepared some remarks on leadership training, which I felt would be helpful. The Saints had been very receptive so far, and I was sure they would appreciate what I had to say. As we sang a song just prior to my remarks, I felt an impression to speak about Joseph Smith and the First Vision. I tried to dismiss this thought. These were all strong members and I felt they needed what I had prepared.

As we sang the second verse the feeling to talk on Joseph Smith came again, only stronger. Again I tried to dismiss the thought and started looking at my notes. As we sang the final verse the prompting of the Spirit came even stronger and I was sure there was no mistake. It is important to prepare well for assignments, but it is vital to leave room for the inspiration of the Spirit (see D&C 46:2).

When the song was finished I stood before several hundred experienced, seasoned members of the Church. I greeted them with love and expressed my appreciation for their great work. I still wanted to give my prepared talk. I stammered a little, then looked again into the faces of those faithful people. They smiled encouragingly. I knew what I had to do. I turned my prepared notes over and said, "Tonight I am going to talk about Joseph Smith, about his feelings and actions, and about the glorious vision he received in the Sacred Grove."

Without really knowing why, I began quoting from the pamphlet "Joseph Smith's Testimony." It seemed somewhat mechanical to begin with, but as I proceeded something marvelous happened. No longer was I quoting from a published account. No longer was I telling the story of a faithful young boy from a third-person point of view, but rather I was explaining what I saw and knew. In effect I was with him.

In minute detail I explained, as a firsthand observer, the moods and reasons and feelings and movements he made, right up to and including going to the Sacred Grove. I needed no text, for I was there. It was an exciting yet sublime experience.

I could see everyone was following my words, every head nodding in agreement, and every face, old and young, wrapped in penetrating attention. I sensed that they were literally drawing the account of these sacred events from me—or through me. I had prepared none of this. I simply explained what I saw and felt and knew to be so.

I didn't learn any new facts. The facts were as written in his testimony. What was new to me was the reality and depth of his feelings. For instance, he stated that he was "greatly surprised" at the behavior of some people he respected. I had not realized before how hurt he was to be treated with contempt by others, especially when Deity had been so loving to him and he was trying to convey that love to others. How I felt for him. I realized what a blessing his family was to him.

Finally I came to a point where the clarity and sureness of what I was seeing and feeling became obscured. I knew I was through.

I understood better than I ever had before the appearance of the Father and the Son to Joseph. I was sure that part of the fulfillment of the promises given to him that day happened right there in Pouono, Vava'u. Faithful descendants of Joseph, who was sold into Egypt, had had emblazoned in their hearts and souls testimonies of prophecy-fulfilling events surrounding the mission of another of Joseph's descendants—even Joseph Smith. Their understanding of and participation in the rolling forth of Zion to fill the earth in preparation for the Lord's second coming in power and glory would continue to be marvelous.

As I sat down I understood more about Joseph Smith than if I had read all the books in the world written about him. I was sure that some of the members present had shared this understanding or vision in a way even deeper than I had. What we know counts only to the degree of fervor with which we accept and act upon that knowledge. I could see gratitude and determination in the eyes of the members. It showed in the glow of their countenances and in the quiet comments they made to me.

Later, at the hotel, a middle-aged man asked if he could speak to me for a while. He had obviously been touched by something. He began by explaining that he had recently listened to our missionaries but was far from convinced of the truth of what they were telling him, especially that "outlandish story" about a boy prophet and visits from God and angels and golden plates and so forth.

The missionaries had told him that they were going to a special meeting at Pouono that evening. "I was curious," he continued, "so as the evening wore on I decided to go to Pouono and see what was happening. I was surprised to find the meeting being held outside. I listened from the road. The next thing I knew I was following a young fourteen-year-old boy and feeling everything he felt and going everywhere he went and seeing everything he saw and hearing everything he heard. It was as real an experience as I have ever had. I knew you were not just talking about something theoretical; you were explaining what actually happened. In a way I never dreamed of, I found myself saying, 'Yes, Joseph Smith really was a prophet of God.'"

Soon this man and his wife and seven of their ten children were baptized members of The Church of Jesus Christ of Latter-day Saints.

As I returned home I knew more surely than ever that Joseph Smith was one of the greatest prophets of all time. I know he has a very personal interest in seeing that the gospel of Jesus Christ penetrates every corner of the globe, including the isles of the sea, and sounds in every ear, including the ears of the descendants of Joseph of old.

50

Please Come

On one of my trips to the islands I was asked to attend some meetings Friday evening and Saturday morning in California, then fly to Hawaii for meetings Saturday afternoon and Sunday. We started our Friday evening meeting with many important items to discuss. Meetings of that nature usually take longer than planned. That night, however, everyone concerned seemed to be in unusual agreement and the items were ticked off quickly. I have seldom felt a better spirit of cooperation and desire to be helpful on the part of so many.

As we neared the end of the rather imposing agenda, I had the impression that rather than meeting again in the morning we should stay a little longer and finish the next morning's agenda as well. When I proposed that we do so, everyone agreed. We then covered the additional items thoroughly but rapidly.

As I offered my prayers that evening and thanked God for His help, I felt that something important would come from this unexpected change of plans. I knew His Spirit was guiding me, but at the time I didn't see just where.

For some reason I didn't sleep well. I couldn't figure out why, as things had gone so well. I tossed and turned and at times seemed almost to be in physical pain. Finally I got up at 5:30 A.M. and began to review the agreements made the previous night. I wondered if I had left something out or if I should not have canceled that morning's meeting. (My plane was not scheduled to leave for Honolulu until noon.) As I prayed for direction I had a feeling that I should call the airline and try to get an earlier flight to Hawaii.

I immediately called and learned that a flight was leaving in forty-five minutes. I reserved a seat and threw my things together. As I ran down to check out, I thought: "This is silly. If I miss the plane I'll just have to sit at the airport for several hours, and if I make the plane I'll just have to sit in the Honolulu airport for several hours, as there is no way to inform those who are to meet me that I am coming early."

Since I had already packed and ordered a taxi, however, I felt I should try. The taxi was waiting, so off we "flew" (almost literally) to the airport. I ran the whole way to the gate and arrived just as they closed the door. It took a moment of anxious explanation, but they finally opened the door and let me on.

As I took my seat I thought: "Well, at least I can sleep on the plane." I was really tired now; nevertheless I still could not sleep. I felt uncomfortable the whole way. Occasionally I thought I heard someone calling or pleading, but I couldn't quite make it out. Eventually I arrived in Honolulu more tired than ever. I took my suitcase and sat down outside the airport thinking I would have a long wait.

Suddenly I heard someone calling my name. I looked up and saw one of my former missionaries, who was now a student at BYU-Hawaii, calling me from his car. "President Groberg," he said. "Have you heard about Sione Vea?" (Sione Vea had been one of my counselors in the district presidency in Ha'apai when I was a young missionary.)

"No," I replied. "What has happened?"

"He just arrived from Tonga and is very ill. He is in the Queen's Hospital, and I was on my way to visit him when I had a feeling to drive by the airport. I saw you sitting there and wondered if you would like to come with me to visit him? Of course, if you have other plans I'll just go on my own."

"I'd love to go," I replied. "My meetings aren't until this afternoon."

We drove directly to the hospital. When we got to Brother Vea's room the nurse told us that he was in critical condition and the doctor had said he was to have no visitors except immediate family. I explained that I was a church leader and in our faith I was his brother and I had come several thousand miles at his request to see him. As I said that I knew I was telling the truth, for I realized he was the one who had been calling. I could now understand in my mind his plea: "Please come, please come." The nurse looked askance at my white skin, but my Tongan companion assured her I was telling the truth, so she finally let us in.

Poor Sione Vea lay on his bed groaning in pain, his eyes squeezed tightly closed and his fists clenched in agony. His body was a very sickly yellow color. I approached his bed, put one hand on his forehead and the other on his hands and said, "Sione, I have come as you requested."

He opened his eyes, looked at me, smiled, and said: "Thanks for coming. I have not been feeling well for quite a while. Finally I came to Hawaii to visit my son, and they put me in the hospital. I don't know anyone here but my son. During this last day or two when I have been in such great pain I felt that you were somewhere near, so I prayed with all my might to Heavenly Father to have you come and visit me and give me a blessing. All last night I exerted my faith and asked that God arrange things so you could come. Thanks for coming. I hope you don't mind. Could you give me a blessing?"

His eyes were so yellow and his face so gaunt that I could hardly recognize him. His voice was sweet and gentle, however, and his smile engaging. I felt calm, as one does when visiting with an old and trusted friend.

I told him I would be happy to give him a blessing. My companion anointed him and I sealed the anointing. I was sure God had a great blessing for him. I started to give him a blessing. But rather than giving the blessing I felt he deserved, I felt impressed to speak of days past and of boat rides together, over rough as well as smooth seas. I recounted times when he left his part-time evening job of selling roasted peanuts and came with me on various emergencies. I recalled our planting coconut trees in his yard. For a while it seemed that we were not in a sterile hospital room in Honolulu but walking dusty dirt roads and sailing elusive sea roads in far off Ha‘apai. I felt his tense body relax. I found myself remembering things and saying things I had not thought of for years.

The words that came were more like a conversation between friends about times past than a blessing for current needs. I talked of the love and support of his wife and family. I talked about his faithfulness and his willingness to do whatever he was asked to do, whenever he was asked to do it. "Now," I said, "because of these qualities, you are being given a special assignment." A more detailed and very personal explanation followed.

As I finished, he seemed totally relaxed, almost as though the pain was gone (though I doubt it was). He took my hands in his, looked at me with an angelic smile, and said: "Thanks for coming. I really wanted to continue my life here and hoped that would be my blessing. More than anything, however, I wanted to know what God desired of me. Now I know. I am at peace. Totally at peace. Thanks for recalling our past times together. It has made me feel good. I feel this has prepared me for what is to come. Those were some of the greatest times of my life. Thanks for trusting me and thanks for asking me to do things that at the time seemed hard. Those are real blessings, you know, especially now. Thanks for hearing my pleas and coming. I hope it wasn't too much trouble. Good-bye."

As I held Sione's hand and saw the glow of faith radiating from his eyes, it seemed as though I was sailing with him—sailing through Ha'apai, sailing to Hawaii, maybe even sailing through eternity. I sensed that these were voyages of faith more than of miles. I squeezed his hand and felt an even stronger sensation of sailing effortlessly over space and time, of being guided by a loving God. Our eyes met. He smiled, and I felt the peace he felt. With deep assurance I said: *"Folau a, Sione. 'Ofa pe ke monu'ia ho folau. Ta toki fe'ilo'aki 'o toe folau 'o a'u ki he ta'engata. Folau a."* ("Sail on, Sione. Have a blessed voyage. We'll meet again and sail through all eternity. Sail on.") He closed his eyes and we left.

I went to my meeting, but before we started I called Sione's wife. Through her tears she told me that Sione had just passed away. I told her that he had begun another voyage with God and he was at peace. She believed me and was comforted.

I hung up the phone and asked to be left alone for a while. As I pondered I seemed to see Sione smiling and sailing. He was happy. In a way I was amazed at the power of love, faith, and prayer in moving people and events in such a way that important needs were met. Yet in another way it all seemed very natural.

Sione Vea had faith. He needed a blessing. He was alone. I was close by. His next voyage was due to start hours before my original flight would have arrived. So the power of faith and prayer took charge and brought me to his bedside, where he was given his blessing, reminded of past events, and sent on his way in peace. It was as simple as that.

When we understand the true power of love and faith and prayer, we will be amazed that we weren't more aware of them and didn't use them in better ways. They contain powers that cut through the apparent limitations of time and space and allow good to be accomplished and blessings to be given as needed. The several small margins of time or space that could have prevented me from being there when needed had little to do with time and space, but everything to do with prayer and love and faith. There are many Sione Veas calling, "Please come, please come." I hope their call will not be too soft, nor our ears too dull. I was glad Sione's cry for help came through as it did.

51

A New Era Begins

In the summer of 1975 our eighth daughter and tenth child was born. We named her Viki Ann, which is the anglicized version of a Tongan expression of gratitude (*viki anga*).

The following December I was released as a Regional Representative. I supposedly now had more time to devote to my family and my business. I found, however, that whatever extra time I thought I had was immediately filled. It seemed to me that uncommitted time was like a magnet attracting stray bits of things to do.

I loved Idaho Falls and wanted to do all I could to make it a good place to live. One Saturday in March I felt a strong desire to go for a ride and see the various subdivisions and other projects we had built. I was impressed with how much those who had purchased the units had done to improve them. There were new trees, new additions, beautiful landscaping, bicycles, wagons, and other signs of families everywhere. I realized that you can provide a house for someone but only through their efforts will it become a home and a neighborhood.

As I pondered for a moment I had an impression to this effect: "It has been a good work. You have enjoyed it. Take a good look, for you will soon be building in a different way." I also had the thought that even more than the work, I would miss the city and its people. It was an unusual impression, but a peaceful one. I didn't know what it meant. That evening when I mentioned it to Jean she sensed something and said that she would do whatever I wanted, but she truly did love Idaho Falls. It seemed strange to be talking and thinking like this, since I planned no move and anticipated no change.

*The Groberg family in the summer of 1975,
shortly after the birth of their tenth child.*

A little later that month I received a telephone call from President Kimball. He said he wanted to visit with me and wondered if I could come to Salt Lake City in the next few days. I said I would be happy to do so. I knew he had just returned from a series of conferences in the islands, including Tonga. I assumed he wanted to ask me some questions about conditions there as he had done on previous occasions.

When I entered President Kimball's office he was warm and gracious. We visited for a few moments and then he came directly to the point. He called me to serve as a General Authority. He then explained what it would entail. It was a very sacred and personal experience which I feel is best to keep to myself. I will mention just one incident that illustrates President Kimball's loving and understanding manner.

At the end of the interview, President Kimball asked, "Now, do you have any questions?" What an opportunity—to be alone with the prophet and be given such an invitation! I was a little too numb to think of anything, so almost by reflex I stammered, "Does this mean I will have to move from Idaho Falls?" It was a silly question considering what I had just been told. But rather than taking an irritated breath and saying, "I've already explained that to you," he hesitated only a moment, then got up from his chair, walked around his desk, and gave me a big bear hug. With a radiant smile, he looked directly at me and said: "I know exactly how you feel. I didn't want to leave Arizona, either. It is good to like your roots. But yes, this will mean that you will move anywhere in the world, at any time, for the rest of your life."

When I returned to Idaho Falls I asked Jean if she would like to go for a walk with me. We talked again about my feelings of a few weeks before. Then I told her about the call, especially President Kimball's last comments. She was humbled, overwhelmed, yet fully supportive. We both knew that whatever the Lord asks is right, and we were willing to do it.

The magnitude of this calling was overpowering. What would this mean? How would the children react? How would this affect their future? And ours? Only our Father in Heaven knew, and we trusted Him. We knew that wherever we went we would have to carry with us our real home—which is our love and testimony. As we did this, God would bless us. We were ready to move forward, placing our lives in the hands of God.

Thus, on April 3, 1976, I was sustained as an additional member of the Seventy. (I became a member of the First Quorum of Seventy when that body was reinstated six months later.)

After April conference the Brethren advised me to return to Idaho Falls and await further instructions. The children were in school and I was working, so outwardly things didn't change much for us, but inwardly we were in turmoil. Our family, friends, associates, and neighbors were full of questions we could not answer. We had many questions of our own we could not answer. We simply had to wait.

Toward the end of May we received our offical assignment. We were to move to Hawaii by the first of August, live in Honolulu, and set up an office for the newly created "Hawaii-Pacific Islands Area." I was to serve as Area Supervisor for the stakes and missions in Hawaii, Samoa, Tonga, Fiji, Tahiti, Micronesia, and, in fact, all of the islands of the Pacific in what is commonly referred to as Polynesia, Micronesia and Melanesia.

I knew I was moving into a whole different arena. I wasn't sure what it meant to serve full-time for the Church for the rest of my life. I worried and wondered where the power to accomplish all that was expected of me would come from. Then oddly enough, from childhood stories I remembered how "The Little Engine That Could" gained power by saying, "I think I can, I think I can," and then eventually, "I thought I could, I thought I could." This caused me to think of the power that comes when we say, "I believe I can." I then thought of the added power that comes from hearing our leaders (and parents) say, "I believe you can." Finally, I sensed the ultimate power that comes from God when we hear His voice, either directly to our minds or through His authorized leaders, saying, "I know you can." I was sure that with all of this, especially God's support and confidence, we could not fail.

With this hope and understanding I was ready to embark with Jean and our children on an odyssey which would begin in Honolulu but, in President Kimball's words, might take us "anywhere in the world, at any time." Another era had begun to unfold.

52

Hawaii, Here We Come

On 28 July 1976 we arrived on the lovely island of Oahu. The members showered us with the true "Aloha spirit." A member family brought us a meal on our first evening in Hawaii. When they saw that we had no chairs, they went home and brought all their folding chairs for us to use. The next day we bought a wooden picnic table and set it up in the hallway and used it as our dining area.

I had previously made several trips trying to find a home to accommodate our family of ten children. It was not easy to find such a place in Honolulu, so we rented a small home for six months, during which time we hoped to find something more suitable.

The rented home had a family room and three bedrooms, one of which had to double as my temporary office. It was fun for the children to "camp out" and explore the yard with its vines and bamboo, and learn their way around the neighborhood. It was interesting to see the children's ingenuity in developing new things to do. We often found them climbing the bamboo to get onto the roof. Our kindergarten-aged boy learned to literally "climb the walls." There was a frame with no door in it between the wide hallway and the living room, and he would go on all fours like a monkey, up the frame, across the top, then down the other side. We had a fun and cozy family experience.

As the novelty of the small house wore off, the realities of too many people in too small a space set in. When Jean discovered some of the younger children being "locked up" by their older siblings for being "too bothersome" she realized that something needed to be done. We liked the schools, the ward, and the general neighborhood, so Jean took a few hours each day, put the baby in the stroller, and walked up and down the streets of the area looking at every available house. Her efforts eventually paid off as she found an ideal home in a perfect setting just shortly before our six-month lease expired. We felt the hand of the Lord in this. (This house is now the Hawaii mission home.)

The children generally did well in school, despite different and sometimes difficult situations. Things had gone smoothly with registering the two older girls in high school, and the next one in junior high. However, when we went to register the next four children in elementary school we were met with an icy reception. There was no question about how the lady taking the information felt about our large family. As we were returning to our car, a local Hawaiian lady came out and said she wanted to talk to us for a moment. She explained that she was a secretary in the office and wanted to apologize to us for the reception we had received. She was one of eight children and she thought large families were wonderful. She mainly wanted to assure us that we would be welcome and that the attitude of the lady we had talked to was not representative of most people at the school. How grateful we are that there are good people everywhere.

The first woman's attitude caused me to think deeply about children, families, and God. I wondered: How many people living on the earth understand why God created it in the first place? How many are serious about learning and keeping God's commandments? How many don't even care?

Our ward was magnificent. The love and help of the members radiated from their deep faith and strong testimonies. The ward had about twenty high-school-age youth. Each day they gathered for early morning seminary before dispersing to several different high schools. They were great missionary-minded youth and helped each other survive and grow spiritually in a pretty "worldly" environment.

Setting up this new area was a fascinating challenge. At that time the area had about thirty stakes, six missions, and over a hundred thousand members, scattered over nearly one-third of the earth's surface. There were few precedents and no previously established budget for the area. Because this was a new administrative level in the Church, I had to carefully develop proper rapport with the local stake and mission presidents who had previously reported directly to Church headquarters in Salt Lake. Fortunately these were men of goodwill and we soon understood each other and were able to work well together.

It was difficult to get the area office set up, as I was constantly traveling all over the Pacific. However, little by little, with some good local help, we were able to rent an office, purchase equipment, hire a secretary, and otherwise organize the area office.

Our home was located about twenty minutes from the airport. Nearly all of my flights left or returned around 2:00 A.M. I didn't feel good about Jean leaving the children, nor did I feel comfortable having her wait for me at that hour. I talked to the mission president, and with his blessing we assigned various close-by missionaries to take me to, and pick me up from, the airport. They were faithful and punctual most of the time. I enjoyed my visits with them and appreciated their efforts. Many sets of missionaries had this "privilege."

Hawaii will always be a special place to us. Our experiences while living there knit the family together in ways that are still a great blessing today. Emily Leilani entered our family October 10, 1977. The events of her birth and the spirit of love and loveliness she brought to our home made her our Hawaiian "flower from heaven."

During our time in Hawaii I had the privilege of baptizing Jean's uncle. Her aunt and uncle had been living in Hawaii for a number of years and were a tremendous help and support to our family there.

Living in Hawaii also gave us the opportunity to renew our associations with many old friends from Fiji, Tahiti, Tonga, and Samoa who had moved to Hawaii. How grateful we are for the warm, wonderful, and extremely helpful Saints in Hawaii. They truly embodied the spirit of "Aloha."

53

Enlarging the
Borders of Zion

Almost immediately after our arrival in Hawaii I was off to conferences, mission tours, and various other assignments. Jean wrote home about one of my trips: "John was gone twelve days. He held twenty-three meetings in five different languages and in six different countries. He spent three nights on planes and in airports, and spent the other nights in six different places. So you see, it is no picnic. Some seem to think so when they roll their eyes and say, 'Hawaii! What an assignment!' But we are grateful to be here and grateful to be involved in this wonderful work."

Throughout these travels I felt impressed to expand the missionary efforts to all the islands in our area. We were well established in Polynesia and had a few members, including servicemen, on Guam. With a few exceptions we had virtually no presence in the myriad islands of Melanesia and Micronesia.

Many of these islands were just emerging from hundreds of years of colonial rule by various powers, including Spain, Britain, France, Germany, Japan, and the United States. Many were only a few miles wide—barely visible on a map. Yet each was inhabited by children of God who still needed to learn of Him and His love for them.

Accordingly we made plans for some exploratory work. As I visited nearly all of those scattered islands I felt an immediate bonding with the people and an urgent desire to take the gospel to them.

We began slowly and sometimes faced intense opposition. However, we were blessed with marvelous and determined missionaries (including many island natives), and eventually we became established in each of the island groups. Today there are members, branches, wards, and stakes all through the area. It was wonderful to watch the Lord's hand as He guided our efforts, opened doors and softened hearts in miraculous ways.

Each island has its own story of miracles and hard work leading to the introduction and spread of the gospel. Let me give a few examples from among many equally wonderful experiences.

Micronesia was originally part of the Hawaii Mission. The mission president and I took some missionaries to open the work on the island of Palau. When we arrived we could find no place for them to stay. Every room on the island was filled, and even the one hotel had no vacancies. Our plane was leaving in a few hours, and we wondered if we should take the missionaries back with us or leave them to fend for themselves.

On a hunch, we went back to the hotel and asked to speak with the manager. He came out and confirmed to us that there were no vacancies and they had a long waiting list. Then he looked at the two elders standing behind us and saw their name tags. His demeanor suddenly changed and he seemed at a loss for words.

The hotel manager was a less-active member who had come to this distant island in an effort to "get away" from the Church. Now he had been found, and his heart was touched. He made the necessary arrangements for the elders to stay in a worker's bungalow. The hotel manager returned to activity and became a great help to the missionaries. Soon the work was moving forward in Palau. The Lord knows His sheep. He knows when and how to find them if we will only listen and take the necessary risks.

An airport contractor on Saipan was an active member of the Church. He presided over the small group of mostly Filipino members who worked there. One day he was notified that he would be transferred soon. His first concern was, "Who can be the branch president when I leave?" He felt that the most capable man he knew of was his construction foreman. The only problem was that this man was not a member of the Church.

This didn't dissuade the contractor. He had lunch with his foreman and explained about his church group. He said that they would need a leader when he left. He told his friend that he felt he should be that new leader. The foreman was smoking a cigar and drinking coffee at the time. The contractor explained that before he could be the leader he would have to become a member of the Church, and in order to become a member he would have to quit smoking and drinking. The foreman thought it was a joke, but he could tell that the contractor was serious. Out of respect for his boss, whom he greatly admired, the foreman began to think about what had been said.

Soon missionary discussions were received, conversion took place, and lifestyles were changed. Before the contractor left he had a faithful priesthood holder ready to take his place as branch president. The foreman became a great leader. Later, he and his family were sealed in the Hawaii Temple.

For several years we had tried to get permission for our missionaries to come into the New Hebrides (now named Vanuatu). We had a few members from Tonga, Samoa, New Zealand, and Australia living there. Our meetings with the government officials about allowing our missionaries in the country were fruitless. At that time the New Hebrides was jointly run by France and Britain. It was necessary that both sides be involved in the discussions. However, because we spoke English we met with the British.

The Minister of Police had the final say in granting visas. On one of our visits he said he was going back to England for a six-month leave and would talk to us when he returned. Six months later, we met with him again. We had been fasting and praying for a good outcome from this meeting. We were a little taken aback when he seemed rather sullen and maybe a bit irritated with us. We talked for some time but his manner remained unchanged. Then finally he said: "Well, there's no sense in keeping you here all night. Let me tell you a brief experience, then I'll give you my final decision.

"During part of my leave in England I attended a special training course in Plymouth. The route I took to my meetings each day went through a rather run-down section of town. As I drove along I noticed a small white building that seemed to stand out noticeably because it was so neat and clean. I wondered what it was and why it was so nicely kept in contrast to its surroundings.

"One Saturday as I drove by I saw a group of young men and women working in the yard, mowing, trimming, cleaning, etc. They seemed to be having such a good time that my curiosity got the best of me. I stopped and asked who they were, what they were doing, what this building was, and why it was so different.

"The young people told me it was a chapel of The Church of Jesus Christ of Latter-day Saints, often referred to as the 'Mormons.' They said they were members of that congregation and came regularly to work on the building and grounds to make sure they were neat and clean and fitting for the Church of Jesus Christ that they represented."

He concluded by saying: "If your church can teach people to be as neat and clean and respectful of property here as I saw among those young people in Plymouth, I will grant you visas for four young men and extend recognition for your church. I have visited with my French counterpart and he agrees, so long as these conditions are met: 1) They cannot be Americans. 2) They must speak both English and French. 3) They must hold a French or a British Commonwealth passport. 4) They must have no criminal record. 5) You must guarantee them to be of the same high quality as the young people I met in Plymouth. 6) You will teach your members here to take care of property like your members in Plymouth do."

We fairly floated out of his office! We returned to the hotel and immediately knelt and thanked God for His help. We asked Him to bless the good Saints in Plymouth for what they had unknowingly done to expand God's kingdom halfway around the world.

We called the Missionary Department and within a few days we had four missionaries assigned to serve in the New Hebrides. They came from Eastern Canada and from New Zealand and met all the requirements set forth.

I have never been to Plymouth, nor to England for that matter, but I often think of a little chapel, well cared for, in an older section of Plymouth, and of some young men and women happily working in the yard and visiting with an inquisitive stranger. Each time I say over again: Thanks, Plymouth!

54

Passport, Please

Because of his broad views and his encouragement of education, King Taufa'ahou Tupou IV of Tonga was to be awarded an honorary doctorate degree from BYU-Hawaii. I was asked to accompany him and his wife to Hawaii.

I had stake conferences in San Francisco, Western Samoa, and Tonga just prior to returning to Hawaii with the king and queen. After my conference in San Francisco I flew to Honolulu. My schedule was so tight that I met the elders at the airport in Honolulu, traded one suitcase full of dirty clothes for another with clean clothes they had brought from Jean, and boarded my flight to Pago Pago, American Samoa.

Being tired, I slept most of the five hours to Pago Pago. It was not until we landed that I came to the startling realization that I did not have my passport with me. I didn't need it in San Francisco or Hawaii or Pago Pago, as they were American, but I would need my passport to get into Western Samoa and Tonga and back into Hawaii. How could I have been so careless? What should I do now?

I prayed about it, but received no particular feeling or direction. I felt an emptiness, almost an abandonment. I seemed to hear my mind chastising me saying: "This is your fault—you shouldn't expect others to make up for your carelessness, or do things for you that were within your control to do."

My flight to Western Samoa didn't leave for several hours. I had to do something, but what? I knew they wouldn't let me on the plane to Western Samoa without a passport, even though I had a ticket. I found a private place and pleaded with the Lord for help and guidance. These were His conferences. I was on His errand. I sorely needed His help. No answer.

There is hardly a worse feeling than sensing you have been careless and must pay the price for it, especially if that price is not being able to fulfill God-given assignments. Those were hours of agony and soul-searching. The feelings of abandonment and terror that came from my own carelessness were deeply impressed on my soul.

Suddenly I ran into a good member of the Church whom I knew. He had just been promoted to a responsible position at the airport. I explained my predicament to him. He invited me to come to his office. We discussed the various options and finally decided the best thing to do was call the Regional Representative in Western Samoa. The Regional Representative said that if this man could get me on the plane in Pago Pago, he would get me off in Western Samoa. How they did it, I don't know. I just know that when the plane left for Western Samoa I was on it. When it landed in Western Samoa I was escorted through a special area by the Regional Representative and we went to our conference on schedule.

We had a marvelous conference in Western Samoa. It was made more meaningful by a heaven-sent discourse on the importance of always being prepared, always having a current temple recommend (heavenly passport), and never allowing carelessness or disobedience to deprive us of that most precious and important possession.

With that conference over I wondered how I would get into Tonga. The phones to Tonga were not working, so I couldn't contact anyone there. I decided I should just go. The Regional Representative in Western Samoa somehow got me on the plane to Tonga. When I arrived in Tonga I explained my predicament to the Immigration officers. Since we were friends, they just waved me through with the good-natured warning: "Only this once. Don't try it again."

Under the influence of the Spirit at the conference I again spoke on the importance of always having our heavenly passports (temple recommends) with us. As I spoke, another incident came to mind, which I related to the congregation:

A year after the 1966 Tongan temple group returned from New Zealand, an older man came to see me for a new temple recommend. I asked him if he was going to the temple again. "Oh, no," he said. "I sold everything I had to go last year. I can't afford a ticket to go again."

"Then why do you want a recommend?"

"Well, I am old. I don't know when I might die. I want to be sure to have a valid recommend when that happens."

I wasn't sure he understood, and I thought I would kid him a little, so I said, "Well, even if you have your recommend in your hand when they bury you, it will just molder in the dust along with your body."

I thought he might smile, but he was very serious. "Oh, President, you don't understand. When I answer all the questions from my heart and you give me a recommend, it is recorded on my heart and that is never destroyed. I know the paper will disintegrate, but my worthiness won't. You see why I want to always have a current temple recommend?"

I saw. He got his recommend that year and the next and then he journeyed to loftier places with a valid recommend engraved in his heart.

This experience was a great lesson to me. I was glad the Spirit brought it to my remembrance at this conference. I sensed a determination among the people to do better. There was a large increase in temple recommends issued in both Samoa and Tonga after these conferences.

I met with the king and queen and we finalized plans for our trip to Hawaii. I had been able to get into Samoa and Tonga without a passport, largely because I knew people there. How was I to get back into the United States without a passport?

I decided to just stick with the king and queen and their party and see what happened. I sent a telegram to my secretary and asked her to send my passport to the airport in case there was a problem. We left Tonga together and no one bothered to ask for passports. So far, so good.

When we arrived in Honolulu we were met by the governor of Hawaii and a whole retinue of high-ranking government and military officials. There was also a representative from BYU-Hawaii. We were ushered into the VIP waiting lounge and the BYU-Hawaii representative quietly slipped me my passport. Just minutes later a government official said, "Passports, please—I will get them processed and we will be on our way."

How simple the whole series of events had been. Yet it was really a series of miracles. God works among men in quiet, simple ways. I am convinced that without His influence those simple things would not have happened.

The investiture service at BYU-Hawaii was outstanding. The king gave a well-thought-out and well-delivered address on the value of education. It fit perfectly with Latter-day Saint philosophy.

The king and queen stayed in Honolulu for several days. I asked them to participate in three specific experiences to help them understand the Church better: a family home evening; some gospel discussions; and attendance at a sacrament meeting in the Honolulu Stake center. They agreed to all three and in return asked that I accompany them to three events: a tour of some military ships and facilities, a large reception given for them by a top U.S. Navy admiral, and one given by the governor of Hawaii. I agreed to go with them. Doing so paid off in at least one way.

A talented Tongan art student at BYU-Hawaii had made a larger-than-life bronze statue of the king. It was unveiled and presented to their majesties at the feast following the investiture. The king and queen were both pleased with the statue, but there was one problem. How do you get a gift of that size and weight back to Tonga?

During the navy reception the captain of a U.S. destroyer ship approached the king and explained that they were going to the South Pacific and he had heard of the beautiful harbor in Vava'u. He wondered if the king would give him permission to stop there for a while on a "goodwill visit." The king hesitated and wanted to consult with his military advisors and see if that would create any problems.

As they were talking, a light went on in my mind and I asked if I could talk to the king alone for a minute. I told him that I could see no harm in allowing the American ship to stop in Vava'u for a few hours. However, to really test their "goodwill" he could tell them that if they agreed to transport his large statue with them and bring it to Nuku'alofa and unload it there, he would give them permission to visit Vava'u.

It was a true win-win situation. They both got what they wanted, so they concluded the agreement with a smile and a handshake. The sculpture was safely delivered to Tonga and placed at the airport in a conspicuous place to welcome all who land in the Friendly Islands.

We had a wonderful family home evening with our family and the well-known LDS entertainers the Osmond family, who were in Hawaii at that time. I felt that the king and queen got a good picture of the importance of the family in our doctrine and practices.

Later we had a great gospel discussion. Hearts were touched, tears were shed, testimonies were borne, truths were taught, and respect and understanding was increased.

The sacrament meeting was marvelous. I explained to the king and queen what we do at sacrament meetings and how, in this meet-

Bronze statue of King Taufa'ahau Tupou IV.

ing, I was the presiding authority, so the sacrament would be passed to me first, and I would be the concluding speaker. I explained about the sacrament and what it represented.

Despite the fact that we had only one small Tongan branch in Honolulu, the tabernacle was filled to capacity with well over one thousand people. Every Tongan from every religion from miles around came. There are not many opportunities to address a sacrament meeting with more nonmembers than members in attendance. I spoke on our belief in the Savior, on the need for authority and prophets, on the Restoration, and on the Book of Mormon.

It was largely a repeat of the discussion I had given to the king and queen a few days earlier. The Lord guided and directed those remarks. I felt impressed to give part of my talk in English. Many people began an earnest investigation of the Church after that meeting and several became good members.

I don't know how many sacrament meetings we have had in the Church in this dispensation with a reigning king and queen in attendance. As I spoke I looked into the eyes of some of our faithful members. I had the strong impression that, though not recognized as such by the world, there are many kings and queens among the humble Saints who have their heavenly passports in order.

55

What Is Important?

Many things are important to the Lord. I am sure it is important to Him that in the deepest recesses of our heart we feel His personal love for us, His complete forgiveness of us, and His all-consuming desire to help us. He wants us to repent, to improve, to love, to forgive, and to experience the joy therefrom. I have witnessed this truth many times.

Because of a misunderstanding on the place to meet in the San Francisco area, a man scheduled to have his blessings restored missed his appointment with a General Authority. I was the next visitor to a stake in that area and was assigned to restore the blessings to this man.

I recognized him as a man I had known years before in Tonga. I was happy he had returned to the Church after a long absence. He had lived in the United States for nearly twenty years and spoke English quite well. I don't think language would have been a problem had he met with the first visitor, but that is not what the Lord had in mind for him.

As we began, I asked him if he would like to speak in English or Tongan. He was silent for a long time. I wondered if something was wrong. Then his eyes began to well over and he replied emotionally, "Oh, President, this is important to me. This has to do with my eternal salvation. My mind understands English, but my heart speaks Tongan. Could we please do everything in Tongan?"

We did. The beauty of forgiveness and love made possible by the atoning sacrifice of the Savior filled every corner of our hearts.

I am sure it is important that we be full of compassion for one another. He wants us to help, bless, and encourage the afflicted, the downtrodden, the helpless, and those in any kind of need. When we do this we feel the comfort and guidance of His Spirit and in turn are helped, blessed, and encouraged ourselves. My understanding of this principle was deepened one weekend in Tonga.

It was sometimes necessary to schedule two and occasionally three conferences a week. The meetings were always wonderful, but at times I felt I was "running faster" than I should.

One weekend I had two stake conferences in Tonga with some missionary meetings sandwiched in between. The meetings began early Saturday morning. The first stake president took me to his meeting then returned me to the hotel, where the second stake president picked me up and drove me to his meeting. After that meeting he returned me to the hotel, where the mission president picked me up for his meeting.

The schedule ran smoothly all Saturday morning, but for some reason I felt uncomfortable. I wanted to do the most important things, as there didn't seem to be enough time to do everything. I prayed for inspiration.

Shortly after lunch I had a strong impression. When the next stake president came to take me to another meeting I told him: "I will not be going to meetings this afternoon. You conduct them yourself. I will come to the meeting this evening and to the Sunday sessions tomorrow. Please give the same message to the other stake president."

He was surprised but nodded agreement and left. I then turned to the mission president and said, "We are going to visit Brother Viliami and his family, and then Sister Mafi and her family. We can be back in time for our evening meetings if we leave right now." He did not question me, although I suspect he wondered whether those people would even be home, as we had made no prior arrangements.

Brother Viliami was crippled. He had a large family and had dealt well with his handicap. When we arrived at his home he was in his garden working as best he could. He quickly cleaned up and came into the small living room of his clean but humble home. We had a wonderful visit. We talked about his health, his family, and the temple. He and his wife and several of their children had been sealed in the New Zealand Temple, but there were still some married children who were struggling to be worthy of recommends. We found that the bishop and other leaders were helping appropriately. He appreciated our concern and encouragement and asked us to leave a blessing in his home, which we did. We were touched by his faith and courage in doing what was right, despite physical limitations.

We then went to visit Sister Mafi, a widow. She was weaving mats as we arrived. When she saw us approaching she quickly put her work aside, invited us in, and spread her best mats out for us to sit on. We asked about her health and her family and the temple. She had been sealed to her husband, and all of their children had been sealed to them. Even though her husband had passed on some years earlier, she and her family were getting along well. She expressed appreciation for her visiting teachers and others who consistently helped her.

We had a wonderful, relaxed visit and gave what encouragement we could. We left a much-appreciated blessing in her home, though we were the ones most blessed by feeling the beautiful spirit there.

On our way back to town I wondered about the value of our visits in place of the meetings I had not attended. Everything seemed fine in both homes. The bishops, home teachers, visiting teachers, and others were helping as they should. I was grateful for the spiritual lift the visit had given me, but I wondered a little why I had felt impressed to visit them.

The conference meetings that evening and the next morning and afternoon were some of the best I can remember. In their respective sessions, each stake president spoke of the importance of visiting the poor and the neglected. They testified that the Savior had healed the sick, comforted those who mourned, raised some from the dead, and given His life freely for all. The quietness, the reverence, and the glistening eyes that followed their words came from people who felt deeply what was being said. I knew that great lessons were learned, hearts were softened, and each soul determined to do better. Because of my experiences of the day before I too was able to share in the rich outpouring of the Spirit.

As I bore my testimony a new vision of the Savior's love and work opened to me. He suffered and died for us here, thus giving His life as a ransom for us. He has also given His life for us from the beginning, from the Creation down to His thirty-three years of example and service in mortality, and continuing on into eternity. I read with new meaning the scripture: "Nevertheless, glory be to the Father, and I partook and finished my preparations unto the children of men" (D&C 19:19).

What is important? Faith in the Lord Jesus Christ and all that entails.

In a way we cannot fully comprehend He is continuing to give His life for us, now and through all eternity. When we have a better understanding we will see that while His atoning sacrifice is the greatest event in the earth's history, there is much more to it than we can even begin to comprehend—much, much more. Think of the Day of Judgment and all that entails, think of the phrase "finished my preparations," and the phrases "worlds without end" and "God's work is one eternal round." To truly follow Him, we must become like Him and constantly serve others with all our heart. Loving service must become our only desire. Indeed it must become "us." Revelation was received and understood by many that day.

As I flew back to Hawaii I realized that what had happened could not have been programmed. It is useless to try to program the Spirit. I always try to follow the outlines given by the Brethren. However, once in a while, in His wisdom and love, a kind Father in Heaven accepts our efforts to abide counsel and gives us unusual inspiration that opens doors for teaching great and important truths more effectively than could be done in other ways. It was reassuring to feel that my assignment had been fulfilled according to His will. That which was important had been done.

56

The Symphony of Life

The year 1977 had been a challenging but growing year. More people had been baptized in every mission in our area than the year before. There were more stakes and buildings being constructed than ever. Thus 1978 began with great promise. I was traveling nearly every weekend because the work was expanding so rapidly. I knew that if we put forth all the effort we could, God would cause things to work together for our good.

While in Fiji on assignment I received a phone call from President Benson. He was warm and friendly and asked a great deal about my family and about how I was feeling and how the work was going. I answered everything as honestly as I knew how. Then he said, "We feel good about the work you have done there the last couple of years. We would like you to return to Salt Lake City this coming summer and take a position with the Genealogy (now Family History) Department. We have some assignments there in mind for you."

He asked how I felt about that. There wasn't much to say, except that my whole heart was to do what the Brethren wanted me to do. We visited for a few more minutes and he concluded with some wonderful words: "I want you to know that this change comes under the inspiration of the Lord. It is right."

It wasn't until I was flying back to Honolulu from New Zealand, after finishing the circuit of meetings on that particular trip, that the impact of the change in assignments began to sink in.

"Leave the islands!" I thought, "How can I do that? There is so much more that needs to be done." Outwardly I tended to fight the thought of leaving, yet inwardly I felt calm. The President of the Quorum of the Twelve had spoken. He had done so with such kindness and such surety that there was no room for doubt. So why was I still struggling with the idea of leaving?

I started making a list of all the things I needed to get done before moving. The list quickly grew far beyond the possibility of its items being accomplished in the few months left. I wondered what to say to Jean. I started to think of some of the practical realities. We would need to buy a home in the Salt Lake City area, and do so soon. We had never lived in Salt Lake, so I had no idea where to look. My spirit was calm but my mind was being pummeled by all sorts of tumultuous questions and concerns.

My flight was an all-night flight. I intended to read for a while and then go to sleep. My mind had been racing and struggling over so many questions and feelings that I was quite exhausted. I started reading in the Pearl of Great Price. As I read about star systems and many other wonderful truths, my mind began to calm down. No matter how great our concerns might appear they are really pretty small when put in the context of galaxies and other eternal things. I read much longer than I thought I would. For some reason I could not sleep, even though I was tired.

I heard a dull drone. It seemed to be coming from everywhere. I opened the shade and looked out. It was the sound of the giant motors as they powered our silver ship through those vast stretches of sky.

I was captivated by what I heard and saw. I noticed the periodic flashes of beacon lights from the tips of the wings. I knew they were important, but sensed how insignificant they were when compared to the vast array of stars vying for my attention that clear night.

I noticed an occasional red glow from somewhere. I looked for a long time before I saw that it was coming from the engines. I was fascinated by the power generated by those engines. I remembered years earlier in Tonga how I had felt our sailboat was going very fast when we had a good wind behind us. Yet by comparison to this plane our speed then was basically nothing—or was it? Maybe at some future time I would look back on what I now thought was rapid plane travel and see that it was nothing. These feelings opened new visions.

Isn't all progress, no matter how seemingly fast or slow, important? Maybe it is direction and progress that counts. Maybe all worlds, skies, seas, heavens, earths, stars, powers—maybe everything is simply the means of allowing us, as God's offspring, to progress toward Him. I had a calm assurance of God's omnipotence. I wanted to rest in the beauty of those serene feelings, but I still could not sleep.

I decided to listen to some music. I turned to the classical music channel just as the announcer said, "We will now hear 'Fantasia on a Theme of Thomas Tallis' by Ralph Vaughan Williams." As I closed my eyes and listened I was literally transported to another element. My ears heard physical sounds but my spirit was hearing something else.

The deep droning of the basses, like the engines of the plane, seemed to be powering me to another destination. These full-measured deep sounds seemed to be the underlying force that held everything together. Then the violins and other instruments took their turns. I heard each instrument and each phrase clearly, and realized that some instruments were playing the same note or phrase over and over again. By itself the instrument or the phrase was quite ordinary, even boring at times, but when put with the others they sounded better. The beauty of the whole could not exist without the mundane repetitious phrases of the basses, the cellos, the second violins, and so forth. In a way they made the beautiful melody of the solo possible, but in another way the solo made them beautiful.

Suddenly, the composition came together in a majestic crescendo of totality. My soul swayed and vibrated to the beauty of the music. I felt tears seeping down my cheeks and a thrill passing through my whole being. It was much more than just a great musical experience. It was a revelation.

I understood that God was pleased with past efforts. The countless voyages, the many storms, the challenges, the repetitions, the triumphs, the disasters, the good times and the tough times—all of these were important parts of a symphony He was creating.

It came to me that God is the great composer and the great conductor. He orchestrates our life. If we will practice and learn our various parts, especially the deep ones—the ones that are repeated over and over again, the ones that often seem to have little meaning, the ones that at times seem boring, the ones that hold everything else together—He will make a beautiful symphony of it. Of course we need to eliminate the discordant sounds, through repentance or change, before the final playing can take place in all its intended beauty.

If we will continue to care for others in need, even though their needs seem never to be met; if we will love others, even though that love seems not to be returned; if we will say our prayers, even when we don't feel like it, or when we don't seem to be getting answers; if we will practice patience against all logic, obedience against all pulls to disobey, faith against all odds, hope against all reasons for hopelessness, and charity against all the world's attempts to disparage, disdain and discredit it—if we do all this we will be blessed and God will cause our symphony to become more beautiful.

Sometimes we might think we are doing these things for others, that no one ever notices, or that our efforts are not important; but the fact is that in everything we do we are but practicing for our symphony. God has composed it and will masterfully conduct it, but we must play it.

Occasionally we may be given a solo part to play, which will be fun, even exciting, but mostly we will be asked to practice the repetitious drones of the basses until we get them just right, for until they are brought into proper tune, the rest—the solos, no matter how dazzling they may seem—cannot reach their full potential.

Everyone should feel that he or she is special—for it is true. We cannot make the progress we are capable of until we feel the assurance of God's love and know of our value in His sight. It is not a feeling of pride so much as of purpose. We must know that we have a special place in the scheme of things, that our life—our contribution to the overall symphony of the universe—is important. Since God is not limited by time or space, the sequence of parts isn't as important as the correctness, proper tuning, and execution of each part.

God will create from our lives a symphony of such rich texture and meaning that its beauty will be beyond our wildest imagination. Then from these individual life symphonies He will create and conduct the most unbelievably beautiful symphony the universe has ever heard. The total effect of that great cosmic symphony will not be complete until our part is right. What we do, hum-drum as it may seem, does matter. Our life and what we do with it is important. We must work with God and practice and practice and practice until we get our parts right, and eventually hear Him say; "That is good. Well done. That part is finished."

The same principle applies not only to individuals but also to families, to nations, and even to worlds. I thought of the Savior: the only Perfect Life, who performed the perfect symphony from the perfect composition—so infinite in its depth and beauty that it could be used by all, to compensate and bring perfection.

Think of His life: "It is finished. Into thy hands I commend my spirit." The greatest of all lives, the most perfectly practiced and executed—never stopping, never failing, till every jot and tittle, every nuance, every prophecy, every expectation, every law, every compassion, all light and life and love were completely fulfilled. The beauty of that life resonates through all eternity. The Perfect Symphony. The Perfect Life.

The Groberg family in Hawaii, December, 1977.

57

Joyous Fulfillment

Even though we knew we would soon be leaving the islands, we were happy that after much effort by many people the Hawaii-Pacific Islands Area was now functioning quite smoothly. I probably hadn't paid as much attention to the temporal side of things as I should have done. My time and energy had seemed fully occupied in trying to keep up with the missionary work and the ensuing training efforts needed to help all the new members who were streaming into the Church throughout the islands. These were busy, joyous times. God had blessed us in innumerable ways. He had fulfilled many of our dreams, but more were to be fulfilled before we left.

I was sure that someday a temple of the Lord would stand in Tonga. I had to be patient, however, for these things happen when the time is right, not necessarily when we want them to. I was completely surprised when the First Presidency called a special meeting of all the stake presidents in my area and announced that they felt the time had arrived for the islands of Samoa, Tonga, and Tahiti to have a temple.

Only those who have worked long and closely with a people, as I had with the Polynesians, can appreciate the emotions that filled my soul. I had watched the Lord move His work steadily forward (sometimes slowly, but always surely) among the Polynesians, and now, this—temples! The Lord had heard the prayers of countless faithful island people. The time had come. What a thrill.

The exact plans and locations of the temples took some interesting twists and turns before they were finally completed, but that is unimportant. What is important is that temples now stand in Tonga, Samoa, and Tahiti (as well as Hawaii and New Zealand). How marvelous to see these blessings come to people whose lives glow with the unquenchable fire of faith.

In June 1978 the revelation extending priesthood blessings to all worthy male members of the Church was received. It was announced at a press conference in Salt Lake City on a Thursday, and the next day the entire First Presidency came to Hawaii for a regional conference and the rededication of the renovated Hawaii Temple. President Kimball had called ahead and asked if I could arrange for him to meet with some of the black members of the Church in Hawaii. What a joyous occasion!

President Kimball invited our family to the luncheon between sessions of the regional conference. He wanted to meet the children. With thirteen of us at the tables next to the prophet we worried about how they would act. President Kimball hugged and visited with each child and held the little ones. What a wonderful man! It wasn't until after he left that the first glass of milk was spilled.

The rededication of the Hawaii Temple was a spiritual feast and as fitting a climax and farewell to our time in Hawaii as we could conceive of.

I received a call from Elder Howard W. Hunter. He said, "How would you like to go with me to take care of items number nine and ten, the last two on your list?"

For a moment I wasn't sure what he was referring to. Then I remembered. When I was released as mission president years earlier, Elder Hunter had asked me to make a list of ten things I felt should happen in Tonga and Fiji to advance the work there. He had kept that list and been working on it. He was now down to the last two items.

"We will create the first stake in Fiji. Then we'll go to Tonga and create a stake in Ha'apai. All of Tonga will then be in stakes."

The creation of the Suva Fiji Stake was a cultural as well as a spiritual experience. The sacred *tambua* (whale's tooth) was presented to Elder Hunter in an impressive ceremony involving many chiefs, both members and nonmembers. How the Fijians revered Elder Hunter, who had done so much for them over so many years. As always, he was gracious and happy.

After completing the organization of the stake in Fiji, we flew to Tonga and on to Ha'apai, where similar ceremonies and feasts were held. It was marvelous to see this beloved servant of the Lord move so easily through the complexities of culture, language, tradition, and family expectations, and still end up with the organization the Lord desired for a solid stake of Zion in Ha'apai.

After the meetings and the settings apart in Ha'apai we walked to a small cemetery by the seashore, where one of Elder Hunter's relatives was buried. This young missionary had died during the influenza epidemic shortly after World War I. We reverently stood before his well-kept grave on a beautiful sun-filled afternoon. We heard the lapping of waves and felt the soft breeze lightly tossing the fronds of the coconut trees. As we looked into the blue of the sea, a deep peace enveloped us. I thought of the joys and sorrows many had experienced in Ha'apai over so many years. Now to be a part of creating a stake in Ha'apai— what joy! What fulfillment!

As though he read my thoughts, Elder Hunter turned and said: "John, this is as lovely a place as there is on earth. This peace is as real as it gets. God is pleased with what has been done here. He is pleased with the sacrifices, work, and love over the years that is represented here today. It is good to be here, isn't it?" How could there be a finer benediction to any list anywhere?

When we are wholeheartedly involved in building the Lord's kingdom in any way, we will experience joyous fulfillment.

Elder Howard W. Hunter (at far left) at the gravesite of a relative buried in Pangai, Ha'apai.

58

Midnight Dedication

Shortly before leaving Hawaii I was assigned to dedicate the Church's new Saineha High School in Vava'u, Tonga, as well as hold conferences in Tongatapu and Ha'apai. I took Nancy and Liz and John Enoch with me. The members loved seeing them. Everything went smoothly until we went to the airport in Ha'apai to catch our plane to Vava'u. We saw the plane coming, but to our great surprise it did not land but kept on going.

Communication was poor, but we eventually got through to the airline office in Tongatapu and were told that the plane had accepted a charter flight to Samoa and wouldn't be back until the next day. I explained that we were scheduled to dedicate a new school in Vava'u and that everyone was waiting. We were already late. They must fulfill their commitment to us. They said they were sorry but the plane was in Samoa and would not be back until the next day. I didn't know what to do.

Then I remembered a telegram I had received from the governor of Vava'u. He said that he wanted to be in town for the dedication, so he had changed his schedule and would be leaving Vava'u the next day. I showed the airline representative the telegram and insisted that he call his headquarters again and explain that the governor was relying on the promises made by them to get me to Vava'u that day. If the governor could not rely on the promises of the airline he might have second thoughts about allowing their company to fly into Vava'u.

Apparently that information influenced someone, for in a short while we received word back that the plane would come from Samoa

as soon as possible and take us to Vava'u. They promised to notify
those waiting in Vava'u of our new schedule.

It was almost dusk when the small plane finally landed in Ha'apai.
The pilot was extremely anxious to get us on board immediately and
only turned off the engine on the side from which we boarded.

Even with the quick turnaround in Ha'apai, darkness was falling
faster than the pilot had anticipated. We were nearly to Vava'u when
he told me he was sorry, but it was getting too dark and he couldn't
land in Vava'u as they had no lights on the landing field, so he would
return to Tongatapu, where they did have lights.

We had to get to Vava'u that day. I knew how important it was for
the future of the school to have the governor at the dedication.
Tomorrow would be too late. I thought of the food the Saints had
cooked and the hours of preparations for their special dances and
songs. They had invited many important people from the government
and from other churches to be there. Not to have this dedication happen as scheduled would be very hard on them now and in the future.

The pilot rightly had to consider the practical danger we all faced.
I didn't know what to do—at least, not for a moment. Then suddenly
the faith and desires and prayers of those wonderful Saints in Vava'u
began to get through to me and I knew what to say to the pilot.

I approached him and said with certainty: "Just keep going towards Vava'u. There are hundreds of members waiting for us at the
airport. They all have lanterns and flashlights and even a few cars with
headlights. Radio ahead and have your people tell them to line the
runway with lights. You will make a safe landing."

He looked at me incredulously and said: "That is preposterous.
Even a few hundred people with lanterns couldn't make a strong
enough light to land by. I can't subject us to this danger. I'm sorry, but
I must turn back to Tongatapu." He began a wide slow turn.

I prayed as hard as I knew how. The more I prayed the stronger I
felt the faith and desires of the Saints from Vava'u coming through. With
deep conviction I told the pilot again: "I understand your concern. We
are almost to Vava'u. Just call ahead and do as I suggested. I ask you to
make just one attempt to land at the airport. If there is not enough light
you may then proceed to Tongatapu and I will say no more."

"Well, OK, one pass, just to satisfy you, but that is all." He radioed
ahead and explained what needed to be done. It took no more than
ten additional minutes to get to Vava'u. As we first flew over the airport only a few straggly lights could be seen. However, by the time the

pilot made the broad turn to head back to the airport against the wind a true miracle had taken place. Now, rather than a few dim lights here and there, there was a veritable double path of flames, as it were. They were as bright and distinct as any set of landing lights on any runway at any airport in all the world.

The pilot was amazed. He said, "Wow! That is some display of lights. I think we can make it. Buckle your seatbelts; we are going in."

As we glided safely into the Vava'u airport I felt another power guiding us. We needed the skill of the pilot, but that night the faith and desires of thousands of Saints ascended to heaven and were responded to by angels with protection and light that guided us safely to earth.

As we disembarked I noticed the number of members there with flashlights and lanterns and the few cars and trucks with their lights on. I realized that all of them put together could not have made even a small portion of the brilliant light we saw lining the landing strip. As the men of Gideon found (see Judges 7:19–22), we also learned that the Lord has a way of multiplying light when needed by those who have faith in Him. As I thanked the pilot for his willingness to try, he just shrugged and said, "It was the least I could do, and it turned out fine. I'm still amazed."

The South Pacific Island Airways plane that landed in Vava'u
for the high school dedication.

In a way, I was amazed also, but in another way it seemed very natural. The faith of the Tongans is strong, and God hears and responds accordingly. How I wished I had more faith. How grateful I was to have the privilege of working with people of deep faith!

We drove to the Saineha school and arrived shortly past 10:00 P.M., eight hours after the original schedule. Those dear Saints had waited patiently the whole time while their feast, which was spread over the entire floor of the new gymnasium, got colder and colder. They were hungry but hadn't touched any of the food.

As we entered the building I saw love and light and joy in every face. No one was impatient or discouraged, they were just happy we were there. The opening prayer was filled with love and gratitude and appreciation for the Church, for the school, and for our safe arrival.

The rather intricate Tongan formalities involving the governor and other guests of honor went forward as though there had been no delay. Then I thanked them for their patience, love, and faith. I said they had waited long enough and could now begin the celebration.

The whole congregation, which up to that point had been sitting in reverent decorum, suddenly exploded with enthusiasm and burst into frenzied activity. The songs were long and loud and beautiful. The dancing and feasting and speech-giving were done with a gusto and an abandon befitting the occasion. In some places this type of enthusiasm might have turned into an uncontrolled free-for-all, but that doesn't happen in Tonga. All of these things are carefully controlled by an unwritten order known only to Tongans. There is a system of hereditary family relationships that allows certain people (and only them) to do certain things. No one breaches the bounds of this complex yet powerful method of social order and control.

The re-warmed food was delicious and the entertainment was marvelous. Once as things got fairly wild—when certain people threw a cake high in the air and then kicked it to smithereens as it came down—I looked around and smiled and was glad there were only "us Tongans" present. This was the type of enthusiasm that has to be understood to be appreciated. I thought of David returning in triumph and dancing in the street.

After an hour or so of feasting and dancing, things began to calm down. I sensed that it was now appropriate to proceed with the dedication. I stood and announced that the time had arrived to dedicate the Saineha school. Immediately the audience returned to a seriousness and a reverence that was as real and as heartfelt as their previous enthusiastic celebrating had been. The profound silence seemed more pure by its contrast to the bottled-up enthusiasm that had so recently been released. Every eye closed and every head bowed in deep gratitude as the dedicatory prayer was given.

Thus, a few minutes before midnight, still on the appointed day, the Saineha school was dedicated by the power of the priesthood of God. The faith and the desires of the marvelous Saints of Vavaʻu had been measured and fulfilled.

As I occasionally look back on that dedication and on the flight into that crude airfield after dark, I can see from a worldly point of view that it was risky, maybe even silly, to try such a thing. Yet from the point of view of the spirit of faith and desire, there was no question and really no alternative. The Book of Mormon records the phrase, "they were filled with desire" (3 Nephi 19:24; see also 28:1). Sometimes the Lord might ask, "I know you have faith, but how much do you desire this thing you are asking for?" The faith and desires of the Saints on Vavaʻu to have their school dedicated that day burned brightly and were strong enough that the plane could land safely. Their desires simply could not be denied.

59

Tomorrow Will Come Soon Enough

As I contemplated our move to Utah I remembered a statement attributed to Brigham Young about the Saints' move to the Salt Lake Valley: "We went willingly because we had to." We didn't want to leave the islands and our friends there, but we did so willingly because we had been asked to by a prophet of God and we knew it was right.

Our six older children had jobs or other activities planned, so they stayed in Hawaii a while longer with friends or relatives, and Jean and I took the five younger children to Utah.

We couldn't hold time back, so amidst mountains of leis watered by an abundance of tears we finally bade "Aloha" to our island home, boarded the plane, and began the long flight to our new home in Utah. As the plane climbed into the sky I gazed longingly at Diamond Head and our nearby home and neighborhood until they faded from view. What memories they evoked. I felt so nostalgic that it hurt. I sensed that one era was drawing to a close even as another one, built on the past, was opening up.

For nearly fifteen years (twelve of them consecutive) I had been given the priceless opportunity of working directly with the people of Tonga and of other Pacific islands. In some ways I had taken this blessing for granted. With this change of assignment I saw more clearly what a priceless privilege it had been. I knew I should treasure it and use it to bless my family and the others with whom I would work. I knew that as we moved into other assignments the important lessons of faith and love learned at home, and in Tonga, and throughout the Pacific, would continue to be the foundation of all that was good and right and according to God's will.

I looked at the family about me: Viki, Jean, and eight-month-old Emily had all fallen asleep. Jennie was deeply involved in coloring in a book. Sue and Tom were reading. I thought of all of our children. Their individual personalities each added to the flavor of our family. I looked at Jean holding our baby. A quiet peaceful thought began to form in my mind: "This is your family." Without any words being said, I was given to understand that Emily would be our last child here. I was taken aback, as I had not been thinking about this, yet the feeling was so peaceful and so clear that I had no question where it came from. It was hard to believe, yet I knew it was true: beautiful, faithful Jean, marvelous mother, incomparable helpmate, holding our last child.

Jean and I had always felt that we should leave to the Lord the decisions about the number of children we should have. Surely He understood our situation better than we ever could, just as He understands every couple's unique circumstances. We tried never to compare or judge, but only to be obedient and do His will as we understood it for us. We realized that after all is said and done it will not be a doctor, a psychologist, a social worker, or an economist that we will answer to when we leave this life. Rather, it will be the Lord. We had long ago determined that since He is the one we will answer to there, He is the one we should listen to here. Now to have this feeling of approbation from Him—it was almost more than I could contain.

Carefully and gratefully I began reviewing the circumstances surrounding the birth and growth of each child. What jewels God had sent us! My heart filled to overflowing with love and gratitude as I thought of the countless sacrifices Jean had made. I wanted to wake her and share these feelings, but when I saw how peaceful she was I realized she deserved every bit of rest she could get. These feelings were from God. I knew He would bless her with the same understanding.

For a long time these feelings, like a beautiful limitless landscape, filled my soul. Then suddenly without warning, like the arrival of an uninvited guest, thoughts about my weaknesses and the things I had done wrong or had failed to do filled my mind. I began to feel more and more miserable. It was such a contrast to the peaceful feeling I had been experiencing that inwardly I cried out: "Oh wretched man that I am." I thought of Nephi and was led to read his lament beginning in 2 Nephi 4:17. As I slowly read and pondered those verses the former feelings of warmth and love began to return.

Finally, as light chases away darkness, these good feelings pushed the painful feelings out and I was once more filled with light and joy. What contrast! What gratitude! For a long time I basked in the warmth of eternal love and forgiveness and felt the approbation of a caring Savior. When we see more clearly everything He has done for us we will realize that what we feel and understand now is but the tiniest part of all He has actually done for us. Our whole desire will be to sing praises to His name forever. How good and forgiving and loving God is!

The words of Isaiah sang in my heart: "He shall feed his flock like a shepherd: he shall gather the lambs with his arm, and carry them in his bosom, and shall gently lead those that are with young" (Isaiah 40:11). I could literally feel the Savior's mercy cover my weaknesses in a blanket of forgiveness and love. I could do nothing but quietly weep and pray and express gratitude.

I felt as though I was not in my body but somewhere else floating in a sea of ecstasy and peace and love, and moving through space and seeing and understanding things in a way I had not previously seen or understood them.

As I moved through this space of warmth I was led to think of the future and understood that there would be many more trials to pass through before this earth's portion of our family's journey was finished. I thought of our five teenage girls. What lay ahead for them? I thought of the younger children, who would soon be entering those challenging years. How would they handle it? How would Jean and I handle it? I thought of our youngest, Emily, and realized that Jean and I would both be in our early sixties before she was out of her teen years. What should we do? How could we best help each of them get through those times of conflict and turmoil, of change and growth?

I thought of the college educations and missions and marriages that we hoped would take place at the proper time and in the proper place. I wondered how we would handle and pay for them. I wondered again at the meaning of President Kimball's statement at the time of my call as a General Authority regarding "going anywhere at any time in all the world for the rest of [my] life." I thought of a thousand other questions that seemed difficult to answer, yet I knew in time I would understand. I realized that the children He had sent us were His choice spirits reserved for the last days. I was comforted by this knowledge. It came to me with brilliant clarity that I shouldn't worry about the challenges ahead, for if we did our best, someway the Lord would see that things worked out. As we now look back and see God's hand in bringing us through great challenges, likewise, whether it be a decade or a century or an eon from now, we will look back and recognize His divine help and feel His unchanging love for us. Our duty is to remain humble and faithful. What a reassuring feeling!

I was led to say (as though I was talking to Jean): "It will take all of our strength to overcome today's problems, so let's not spend any of today's energy worrying about tomorrow's problems. Let's just handle today and keep the Spirit of the Lord with us and move forward in faith, and somehow things will work out. They have in the past and they will in the future." I thought of the scripture: "Take therefore no thought for the morrow: for the morrow shall take thought for the things of itself. Sufficient unto the day is the evil thereof." (Matthew 6:34.)

We could move forward in faith; even into uncharted waters, if necessary. We need not fear, for God, unlimited by time, is already there.

I looked again at my beautiful wife and our youngest daughter. I thought of each of the children in Hawaii and marveled at how special each one was. I looked at precious Tom and Sue and felt their goodness. I looked at Viki, so tired yet so full of promise. I looked at Jennie and tousled her hair. She looked up and smiled, then settled back to more serious coloring.

I felt a thread of tiredness. I closed my eyes, and as I began to drift off I heard, as it were, a voice saying: "Go ahead and rest for a while. Tomorrow will come soon enough."

Index